W9-ACM-694

Faded Pictures from
My Backyard

Ballantine Books

NEW YORK

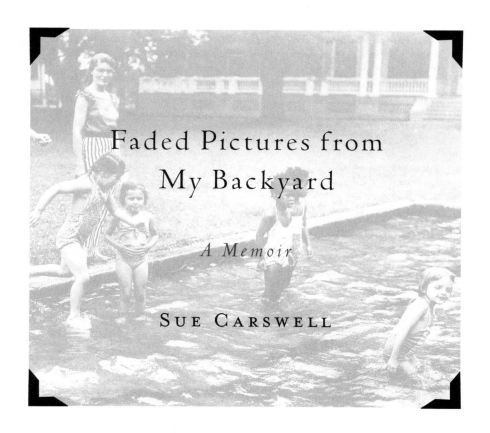

Faded Pictures from My Backyard

A Memoir

SUE CARSWELL

While all of the incidents in *Faded Pictures from My Backyard* are true, some of the names and personal characteristics of the individuals involved have been changed in order to protect their privacy. Any resulting resemblance to persons living or dead is entirely coincidental and unintentional.

Published in the United States by Ballantine Books, an imprint of The Random House Publishing Group, a division of Random House, Inc., New York.

Ballantine and colophon are registered trademarks of Random House, Inc.

LIBRARY OF CONGRESS CATALOGING-IN-PUBLICATION DATA

Carswell, Sue.
Faded pictures from my backyard / Sue Carswell.—1st ed.
p. cm.
ISBN 0-345-43856-6
1. Orphanages—New York (State)—Albany—Case studies. 2. Carswell, Sue.
I. Title.

HV995.A32C37 2005
362.73'2—dc22   2003063865

Printed in the United States of America

Ballantine Books website address: www.ballantinebooks.com

2 4 6 8 9 7 5 3 1

First Edition

Book design by Dana Leigh Blanchette

for

my mother, all mothers, and the children they've left behind who still feel their passing like it was yesterday. This is a story about children's ties to their mother, no matter the circumstances. Every day is our mother's day.

for my nieces and nephews, MaryBeth, Catherine, John, Allison, Maggie, Megan, Madeline Elaine and William James Carswell, and Kirby John and Henry Watson Heffernan. I wrote this story in memory of your grandmother, who, in her final days, lamented that she would not live to see you grow, as she had the many generations of children who lived in our old backyard.

and for my sister, Amanda Smith, your time will come. Be patient, as she would say. Keep lighting candles.

finally, to Claudia Cross, my trusted agent, adviser, and loyal friend, your benevolence through all these long years often reminds me of my mother's kindness and goodwill.

—Sue Carswell, New York City, 2004

Prologue

All that is me goes back to my yard . . .

It is close to midnight on New Year's Eve, deep in the chill of winter. I cannot recount the story of my childhood backyard and its everlasting effect on me until this year has crossed into the next. As it is not yet midnight, I make myself wait until the aged year passes into oblivion. Only then do I let my mind embark on an imaginary train ride. Horn at full blare, my thoughts drive a locomotive closer to that North Wind. Beneath the illumination of a fair moon, I ride the rails along the Hudson River. Its final destination, my hometown: Albany, New York.

I think I know what Franklin D. Roosevelt meant when he said, "All that is within me cries out to go back to my home on the Hudson River."

The Hudson flows from high, starting at Lake Tear of the Clouds in the Adirondack Mountains, past the quaint homes of Glens Falls—the small town where my father grew up—down through Watervliet, where as a child, my mother lived next to an arsenal that manufactured cannons for World War II. The river travels south, making its way through the Port of Albany where each spring the waters threaten to flood the city. The Hudson continues past such picturesque towns as President Roosevelt's Hyde Park, into New York Harbor and New York City, where I live. Eventually, it flows into the Long Island Sound, where it romances the Atlantic Ocean. The mercurial Hudson will always be a symbolic link between my past and present.

Just as FDR's life was defined by the Hudson River Valley, who I am and who I have become is defined by the diverse backyard of my childhood at 60 Academy Road—where my family lived for twenty-five years on the grounds of the Albany Home for Children. While my tale is not one of some tragic foundling like Oliver Twist, much of my childhood was lived among a community of such children—whose faces, although now fading, I remember to this day.

The clock has yet to strike twelve. Turning from the flickering screen of my computer, I peer through my apartment's antique stained-glass window, its frame chipped and weathered by time. Below a traffic-filled avenue courses through Manhattan's West Village.

This window was a gift received just days before, when I joined my family upstate for Christmas. Something about the glass touches me—me, still raw from having, months earlier, lost my mother, our indomitable Mother Goose. This was our first Christmas without her, and her absence was felt everywhere. Unlike the joy-filled holidays vivid in my childhood memories—with carols, reindeer on the roof, and a decorated chimney—none of the gaily wrapped presents piled beneath the exquisitely adorned sixteen-foot Fraser fir in my father's living room mattered much at all.

Over the past few days after returning home, sitting alone in my apartment, I have wondered whether this simple window might act as a spiritual catalyst for me to move on—despite my grief and all my fury. Three metal rods vertically cross translucent panes of glass. In its center, a vibrant green stem embracing an orange bud attempts with all its might to burst through the lead.

I lean forward in my chair, my nose brushing the lightly frosted pane. Squinting through the tinted glass, I remember a visit to St. Patrick's Cathedral when I was just five years old. My mother clutched my tiny hand in one of hers and a crisp dollar bill—freshly ironed with starch for this deeply religious occasion—in the other. Money, when pressed into a bronze collection box, entitled one to light a white votive candle and say a prayer to the giant marble saints looming over the vast sanctuary's perimeter. Back then, I thought these saints were long-dead family members: Andrew, Paul, Matthew, John . . . and Teresa, my mother's favorite, and thus my very special aunt.

The din from holiday revelers drifts toward my window from the street below. There is a distant muffled boom of fireworks, while closer by, "Auld Lang Syne" filters through the midnight air. Noisemakers explode as the twelve chimes from the clock tower of the nearby Jefferson Market Library signal the start of my pilgrimage to the past.

I look to my computer screen, and rushing back are all the confusing shadows of my childhood's haunted landscape.

> I have more memories than if I were a thousand years old.
> —*Charles Baudelaire (1821–1867)**

---

* Baudelaire was six when his father died.

Welcome Home

In September 1989, I was working as a reporter for *People* magazine and was assigned a story on an orphanage having a reunion some fifty years after the now grown-up children had left it behind. It was the story of my extended backyard on which lay the grounds of the Albany Home for Children. On the day I returned to the running fields of my childhood, I met a man named Bob Wygant, whose enthusiasm for life was immense, despite the loneliness he had endured as a child. I instantly knew that I wanted Bob, then sixty, in my life forever as my friend. Our stories and reasons for growing up on the grounds of the Albany Home for Children were as different as they could be. And in those days of coping with my own mental fragility as an adult living in Manhattan, I looked to Bob for inspiration. Perhaps one day my own unquiet mind might achieve a similar state of tranquility.

At the reunion of orphans, when I wasn't busy taping their recollections on a recorder, I would sneak away to look for my mother. That day she strolled the grounds of the old Albany Home for Children clutching my father's hand. I wanted to make sure she was okay, that she wasn't crying because she found this reunion too wrenching. I wondered whether each orphan's eyes she looked into caused remorse over her own past, even though that, too, was a story laced with childhood sadness. The sight of my mother crying broke my heart, so perhaps, knowing I had to stay focused on this day, she simply beams at me with that look of everything is fine. When I catch a glimpse of her, there is a glow around her. The white crepe dress she wears, full of stitched-in vibrant blue, purple, and orange butterflies, seems to come alive. It's as though the butterflies move her forward so that she doesn't have to look back.

My mother hated looking back.

This was a deep contrast to Bob Wygant's worshipful memories. He had come to terms with it all. And so my story, or rather the story of a reunion as told by a journalist, unfolds. Perhaps the telling of my personal story, the journalist looking at her own childhood, also began on this day, but it would take my own orphaned heart, years later, to examine it more fully . . .

They came from all parts of New York State and as far away as Florida, South Carolina, and Michigan. One hundred or so Depression-era orphans—now in their fifties, sixties, seventies, and even their eighties, many with their spouses, children, and grandchildren—journey back in time to their beginnings, to the place that had been their childhood sanctuary.

On this afternoon in the middle of September, they converge on the grounds of what once had been the Albany Home for Children, one of the country's oldest continuing orphanages. Most of the people visiting the Home had lived on the larger portion of my childhood backyard between the 1930s and early 1950s, in the cottages now occupied by the Junior College of Albany.

Their reasons for returning vary. Some came out of curiosity, or affection for one another, or to see if Coach would be there, or perhaps hoping to say thank you to a kindly housemother who read bedtime stories to them many years ago. Others came to show their families where they had grown up. Many had been as young as three when they were placed here.

Throughout the day, the alumni, some of those who lived there when it was known as the Albany Orphan Asylum, share their memories as they walk

arm in arm with a long-lost brother or sister around the quad of their old campus. The early-autumn sunlight filters through the trees, casting golden halos
over the heads of these now older orphans. They are the special ones, at least
for today. Or perhaps it is a gift from a higher power, a gift from their parents
who long ago left them on the orphanage's doorstep.

After leaving the Home, many of the orphans tried to locate their parents.
For some, this search took years, for others, decades. And, of course some
never found what they were looking for. Those who finally did track down a
parent heard endless, remorseful excuses.

Your father died and I had no money to take care of you and your sister . . .

Your mother died and I had no place to turn . . .

Your dad drank away all our money . . .

*Your father abandoned me, and I tried to kill myself and so you see the police took
you away from me in the middle of the night . . .*

Times were tough, please understand . . .

Your mother was mentally ill . . .

It was the Great Depression . . .

We were in the middle of World War II . . .

I could keep only one of you . . .

I was too ashamed to visit . . .

I got pregnant . . . it was a mistake . . . but I always thought of you . . .

I had no place to turn . . .

This was the only place you could go . . .

I didn't want you to live with me on the streets.

Whatever stories these orphans had to tell, what matters most to them on
this glorious day is that they are together again.

Laughing at their long-gone innocence, their eyes well with tears when
they recall what, at times, was their sorrow: These orphans rarely experi-

enced the spontaneous hugs and kisses and the unqualified love of a mother or father. Clearly this has separated them from their spouses and, obviously, from their own children, who have never lacked a parent's touch.

Many of the orphans admit that they were not able to get love right after they left this haven. Sometimes they loved too much, or too little. Few had a clue about how to express their emotions. For several, it took more than one marriage to decipher the raw complexity of love.

I couldn't wait to start life, Caroline Commisso exclaims, taking hold of my tape recorder as she holds her sister Edna's hand tight. My first husband and I had seven babies in eleven years, and I made sure to let them know how much I loved them—even if it was just a hug—when they left our house, and a kiss when they came back in.

Even the boys had little preparation for love, marriage, and parenthood.

As one orphan shows his wife where he had lived as a boy, he says, All of us grew up without love. We didn't even know what love was, but we certainly yearned for it.

Strolling the grounds of their old home, alumni point to the cottage windows where, as girls, they looked above to the clouds and daydreamed about their futures, or as boys, they clamored down the brickwork on the corners of their cottages for after-curfew revelry with their friends. As they show their children where their gardens had flourished and where the duck pond once was, they fondly reminisce about sipping hot chocolate together after a night of ice skating on a frozen pond. They go on to recall the thickness of their toast, and the gleam of their cottage's hardwood floors.

These once agile young athletes—now retired, fathers and mothers—share memories of the annual Lawn Festivals, when neighbors once watched them show off their tumbling skills on the grass between the cottages.

Others, with eyes sparkling, relive stepping into the spotlight in the plays they performed, including their biggest hit, *Snow White and the Seven Dwarfs*. They were directed by their former activities director, Coach Ronald J. Huddleston and his wife, Swannee, and wore splendid costumes made for them by the Home's handyman, Mr. Keck. On that faraway day, they had felt like stars.

The former boys of Wasson Cottage now stand in front of their old home, amazed that it has been transformed into the art building of the Junior College of Albany. A still-fit and handsome man, recently turned sixty, simply can't grasp the notion that an easel splattered with paint could be standing in the very place where his bed once was. *An art building?* He shakes his head, standing by the back door where he once jumped aboard a bus in his Sunday clothes to head off to church. Today he wears an impressive lavender suit—making sure that he stands out in the crowd. This is to be my new friend. Bob Wygant is also the one who spearheaded this grand day, along with the organizing committee, which included friends from when he was just a young boy and girls he thought of as sisters.

Trading memories and renewing friendships with the compatriots of their youth, most of the returning orphans express gratitude for having had a safe, secure place to live. Neither names nor even faces have been forgotten over the years. Images of callow boys and hopeful girls radiate from the wrinkled faces of men with thinning hair and women with permed white locks.

As the afternoon moves on, these elderly girls tentatively walk toward the chain-link fence, the line of demarcation separating their old home from what is now known as Parsons Child and Family Center. They touch the metal fence with one hand, aiming cameras through its diamond openings to snap pictures of what had been their home, Parsons Cottage. It is now on the other side, where the new Albany Home for Children was built after the rest of the campus—the part where most of them had lived—was sold to the Junior College.

Soon the former Wasson boys gravitate to them, standing at the fence alongside the now grown-up girls, peering across the way at the Van Alstyne Gymnasium, the scene of many childhood pleasures.

When an older man with a ready smile and wire-rimmed glasses joins them, he sadly shakes his head. The stand of birch trees the boys cut through to sneak into the Albany Academy football games was gone. They had been cut down to make room for the more practical single-story cottages that now bore the honorable names these orphans had known so well—Rathbone and even Wasson. In the far distance, they can see only vague figures of children at play.

Such a shame, someone laments to the older gentleman, as everyone nods in agreement. They cut our old home in half.

This particular man is one of the most welcomed faces in the reunion crowd. Coach Huddleston has returned to Albany from Sarasota, Florida, for this occasion. Retired, Coach works as a consultant to the Boys Club in Sarasota. In 1955, Coach and his wife, Swannee, and their children left the Albany Home when he accepted the position of superintendent of the nearby Charlton Home for Girls. Only a day after Coach's departure from the Albany Home, a little boy from Wasson Cottage named Jamie took a sheet from his bed, scissored out two eyeholes, and covered the head of the Home's horse. Then straddling his trusty steed, Jamie rode through the night to Charlton, where he knocked on their door. Coach and Swanee let the boy stay the night, but the following morning, Coach explained gently to him that this was a girls' orphanage and that he would have to go back to his home.

By the mid- to late 1950s, government-assisted programs to keep children with their families or in foster care began to make conventional orphanages obsolete. In keeping with this trend, the Albany Home for Children was on its way to becoming a treatment facility for children with behavioral and emotional problems. The orphanage—as it had once strictly been—was closed in 1959.

Coach's eyes well with tears at the changes he sees today. Bob Wygant, in his lavender suit, puts his hand on Coach's shoulder and says, Our history is on this side of the fence, yet our legacy is over there. One day, Coach, maybe you and I should go over and meet the children who live in those cottages.

I think we should do exactly that, Bob, replies Coach, smiling at the man who was his favorite orphan and now, all these years later, is his closest friend and confidant—even more so since he lost his love Swanee two years earlier.

For this reunion day, Bob Wygant chose his lavender suit with care. A week earlier, he and his wife had seen a Steve Martin video in which the comedian wore a pink suit while he made colorful animal figures out of balloons. If Steve Martin could wear pink because he was a wild and crazy guy, Bob figured that he would wear lavender to show everyone that he is a most happy fellow.

Before the group walks away from the fence, someone calls attention to the beautiful flowers, still blooming in the garden around one of the two identical ranch houses that mark the entrance to the newer Albany Home for Children.

Oh, that's where the executive director and his wife live, Bob says. I understand their five children grew up on the grounds of the campus, but they're all grown up and moved away. Then he turns around and winks at me. Except for the one who has come back to interview us for our big day.

...

As the older orphans and I stare onto the grounds where I once played kick-the-can under the twilight of the evening and swam in our beloved pool for so many years, my father leads my mother in our direction. He answers questions from Bob, Coach, and their friends about how their long-ago Home, as they knew it, grew into a large agency, over time treating thousands of emotionally disturbed and orphaned children. And just like the children who lived next door to me in the cottages during the almost two decades when I lived there—the ones who often asked my father why they were there—the orphans of the past also reach out to him, still seeking answers as they try to comprehend their history.

Unfortunately, my father offers a startling fact: Most of your files were lost when your half of the backyard was sold to the Junior College.

Without records, they were anonymous orphans to this new modern-day Home. They were strangers to their old backyard, in the same way I had always felt, as a kid, that I was, too.

PART ONE

The Children's Yard

"It's no use talking about it," Alice said, looking up at the house and pretending it was arguing with her. "I'm not going in again yet. I know I should have to get through the Looking-glass again—back into the old room—and there'd be an end of all my adventures."

—Lewis Carroll, *Through the Looking Glass*, 1872*

* Carroll was orphaned after his mother's death when he was an infant.

Pause

Even when I was young, I knew there were two things my mother hated. She hated leaving her five children and she hated when the big brown cardboard boxes had to be packed up—signaling a move from one home to another. They were *homes* to my mother, not *houses*. On the day we headed toward our new home on Academy Road in July 1968 where my father worked with children who, as my mother explained to me, needed to feel better before they went home again—just like little birds whose wings needed to heal over time, or perhaps even find new parents to be loved by—my mother cried the entire ride. Her tears steadily dripped onto the bald head of my baby sister Sarah, whom she clutched in her lap.

Right before my mother got into the car, she stood outside our garage, the sun beating down on her curly red hair, and looked over the roof toward my father with her piercing blue eyes, shaking her head, and with a voice choking back tears, she said, John, I can't help it. You know how much I hate change.

Car rides became so stultifyingly quiet and places became so far away when my mother cried in the front seat.

Unlike my mother, I wasn't sad about the move because our old house—which was really a rather beautiful barn-red house—was just too similar to the first house we had lived in. Both had made me feel spooky inside. I was happy about our move, and my breaths no longer had a nervous twitch behind them. I felt as lucky as a helium-filled balloon that had finally popped and could let all its tense contents out. I think balloons stayed intact just to make kids like me smile, but they would have really preferred to pop and let out their long deep breath, too.

I did feel sad, however, that my best friends, Cammy and Brad, had to move away from their home because we were now moving into their house. I would now be sleeping in Cammy's bedroom. My father had a new and better job at the place where all the children played, as I saw it, and now we had to live there because my mother said it was a big job and my father was going to earn almost ten thousand dollars a year. Sometimes you move to new houses in order to become rich. Cammy and Brad's dad, Mr. Cordes, had taken a different job working with children in St. Louis, which was very far away.

When I had asked my mother, a couple of weeks before our move, where Cammy and Brad were going, she walked right over to the large map she had tacked up on the wall in our playroom because my older brother, Jimmy (and that was only one year and one month to the day, so he really wasn't older like Wally on *Leave It to Beaver*), and I were trying to learn the names of states. She put her finger on the red dot that stood for our house, then she slowly moved her finger through state after state until it reached the halfway mark on the map in between our dot and the long, thin state, California. Just to get an idea of how far away that was I asked, Where's Cape Cod again? Cape Cod was as far away as I had ever been. But at the end of a long car ride, which would begin even before the sun came up and in which Jimmy and I slept the entire way in our pajamas, when we woke up hours later, there it would be—the magical sight of little green waves tipped with foam that looked like Mr. Bubble washing onto the off-white sand. Cape Cod was the yellow dot on the map, the place where the sun baked us in our bathing suits and where Jimmy and I spit salt water as we dodged cool waves. Red was where we lived. No matter where we went, all trips came back to the red dot, the stop sign color that signaled our home. My mother put a green dot on the state where Cammy and Brad were moving. She said someday we would visit and play with them again. Green meant go.

When we left our house, driving only a few miles to my father's workplace and our new house, Jimmy and I sang the *M-i-ss-i-ss-i-pp-i* song the entire way in honor of Brad and Cammy, since we didn't know any song for Missouri. My mother said that the Mississippi song was okay because the two states were friendly neighbors.

In our new blue station wagon, Jimmy and I always sat in the way backseat—the best place to sit because it looked out the rear of the car and not the front. Instead of looking forward to see where we were going, we looked at the places we were leaving behind.

When we finally pulled into our new driveway, hopping over into the middle seat, Jimmy bolted from the car and headed toward our new front door. But something kept me from moving and exploring our new surroundings. I was mesmerized by one of the movers: an older man with a bald head who smiled at me and kept taking his finger off and then putting it back on his hand. Each magic move he made began with this abracadabra wave of his hand behind a blue kerchief and then he would lift his thumb off his left hand, creating the impression that only a stump remained behind. The escaping thumb would then be miraculously tucked inside his right hand, raised into the air until the moment when he placed it back on the lonely stump again. When my father opened up the back of the car, the moving man came over and sat on the ledge, doing his trick over and over again—taking his finger off and putting it back on. I was so impressed by this that nothing else mattered, even our biggest moving day.

We were a large family and there were a lot of kids, so it was nice to feel like I was someone special, at least to the moving man. And that I didn't have to worry about my mother, father, Jimmy, Billy, Mandy, and now Sarah, because in this new house we would be safe and there wouldn't be a cemetery, slaughterhouse, and ghosts, like there were in our first backyard, or fast-moving trains plowing through the night like they always did in our second backyard. I could just be a regular kid without the fears that had been growing inside of me ever since right before I turned three and my mother had gone off to the hospital for what I presumed was forever. I didn't understand days or tomorrows. I only understood gone. When she came back seven days later, instead of bringing toys my mother brought us twins that cried a lot.

While I was looking forward to having fun, riding my bike, and creating new kinds of cakes in my Easy-Bake Oven, I wasn't going to let go of this moment of freedom. I sat in the backseat of the car almost all day, watching the moving man unload all our boxes. When he could sneak a break, he would come over to help me improve my own magical abracadabra style.

It was late afternoon when the moving men finally pulled away and I entered our new house. I headed for my bedroom, where my mother had already unpacked my things and made my bed with flower sheets and a new yellow blanket. I had played in this room when it was Cammy's, but I never looked at its walls or the sliding-door closets, and I had never even looked out the window. Now the newly painted pale yellow room was mine. I was drawn to its window. Looking out my window on that first day made me feel happier than I had ever been.

My bedroom inside our redbrick ranch-style home, which was shaped like the letter *L*, was sandwiched between my parents' large bedroom and Mandy and Sarah's room, which was right next to Jimmy and Billy's bedroom. My brothers' room had three windows, one facing the direction mine did and two others that faced our new street. Their room was two doors down from mine. My parents' room had the only windows that also looked out onto our big backyard. Nineteen acres, my father told me and Jimmy, made up the size of our new playground.

From all our bedrooms, we shared a view of the four little houses my mother called cottages. Sad children, she told us, lived in three of these cottages. Our windows faced the back entrances of the cottages as well as a parking lot where the people who worked inside with the children left their cars. My father told me that some of the workers were there all night long to make sure nothing bad ever happened to the children. I decided this move by our family was the safest thing we could ever do. Looking out my window, I imagined the child care workers were the night police. I hoped they would watch over our house, too.

Being in our new house felt a bit off. Jimmy and I had been practicing before we moved that day how to say the name of the grounds where we now lived. It was called the Albany Home for Children. The words were painted in gold block letters on a small blackboard sandwiched on an island full of flowers. Our home, my father explained, was separate from life in the cottages with the other children. Still, we all shared the same address, 60 Academy Road, and large elm trees planted closely together in the front—and a fence on the left side of our property—kept all of us snugly together on the property.

When we eventually started at our new school, we were to tell our new friends and teachers that we lived at 60 Academy Road. We were *not* to say we lived at the Albany Home for Children. I don't know why we couldn't say we lived at the Home: I liked the sound of it. It felt like a place where we had the biggest family imaginable. All my eventual classmates would want to live where I lived, too. Who wouldn't want a rainbow full of children living and playing in their big backyard? For the first time in my life, I didn't want to say exactly what my father told me I should. If anyone asked me where I lived, I would tell them my own way, and I would invite my new friends to come home and play with me and Jimmy and all the other children who lived in our backyard at the Albany Home for Children.

A Little Boy's New Home

Now for a moment I will ask leave to remove my own insignificant personality and to describe events which occurred before we arrived upon the scene by the light of knowledge which came to us afterwards. Only in this way can I make the reader appreciate the people concerned and the strange setting in which their fate was cast.

—Sir Arthur Conan Doyle,
*Sherlock Holmes: The Valley of Fear**

Long ago on July 4, 1932, *The New York Times* reports that President Herbert Hoover had left Washington to divide his holiday time between work and rest at the presidential retreat near the Rapidan River in Luray, Virginia. Other important news, also covered in every newspaper around the country, was the whereabouts of the Democratic presidential nominee, New York's governor Franklin D. Roosevelt. Roosevelt had just defeated Alfred E. Smith at the national convention in Chicago, and when asked about his holiday plans, he said, "I am going back to Albany!"

By early afternoon, the newly named candidate arrives at Union Station in

---

* Along with his six siblings, Arthur Doyle grew up in poverty. His father suffered from depression, alcoholism, and epilepsy. Charles Doyle was later institutionalized.

downtown Albany. Thousands of local residents eagerly wave placards and signs smeared from the rain as they rush to greet his train. They then follow his entourage to the Governor's Mansion on Eagle Street.

On the same day but earlier in the morning, another journey takes place in Albany. It, however, goes unnoticed by the newspapers. Robert Wygant, celebrating his third birthday, is leaving an orphanage for infants and babies.

As Bob walks away from the gate of St. Margaret's House and Hospital on the corner of Elk and North Hawk Streets, the little boy tightly clutches his nurse's hand. He has never been this far away from the big house that has thus far been his entire world. He has never put his soft leather soles outside the huge fenced lawn onto the cobblestone street. To the boy, the feeling of paved stones feels funny, like bumps against his feet, hard bumps that he cannot squish down like the bumps he makes with his pail and shovel in the giant sandbox where he and the other boys and girls who live at his house play. With the nurse, Bob climbs into an old black delivery van.

As he and the nurse continue along, he cannot believe he is sitting in an actual car, so much bigger than the toy cars he is used to playing with as he and his friends race them across the polished floor.

Through the back window of the moving black van, Bob looks back over his left shoulder at the smaller and smaller St. Margaret's, the place where he has slept in a walnut wood crib his whole life. He doesn't know this nurse sitting closely beside him any better then he knew any of the other fifty nurses who have bathed and fed him since that morning when he was placed there on the front stoop. Still, he feels safe. Surely she knows how to get them back where they belong once this exhilarating car ride has ended. Although it is fun for him to see streets he has never known of, Bob is also apprehensive.

So far, Bob's life has been warm and filled with affection. He knows nothing different: a world of babies and nurses. The kind nurses, all so young and pretty, wear starched white linen uniforms with gathered skirts that almost touch their white laced shoes and blouses buttoned all the way up their long necks. Their caps look just like the boats that capsize in the waves he and the other children make when they splash the water too hard in the spotless metal bathtub.

Occasionally, the boy noticed that before he went to sleep at night, after a nurse had read to him and his friends from the big *Mother Goose* book, he would stand up in his crib and see that another baby—perhaps one he had come to believe was his friend—wasn't in his crib that night, or even the next night, or the night after that. The crib of Bob's friend could, without warning, suddenly belong to a new baby. Perhaps the stork that brought the new babies decided to take the bundles back.

The nurses had told him he was a big boy when they hugged him earlier that day before he left St. Margaret's. He received so many squeezes and kisses that he lost count. He felt bad when one of the nurses cried as she waved good-bye. But Bob knew she would feel better as soon as he returned to his house. He would hug her first.

It is a hot day, and the nurse rolls the window down halfway, so that he will feel, as she says, Cool. He loves the fresh air and breathes it in and out copiously. It is not the same air Bob is used to breathing, so he opens his mouth wide and sticks his face as close as he can to the window, catching the air as it drops sideways onto his tongue. He blows it out slowly like he is blowing out a candle on a birthday cake. When he thinks about why he likes the air so much, he has sketchy memories of nurses wrapping him in a blanket, warmed by hot-water bottles, as he was carried outside on the porch. They sang lullabies to him, even in the wintertime when snowflakes make funny, chilly freckles on his small red cheeks.

He knew of snow, he knew of the warm feeling of the sun, and he also knew of rain. Rain felt just like the water when he wet his cloth diapers, until a nurse changed him. But the joy of experiencing rain was brief, because when he and the other children played outside, sometimes on their tricycles riding around a little loop, the nurses called for them to hurry back inside at the sight of the first sprinkle.

But on this day, a ripple of rain begins. Before the nurse is able to close his window, rain pours into the car and falls on Bob's cotton shorts. It seems to him that it's time to end this adventure and return home. Instead, he and the nurse keep moving along.

The boy is amazed at how many people with children holding their hands are walking on the sidewalk as he passes by, and how many more ride in the big toy cars that roll all over the street. They are honking their horns and waving flags and smiling happily as they make their way to what the nurse calls, Downtown, Governor's Mansion.

Isn't this an exciting day? the nurse asks as she waves from her window at the growing crowds passing by.

The boy smiles, too. He has finally figured out what this is about. These people are blowing their horns and colorful tin toots because it is Bob's third birthday—obviously an important number, considering that for a gift he also gets a real car ride.

He thinks back over the day so far: First, all the nurses hugged him, and now all this commotion. He jumps up and down in the car until he realizes that something is missing.

He looks up and asks the nurse, Where is the Robert birthday song?

The nurse smiles. She doesn't answer him, and he's not sure why. As he glances over at her he sees she has pulled an envelope out of her bag and now carries it in her hand closest to his. Inside the envelope are his transfer papers, which clearly state that the beautiful little boy with light brown hair and expansive brown eyes, so wide with wonderment, is not available for adoption. His papers had been stamped in bold red ink with the word NEVER.

But he does not know that.

As the boy and the nurse pass through the giant entrance to the Albany Orphan Asylum—as it was then called—at 140 New Scotland Avenue, he cannot believe his eyes. This place is huge. He can see there are six large red-brick houses with tall white columns, shutters, and porches, all facing a giant wading pool a hundred times bigger than the bathtub at his house. He is dazzled by the vision of another world of children before him. Instead of just babies like he has always known, there are boys and girls. Some look his age, but most look older.

Maybe he really is a big boy now. He is pleased to think that three birthdays means that he is old enough to take a trip to look at new children for his special day.

The nurse opens the car's door and leads him into the largest house, where he sees another nurse. Her white dress is different from his nurse's and she does not wear a boat cap. Her hair is not yellow, brown, black, or red—the rainbow of colors his nurses have. Instead, her hair is gray and her forehead has been etched with little lines. Her skin resembles a giant raisin.

While the nurses talk, Bob smiles at them both when he hears them say *birthday* and *Robert* but as they continue, they seem especially enchanted with the word *Roosevelt*. When they finish speaking, his nurse says, Good-bye. The little boy follows her to the door, but the other nurse bellows his name as if she were a train conductor.

Raaaaaaah-berrrrrrrrt!

Ah, yes. He did not remember the rules. He cannot believe he forgot his manners, but it has been a strange day. Quickly, he scampers all the way back to where the new nurse is standing and waves at her and says, 'Bye. Then he turns and runs toward the front door, hurrying to catch up with his nurse.

But by the time he gets there, he sees her through the window in the now closed and locked door. She is walking back the way they came in. She has left him. She has made a mistake. She forgot to take his hand, and Bob cries out.

The new nurse kneels down to be closer to him, and he hears her say, among other things, New home.

He stammers through his tears and says, No, my house.

The boy flattens his hand on the windowpane as the rain begins to fall again and the children outside race back to their cottages from the yard. He has never had such a miserable birthday. It rains outside, it rains from his eyes, and it feels like the rain is everywhere.

He wonders to himself, Where *is* Robert?

A Mother's Cradle

It is cold outside in the small town of Watervliet, near Albany, as two adults and two young girls exit the front door of their house on Broadway. There it is: the gray-shingled box house with a red door. The older woman leading the way is my great-grandmother, Mrs. Ella Primmer. She has dressed her two granddaughters, Elaine, now three but ready to turn four in less than a month's time, and Mary, older by a year and two months, in their Sunday finest. Along with their grandfather, Mr. Reed Primmer, the group walks toward Third Avenue, after first passing First and Second Avenues. On Third Avenue, they will catch the Number 22 bus before it transfers at Fulton Street in order to get to Oakwood Avenue in Troy.

Mary and Elaine are excited. They have been visiting with their grandparents and now they are going to visit their mother. Their father will be there, too. They've seen very little of him since their mother went away. They can't help but be anxious, as it has been a week, or maybe longer, since they last saw her. It feels like much too long of a time and they miss her. They miss her kisses on their rosy cheeks. They miss when she bends down and picks them up in order to be clutched near her breast where her warm face touches the cove of their necks. They want to build snowmen with her. As she impatiently waits for the bus, the fierce wind rushing across the frozen snowdrifts on the banks of the Hudson River only a few blocks north knocks Elaine away from the snowman she has started to build. She falls to the ground, and her coat is now dusted with snow.

Elaine, come to Grandmother. Let me wipe away the snowflakes. There, there. You needn't cry. Mary, please take your sister's other hand so she doesn't fall again. Grandmother sees the yellow-and-red bus coming. Elaine, start counting, one, two, three, and the bus will be here in no time at all.

Their grandfather, Boppy, has always been quiet, but he seems even more so today. Elaine thinks maybe he doesn't like buses. He wants to drive his car. But the snow is too heavy and the winds are too powerful. Hardly any black cars are on the road today. This is fine with Elaine. She loves the bus, as does Mary.

The bus is more fun than a car ride, and Boppy bought his first car only that summer. On the bus, you get to look at all the other people sitting with you. The bus riders always smile at Elaine and Mary. Today, the sisters know the passengers will look at them and comment on how pretty they look in the beautiful dresses their grandmother just made them on her sewing machine. Mary and Elaine will open their coats to show the riders their outfits, considering their grandmother worked so hard on making red-and-green woolen dresses for today's special occasion.

With their grandparents seated behind them, Elaine and Mary look around at the faces of everyone now traveling with them. And so it begins . . .

Little girls, you look darling in your dresses. Did your mother make those for you?

No, Mary says, Grammy did.

Mommy made my birthday dress, says Elaine.

She puts up four fingers into the air and raises them high trying to reach the top of the bus, and says, January, Elaine birthday.

The bus moves cautiously through the streets of Watervliet and then into

Troy. There, they transfer to a second bus that slowly moves down the icy streets across town. On this late afternoon, Elaine and Mary, with their grandparents, are making their way to St. Mary's Hospital.

It is two nights before Christmas Eve, and Santa will be at their house in just a few days, hopefully with new dolls for Elaine and Mary to rock in their shared wooden cradle.

Remember what I have asked of you, says their grandmother upon their arrival at the hospital. Make your mother proud. Let her hear your beautiful voices.

Elaine and Mary walk down the polished sterile-smelling hallway of St. Mary's, following in the steps of their grandmother. Their grandfather lags behind. The doors in front of the rooms where people are sleeping are decorated with Christmas cards. Before they enter their mother's room, they see taped on her door all the Christmas cards that they have made with construction paper.

They enter her dimly lit room, running to the sides of her bed and both of them asking if they can crawl in bed with her. Their father is there, but he does not look at them. He stands off to the side now with Boppy, both men with their hands holding their caps, looking downward toward the polished white floor.

Their mother is sleeping. She has never been this quiet. But when Elaine and Mary pull on her flannel nightgown, she opens her blue eyes and looks at them with a sad smile. It's not the happy smile Ora Kirby normally gives her two daughters.

Sitting on her bed, Elaine holds her mother's dainty fingers with her wedding and engagement rings while Mary holds her mother's other hand.

Mommy, come home, says Elaine.

Mommy, it's almost Christmas. Can I help you bake cookies? asks Mary.

Now is the time, their grandmother says. Mary, you know the words and you are the oldest. We've been practicing this. You start, and Elaine will follow.

And so Mary begins in a strong voice as if she were the one leading the shepherds on a procession to Bethlehem.

Silent night, holy night,
All is calm, all is bright . . .

Elaine catches on. Just as expected, she begins to hum, and sings some of the words from the simple verses. While the sisters sing to their mother, who has closed her eyes again, their pure voices trail down the long corridor. At the door, doctors and nurses have gathered to listen to their singing.

Why does their singing make all the grown-ups cry—even their father, Grammy, and Boppy? When they practiced the song at their grandmother's house, no one had cried. What is different now?

Kiss your mother, says their father quietly as he walks over in order to lift them down from the bed.

Say good-bye.

Later that night, their young mother, just twenty-five years old, went on her journey to heavenly peace, alone, without her two little girls.

It is Christmas Day, 1936. Elaine and Mary's grandmother seems to be preparing food in the kitchen for a party. Beside the Christmas tree surrounded by toys is a wooden box just like a cradle but bigger. Inside it is their mother dressed in a new white lace nightgown. Her coffin has been placed by a large bay window looking out onto their street, beneath a ceramic statue of the Infant Jesus of Prague with its beatific smile, childlike innocence, and purity of soul.

Not long after my grandmother's death from peritonitis, my aunt Mary and my mother were abandoned by their father. He left his young daughters without even saying good-bye. He walked into the snowy winds, leaving them behind to be orphans. And they could have been sent to the Albany Home for Children, had not fate stepped in and wrapped the two little girls in its loving arms.

> *Oh! hush thee, my baby, the night is behind us,*
> *And black are the waters that sparkled so green.*
> *The moon, o'er the combers, looks downward*
> *   to find us*
> *At rest in the hollows that rustle between.*
> *Where billow meets billow, there soft be thy pillow;*

Ah, weary wee flipperling, curl at thy ease!
The storm shall not wake thee, nor shark overtake thee,
Asleep in the arms of the slow-swinging seas.
—Rudyard Kipling, "Seal Lullaby" from
The Jungle Book*

---

* Kipling's foster father died soon after Kipling was placed in their home. In his later works, he referred to his foster mother as "The Woman," her son as "The Devil," and their home as "The House of Desolation."

Flip-Flops

As I walk around the inside of our house, I fall in love with a small area attached to our living room, which has a sliding glass door directly in front of the formal dining table. There we would one day eat our Thanksgiving, Christmas, and Easter dinners, and blow out the candles of our birthday cakes; my parents would sip their coffee at that table every morning before my father went off to work.

Looking through the door, you could almost see my entire backyard—all its acres, all its yards, and all its many feet. I immediately felt that the children who lived on our property were my new goldfish to watch and study through this glass door—even if I didn't get to choose my favorites from the tank like I did at Woolworth's by scooping out the most beautiful ones until they wiggled their way into a plastic bag. I had always been the protector of our goldfish bowl. Perhaps now I would be the protector of the backyard children's bowl.

That first late afternoon in our new house, the sun is not yet ready to fall from the sky, just slightly drooping and rose-colored at its rim, as Jimmy, Mandy, Billy, and I stand outside on our patio. My father wants us to walk over to the Home's pool as a family. He wants to lead the way that first day, even if we had driven over from our old house to swim in this same pool countless times before, ever since Jimmy and I first learned to flap our wings in the water. We would inch farther and farther away from our mother who, when we were younger, would sit on the stairs leading down to the water, wearing her pink bathing suit with the frilly white apron attached to it and a matching pink-and-white cap on her head because Jimmy and I used to splash too much and she didn't want her hair wet like ours.

Because we now lived at the Home, our swim time would be from noon until one o'clock and then again from five to six. It was our swimming pool, but not really. We shared it with the other children who had their own time slots. We could start our walk over to the pool no sooner than five minutes before our hour, which seemed unfair because if you see a pool, you want to be in it, just like the ocean. You want to do cannonballs and belly flops and hold your breath underwater until you just about explode. I didn't understand having a specified time slot to swim. Since we were all just children either living in our house or in the cottages next door, it didn't seem right that we couldn't all be frolicking there together morning, noon, and into the night. And when it finally got too cold to swim, then you made the decision that you wanted a dry towel around your shoulders and it was time to put your flip-flops back on and leave.

While we wait, Jimmy and I whip our towels against each other's legs, making a snapping sound like a Thanksgiving wishbone breaking into two. The twins Mandy and Billy keep running away from the cement patio, with its different-colored slate stones sandwiched inside the place where our father told us to stay. They head toward the small woods outside our bedroom windows, which are difficult to see from the patio. My father hollers for Mandy and Billy to come back. We didn't dare leave because the sound of his holler is much more powerful than Jimmy and me combined, but the twins don't seem to feel the chill of his roar. They giggle, run, and don't return until my father darts to the right of our patio and brings them back, one draped over each shoulder, like little fearless weighted pillows, still giggling away because every-thing made them laugh. Everything was funny to them.

Jimmy and I had never been that carefree. We wonder about this new place. Jimmy thinks all the boy children at the Home will be his new friends, and I hope all the girl children will be mine. We want to go to the pool so that we can talk to them and figure out who will be our best friends and then de-cide who will be just a friend—a notch below best friend. Best friends slept over. Friends just came to your birthday party and brought new toys. You were always nice to those kinds of friends on your birthday because you wanted them to come back to your party the following year with another wrapped gift. Still, they would not be among the select with whom you would share your pillow and blanket. Jimmy and I are both on the lookout for new best friends, and it seems that just outside our window we have a whole dime-store-ful to choose from.

Right before five o'clock, we make our way over to the large swimming pool. We walk away from the patio in a single file, all wearing new swimsuits that my mother chose to match the colors of our new blankets atop our beds. Jimmy wears blue trunks, Billy wears green, and Mandy has on a one-piece red Speedo. I wear yellow, and Sarah wears pink, the color that also defined my youngest years. Slung over our shoulders are new colorful towels from my mother's shopping spree at Sears. Our parade of matching-colored flip-flops shuffle across the grass toward the pool.

As he leads the way, holding Sarah in his arms, my father looks taller than he really is. His new job makes him look taller. My mother decides to stay home to arrange—and then rearrange—the pots and pans in the kitchen. She is very quiet that first day. It hurts my heart to see her cry as she scrubs each pan with a Brillo pad before putting them away in the new cupboards. My father asked me and Jimmy to be gentle with her. I don't think Jimmy and I knew how to be any other way, but we left her alone, occasionally peeking at her through-out the day to make sure she hadn't gone away because of her sadness. It was like we had moved into our new house, but she hadn't moved in yet. Hopefully, she would move in tomorrow. Our mother was everything to us.

It seemed as though my mother and father had traded places and smiles that first day. I don't recall ever seeing my father that cheerful. Something in his blue eyes behind his brown horn-rimmed glasses twinkled like the stars

Jimmy and I stared at through the lenses of our telescope made from a Charmin toilet paper roll. My father had a wide smile on his face that looked like he was the happiest, luckiest man in the world—all because we had just moved into a new house and his job was right in our backyard. He said, I promise you, kids, this is our forever home.

I wonder if, in all his excitement, he forgot to say those same comforting words to my mother. My mother loves the word *forever*. She uses it in every story she tells us, and it is in the last phrase she says to us before she tucks us into our beds at night after reciting our favorite nursery rhymes. I love you forever. How far is forever? Forever is even farther away than Cape Cod.

We stayed close to our father as my brothers, sisters, and I walked diagonally across the lawn, passing the brick gymnasium on the left side. Jimmy and I knew it contained a big blue trampoline. My father promised that at some point soon he will bring the trampoline out onto the lawn. Jimmy asked my father if he could jump to the moon. Jimmy was getting kind of weird.

It wasn't until we passed the gymnasium that our flip-flops finally touched our favorite part of the driveway that wound through our backyard. We used to be so jealous whenever we were at the Home and saw the children riding their bicycles around and around the loop, like a colorful bike carousel.

We knew all about the twists and turns of the driveway from the many times we drove over to the pool or visited Cammy and Brad. When you drove in, your car immediately had to go slow once it went over the speed bump. It was more fun when my mother was driving, because she always forgot about the speed bump and our car would fly through the air. It felt like we were on the roller coaster at Hoffman's Playland, where we went whenever my mother said my father had saved enough money. My father had been working at the Home since I was six months old, and he never forgot the speed bump. He went superslowly over the bump. After the bump, the steering wheel had a choice of turning right or going straight past the sign surrounded by flowers, which read: THE ALBANY HOME FOR CHILDREN. The car couldn't turn toward your left hand because then it would plow through the small woods and end up in my bedroom and I would be dead.

If your car went to the right, it meant you probably worked with the children, because the driveway went all the way back to the last of the ranch cottages. Each had its own name. There was Winnie Cottage, like Pooh, and then there was Lansing, Rathbone, and finally Wasson Cottage. Past the cottages there was a small hill where my father taught Jimmy and me how to ski the winter after we each turned three and four. On special nights he sometimes drove us over so that we could run our sleds down the snowy slope. Our house looked like a smaller version of the cottages, but it didn't have an official name. That was okay because my mother said it would be called Carswell Cottage after our last name.

If you didn't drive to the right toward the back of the cottages, the driveway kept going all the way back past our favorite loop. Your car could go around and around the loop all day if you wanted. I vowed that when I was old enough to drive, that would be the first thing I would do. I would do it as often as I could, driving our family car around and around our backyard loop, faster and faster until it melted into whipped butter like I once saw on a cartoon.

After the loop, if you decided to go straight, your car passed the pool on the right and the giant swing set on the left. You would be headed to the area in the back near the marshes. Jimmy said the marsh was full of yellow and black snakes. At the edge of the marsh was an old brick building where Jimmy said a mad doctor dissected people's heads and bodies, and put their hearts in large sealed jars just like you would do with huge dill pickles. That scared me especially because when Jimmy told me the story in front of my father for like the one hundredth time, my father said it was sort of true. Usually, my father told Jimmy, Stop telling fibs to your sister.

The loop was kitty-corner to the gym and right in front of a big old three-story building that didn't look like it belonged on our property at all. My father explained this was the building where the children went to school, and where some of the people who worked on our property lived—including Miss Mary Fundis, the beautiful cook who always wore a dress with a neat white apron tied around it and a matching hair net. Brent lived in the same building, too. He was a friendly and handsome man who played with the children during the day and had a little brown hot dog named Marnie. My mother loved to kiss Marnie smack on her black poop nose.

The old tall building, named Parsons Cottage, looked lonely. It seemed as if it should be on the college property next door. Similar to the college buildings on the other side of the simple diamond-linked fence, it was like each building could look at itself in the mirror and see they were twins. Not twins like Mandy and Billy, who neither looked alike nor dressed alike, but like the twins in my favorite movie, *The Parent Trap.* You couldn't tell Hayley Mills from the other Hayley Mills.

I felt bad for that lonely building. It missed being with the other buildings it seemed related to. The more I thought about it—and my mother and father said I thought way too much about things—I think someone must have made a mistake when they put that fence up, leaving Parsons Cottage behind. The fence men had forgotten to put it on the college side and now the cottage was left on our side.

When I asked my father why it was there, he simply said to me, History, Susan. It was good he kept the history subject short, because we had been learning the names of presidents in our first-grade class right before school ended for the summer and I had gotten confused about all the names and who had come first and who went last and why anyone would kill that man on TV, considering he had been a president, which was such an important job. The president, God, and now my father were the ones with really big jobs. Anyway, history was school's hardest subject, and I certainly didn't want to study more of this unpleasant subject at home just because it was a building living in my backyard.

As we continued walking to the pool that first day, my father promised Jimmy and me that we could ride our bikes around the loop for as long as we wanted the next day right after church—or the Quiet Place as we once thought of it. Now Jimmy and I just thought of church as the Boring Place. We would have preferred it if St. Ronald McDonald had his own church for bored children.

Our flip-flops move closer and closer to our pool, and finally we are at the meeting place where Jimmy and I will soon choose our new best friends. As we approach the fence, the children standing on the inside while we stand on the outside look right into our eyes. Suddenly, they start shrieking and screaming like they were seeing ghosts.

New best friends don't usually act that way.

A Loop of Our Own

Some of the kids at the pool look like they are my and Jimmy's age, but a couple look younger. No one is a baby like Sarah. I don't know what makes them cry like this. Jimmy and I don't cry like that. It's kind of a howl, like wolves baying at the moon. The children's teeth chatter. Is it from fear, or because they just got out of the cool water? I don't ask my father because he doesn't understand children the way my mother does. He just seems to be a really good boss of kids. Maybe some of the black children scream because we are white. But that doesn't make sense because just as many of the white children and the light brown ones are now screaming as well. There must have been about fifteen children getting out of the pool as they first lay eyes on us and we on them. Only four are girls—which means Jimmy has more to choose from for a best friend, at least in this group.

Thankfully, though, there are other nonscreaming children and lots of them. Directly behind the pool, I see them playing on the swings in front of their cottages. Some are being given hot dogs in a roll by Miss Mary Fundis. She cooks them on the grill in the middle area of eight picnic tables, which are painted the same barn-red color as our old house.

It seems that for every five children there is one grown-up who watches over them like a mom or a dad. But on this early night as some of the Home children eat their supper and the others get out of the pool, it's like our backyard has become a place where everyone yells, cries, or stands completely scared like we're hungry grizzly bears that have finally hunted them down. I try to put my hand through the fence toward a girl with blond hair like me, to let her know I am friendly, but my father looks over at me sharply and hollers, Susan, no!

Now I feel scared, too. I fear his yell. Am I becoming the one he thinks of as the bad one? Have I tired him out with all my fears and sleepless nights? Maybe I have exhausted him by being me. But I am not yet even seven, and we will be spending forever together.

I am reminded of a day just a month earlier. My brothers and sisters and I were playing in the sand in Cape Cod and started to fight over the new pail. Sharing a pail didn't make sense. We didn't listen to our mother when she told us to stop. She had to call for my father to leave the porch of Hopkins Cottage—where we vacationed each summer—in order to break up the fight. My father had been drinking gin with Half & Half soda (which tasted even better than lime Kool-Aid because it had this instant kick). With him was my mother's sister, Aunt Mary, Uncle Ed, my grandmother with a beehive hairdo, my very nice grandfather whom my grandmother called Wat (you know, like *What*, but spelled *W-A-T* because his name was Watson Carswell), and Aunt Helen (although she wasn't an official aunt but rather a cousin but she was old like my grandmother so it seemed awfully weird to think of Helen as a cousin so we called her an aunt). My mother would often make my father break up our nastier fights. She did not have the yelling power in her lungs to do the job as well as he did.

In the way that it was hard back in Cape Cod to calm us down over a pail, it now seems that the adults at the pool are having the same problems with the children. Pretty soon more of the adults leave Miss Mary Fundis's hot-dog-grilling area and run toward the pool, opening the gate to help out.

I'm so sorry, Mr. Carswell, some of the adults say to my father.

All I want to know is: What is happening?

Jimmy's frown gets all crunched up and his head tilts downward toward his right shoulder—the look he uses whenever he can't put together a word for Scrabble and my mother has to help him. Mandy and Billy start to cry so hard that they each drop to the ground and crawl under my father's legs like he is their green pitch tent without the hiding cloth.

My father points for Jimmy to take the twins, and for me to carry Sarah back to the grass by the bicycle loop area. We are to wait there until he says we can come back to the pool. The twins continue to cry, and Sarah is heavy in my arms. Finally, I have to let her down, keeping hold of her diaper so she won't run away and get killed by a car on Academy Road. That's the way my mind naturally wanders, right toward car crashes, blood, and gore. We look back over to the pool and listen in shock as my father yells at those children in a way that he has never yelled at us. Perhaps it is three times louder than the yell we got because there are three times the amount of kids at the pool.

But just like the paralyzing spell he has over us, when my father yells at the other children they stop their screaming as quickly as the speed of a snap. The children wipe away their quieter tears with their beach towels instead of wiping the wet pool water covering their bodies and their messy hair.

When my father opens the gate, our new best friends slowly shuffle away from the pool in not-so-brand-new flip-flops (like the ones we have). Some are even broken at the exact part where the plastic stem separates your big toe from the second biggest one. Single file, they head back to their cottage, teeth chattering and goose bumps covering their bodies, turning back as they walk in order to stare at us. We stare back. The only difference between our stares is that the children's mouths neither smile nor look sad. They are frozen in place like a Popsicle stick that hasn't yet been touched by a warm tongue.

It seems like they fear us, but Jimmy and I still smile back at them. We are full of hope. We look forward to the time when we will be invited over to their picnic tables and handed hot dogs in a bun cooked by Miss Mary Fundis. Maybe we will even get to spread as much butter as we possibly can on the corn on the cob, like the time my mother wasn't looking and Jimmy took a whole stick of butter and swabbed it around and around his ear of corn until there was none left for anyone else. Jimmy got in so much trouble for doing that. My father said to my mother, Elaine, this wouldn't have been so costly if we bought margarine.

Horror had filled my mother's stormy eyes then, and she had replied, *Jesus, Mary, and Joseph, John*. I will not save our money when it comes to buying butter.

The children walk into their cottage with the red door, and the shiny brass doorknob closes behind them. Only now does my father signal me and Jimmy to bring the twins and Sarah back over to the pool. Jimmy and I are careful about standing too close to our father that first night we swim in the pool. We don't want any of the other children—who are still eating more and more of Miss Mary Fundis's hot dogs in a bun and staring over at us every time they take a bite—to think that just because our father is with us doesn't mean we yell the same mean way, too. We want those children to see that our father is just this guy who brought Jimmy and me over to the pool, like a tough, yelling babysitter, and we don't actually know him that well. We are on their side. Kids stick with kids, and adults stick with adults. Except maybe my mother: She doesn't yell at children with the commanding voice my father does. She is very in between.

We swim for an hour. It isn't even a good swim on account of the fact that our mother isn't there to watch and clap her hands whenever we try some new trick. The lifeguard now blows his whistle to signal that our time is over. Our mother would have said to the twins, Pool needs to go Night-Night, but our father just says, Time's up. Out. Towels and flip-flops. Let's go.

We make our way home—kind of a weird thing to even think because it's strange that we had one home this morning and another a couple of hours later. I ask my father when we can have a party and cookout with our new friends so that Jimmy and I can pick out our best friends.

Best friends? He repeats this in the same tone of voice he used when I once asked if our whole family could go to Disneyland for the entire summer. Then he shakes his head and says, Sue, those children will never be your best friends.

His answer to my question now is as baffling as the no reply he gave me when I asked him about a Disneyland summer. Why not? I ask.

Because you'll make other friends.

But I want those friends. I point to the children now watching Miss Mary Fundis scooping out ice cream to make sundaes.

It won't happen. That's all my father says, meaning he now thinks the subject is closed.

Will happen, I shout back at him, but he is now running after the twins. They are heading toward the small woods again instead of our patio.

I continue to walk, holding Sarah's hand, our flip-flops passing the loop and making their way across the freshly cut grass on our side of the backyard. I try to ignore in my head what my father has said, although it's hard to stop my thoughts. I refuse to believe that not one of the children will ever lie right next to me in my small twin bed and share my soft pillow. I can't believe that we will never have the chance to stuff as many kernels of Jolly Time popcorn in our mouths as we can, or giggle together about Jimmy and that dinky thing growing in his underwear before we go off to sleep. Aren't they just children like me and Jimmy? Since when does anyone's father pick out their best friend?

The next morning as our family sits in the middle pew at St. Teresa's Holy Holy Holy Catholic Church on New Scotland Avenue, Jimmy and I look for the children's faces we got only a sneak peek of at the pool. We can't spot any of the children in the crowded church. We see only mothers and fathers with their children, all of whom are well behaved. Throughout the entire Mass, we continue to try to look for any of the children who live in our backyard, because it is much more fun than listening to the priest talk about the Lord. Amen.

Jimmy and I finally figure out that none of the children in our backyard are at St. Teresa's Holy Holy Holy Catholic Church when it dawns on us that not one black boy is sitting on the hard seats or kneeling with his bumpers touching the pew in the way we did. Nor is there one black girl with colorful barrettes sitting in any pew, in all the many aisles throughout the big church, which is rather dark except where the sun has slipped past the stained-glass windows full of pictures of God and Jesus and Mary. Jimmy says God, Jesus, and the Lord are the same people, but he's wrong because they are three different men, just relatives like Aunt Helen is to us.

As soon as we drive home from St. Teresa's, Jimmy and I immediately change out of our dreaded Sunday church clothes. We really hope no one saw us in them, because that type of clothing could quite possibly keep me and Jimmy best-friend-less for life. We put on our play clothes and are hoping we can share the loop with the Home children today. Hopefully, without all that screaming.

After taking our bikes off the rack in the garage attached to our house, Jimmy and I pedal over to the right of our house, down the small path of the woods outside our bedroom windows, and make our way to the loop.

Not one other child is there.

Jimmy and I must have really bad luck.

I ride my purple bicycle around the loop, leaning my bumper far back on the white vinyl banana seat, which slopes upward. I put my left hand on the three-speed handle. My right hand loosely holds on to the metal brake. I extend my back almost three-quarters of the way to the rear, the same position I would be in if I was lying on Uncle Ed's La-Z-Boy rocker with its leg rest up.

I always sneak onto his Holy Chair, as my mother calls it, whenever Uncle Ed takes a bathroom break from the Sunday-afternoon football game on our frequent trips to visit him and Aunt Mary and our cousin Laurie who is six years older than me. Jimmy and I think she is cool. She is very pretty with long dark brown hair. She looks just like Mandy, but my mother said that Laurie was adopted so it was just coincidence that she and Mandy looked like sisters.

Mandy is the only one of us who doesn't have beach-looking blond hair, so every now and then back in our old house Jimmy and I would make Mandy sit down in a chair, and as we held her prisoner we told her that she was an orphan so we adopted her, and that was why she had brown hair. Mandy didn't understand this game so she cried, then my mother came into our old TV room and immediately turned off *Batman* even though it was right in the middle of the show and not on a commercial break. She said to Jimmy and me, You two can be very, very nasty children. I want you to talk to God about this in church on Sunday. Then she stormed out of the room, scooping brown-haired orphaned Mandy up into her arms and wiping Mandy's tears away with the side of her cheek.

With just my hands on the handlebar to protect me from doing a somersault off the rear of my bike, I ride around the loop until I count one hundred circles. Still my new best friends have not come out to play. I wait and wait and play the orphan game in my head. I pretend my parents have been killed in a car crash and—although of course I am sad—I will live in a world of children and toys and games, minus adults. We will live together in a big home and laugh with no one to yell at us.

Finally, however, I see them.

Dressed like they are going to church, the Home children come outside. A couple of them walk together past their cottages and stand right on the grass strip that is in front of the empty parking slots lined with thick yellow marks. When they get to the spot where the grass ends, it is clear that they are not to put their foot an inch farther onto the pavement. The boys slip their hands in their pockets and stare at me and Jimmy as we continue riding our bikes. A couple of times the black girls in barrettes come over in their Sunday dresses.

A girl who looks a lot like Mandy with big brown eyes, long, dark eyelashes, rosy pink cheeks, and short hair framed with curls tries to cross the line, and I hear an adult scream out to her, Jodie, you know the rules. Reluctantly, she takes a tiny step backward.

Jodie. What a cool name. Jodie will be my new best friend.

Unlike Jimmy and me, the children and the one named Jodie stayed in their Sunday clothes the entire day. Occasionally, a car slowly entered and passed the ALBANY HOME FOR CHILDREN sign and some of the kids ran over to the space to see who would get out. As soon as they could see the face of the visitor, one of the children would run to the car and melt into the arms of whoever had arrived, in the same way we ran into my mother's arms when she went away to the hospital only to come home and give us Sarah.

My father had once explained to me and Jimmy that forty-eight children lived in the cottages, which meant sixteen kids slept behind each red door with the brass doorknobs. Still, on that first Sunday only three cars drove up and parked next to the sign that read, VISITORS ONLY. Only three children jumped into the arms of their mothers or fathers or whoever they were, and so that meant that the others I saw just looked like they were getting sadder as the day grew longer and the sun began drooping in the sky. When I looked at the sad children, those who remained looked like they had glued their hands together. I think they were praying.

But no more cars came.

Right before it was time for Miss Mary Fundis to cook their supper, several kids made a last-minute dash to the VISITORS sign, turned toward their left, and waited on tiptoes for someone to drive through the entrance and bounce over the speed bump so that they could jump into someone's arms as well.

It didn't happen. Instead, they were called to eat dinner by Miss Mary Fundis, who sang the word *supper* the same way you would sing a beautiful Christmas song like "Rudolph." The children made their way back toward the picnic tables only after they took the hand of one of the adults who had to go over and get them, one by one, and help them stop crying. It was the first time I saw the children taking the hand of an adult all by themselves and not having to share an adult like they did at the pool. Perhaps it was their special treat for the day since God hadn't listened to their prayers for a visit from their mom or their dad.

On that first Sunday night, we had our first family picnic at 60 Academy Road. For dessert, we had a chocolate birthday cake with candles to celebrate our new life in our new house.

The day before, my father had placed our old picnic table on the patio outside the sliding glass door. When I asked my father if we could move our picnic table next to the other children's picnic tables, he said, No. Stays here.

My father was smart and all, but even fathers get things wrong because today—which Jimmy and I counted as the day our mother really moved into our house because her tears were now gone—she made my father move the picnic table to the left side of the patio so that our family could have more privacy from the peering eyes of just about anyone who cared to look over at our house.

When she first saw where he had placed the picnic table she looked absolutely horrified and said to him, Oh, John. It shouldn't go there. Honey, what were you thinking?

After eating our moving-day birthday cake and while my mother cleared away the dishes, I asked my father why the children weren't at church that day.

They have their church right in their cottages, he explained.

But then that's not church, I said. Who wouldn't want to stay home and watch cartoons in their pajamas at the same time as having church?

It's not like that and it's not what you think, he said. Most of these children are not used to going to church. It would be difficult for the staff to make sure they behaved.

Who were the people who came for a visit today? I asked.

Some were visited by an aunt or uncle, he said, now getting up from the table because sometimes I knew he just wanted to avoid my relentless inquisition and he would prefer to be with my mother even if it meant doing dishes with her. Then he said, A couple of them saw their fathers. I think I saw a mother.

When I asked why all of them didn't get to have a visit by their mother or father he thought about my question a while and said, Because it's safe here. Most of them were never safe living with their mother or their father before. Some will never go home. And then my father walked away.

I wondered to myself, how could that be? At the end of every good story everyone goes home.

Perhaps the orphan life I had imagined for myself while riding my bike was not too far from the truth for the children in my new backyard. But my father wouldn't tell me. By myself, I would have to figure out this increasingly complicated riddle of where I now lived.

Someday Sundays

For the first two weeks at his new residence, Bob Wygant is confined to the Albany Orphan Asylum's quarantine quarters on the second floor of the administration building. The nurses wash him down in a vinegar bath and shave his brown hair while also checking it for lice. Even though he came directly from St. Margaret's, all orphans and abandoned children arriving at the Asylum go through the same admission procedure.

Only after he has been thoroughly examined by a physician and several medical students for signs of contagious diseases and vaccinated for smallpox is Bob moved into Lathrop Baby Cottage, which houses orphans between the ages of three and six. Lathrop is the only house where boys and girls live together. When a child turns six, he or she is moved into the appropriate all-boy or all-girl cottage.

For days, Bob searches for another child to cling to in his new world. At his other house, there had always been a kind nurse to give him a smile or a hug. Here, things are different. Everyone is busy. There are so many boys and girls in Lathrop Cottage, and at least a hundred others—the bigger boys and girls—living in the other four cottages. There aren't enough grown-ups to go around.

Lathrop's housemother, Mrs. Dugan, is a kind older woman, a widow who understands inconsolable loss after losing her husband so young. She wears colorful floral dresses and plays with the children. Mrs. Dugan is assisted by several young housemistresses-in-training, as well as older girls from Parsons and Rathbone Cottages who often help out in the baby cottage to earn income to supplement their weekly allowances.

At night, Mrs. Dugan reads the children story after story before, with maternal solicitude, she tucks each of them into their little white cast-iron beds.

Not all the other housemothers are as nice as Mrs. Dugan. Bob has heard that one housemother whipped some of the older boys who misbehaved. Another housemother, it is said, counts every raisin each night and if even one is missing, the girls in her cottage are forced to stay awake all night, or until the raisin thief confesses her guilt.

Mrs. Dugan isn't like that. While Bob and the other children in Lathrop Cottage learn at an early age that they must do chores, she teaches them how to wax the floors with their heavy socks by skating through the kitchen, dining, and living rooms downstairs and bedrooms upstairs to make the floors sparkle.

All the boys and girls who are too young to go to elementary school attend kindergarten on the first floor of the administration building. Every day after classes, everyone—even the little ones—has chores to do. Afterward, there is time to play.

In cold weather, the water freezes in the large circular wading pond that had so attracted Bob that first day when he came to the Asylum, providing the children with their very own skating rink. Every cottage has its own sets of skates for each boy and girl. The Lathrop children take great joy in pushing Mrs. Dugan around the icy surface on her wobbly skates.

In the warm months, Bob and his new friends, with their housemother standing by, play on the swings, pushing themselves higher and higher in order to get the best view of places beyond the orphanage's horizon. Mrs. Dugan also teaches the boys in her care how to play kick-the-can, the most popular game during their growing years. And although she refuses to climb up into their tree forts, Mrs. Dugan waits patiently below, with her arms outstretched, should someone fall.

She teaches them about nature when she leads them to the two gardens at the orphanage, one for the older boys, the other for the older girls, telling them about the life cycles of the flowers and vegetables. She explains how seeds grow and thrive, blossoming as flowers or maturing into fruits and vegetables. She promises the Lathrop children that they, too, are tender shoots who will grow and flourish. But, she assures them, unlike flowers, when the cold winds come, little boys and little girls will not die.

With so many children in her care, Bob thinks that Mrs. Dugan is very much like the lady who lived in a shoe.

On the day he turns six in 1935—the same year the orphanage is renamed the Albany Home for Children—Bob Wygant makes his way from the baby cottage, across the lawn, to Wasson Cottage. Bob has grown tired of crying babies. He will be starting first grade in the fall and is too grown up to live in the baby cottage. He is thankful on this day as he walks up the steps to Wasson Cottage to join the bigger boys. Still, Bob will always miss Mrs. Dugan.

Mr. and Mrs. Scott, his new houseparents, welcome Bob formally, certainly not as warmly as Mrs. Dugan had when he went to live at Lathrop. The couple lead him upstairs to one of the two large bedrooms. Each has sixteen cast-iron beds placed side by side in two rows.

Bob is assigned a corner bed. Beside it is an orange crate for him to place his favorite things: his Buck Rogers disintegrator gun, his flashlight, a yo-yo, a Santa Claus figurine that a housemother-in-training once gave him, and his shiny harmonica. Most of these prized possessions are gifts from Christmases past. That is the only time the orphans get presents. While those who have relatives may receive birthday gifts, there are too many children living in the orphanage and not enough money in the annual budget for birthday celebrations for everyone.

Folded neatly on his bed are a new Sunday outfit and enough clothes for a complete school year. The clothes are hand-me-downs. There is also a new day uniform—a one-piece gray, white, and red jumper. After he puts it on,

Bob walks downstairs where one of the older boys asks him if he wants to play ball.

An older boy, asking him to play. He cannot remember ever being singled out this way. The only other time he remembers feeling special was on his third birthday when the nurse took him for a car ride—the only car ride he has ever taken—and brought him to the orphanage. Outside, George Myers teaches Bob how to catch a real ball—not the big red rubber balls he has always known. When lunchtime comes, George asks Bob to join him at his table. Bob feels like he has been adopted.

But Bob knows what he really is. He now understands the meaning of the word *orphan*. He understands what happens every Sunday afternoon when everyone—even children like him who have no known relatives—have to wait in their cottages in their best clothes in case someone comes to visit.

Bob hates that day of the week. He can't wait for Sunday's interminable afternoon to end so that he will no longer look with hope toward the entranceway to see someone, anyone, who might be coming to visit him.

Bob is hardly the only orphan who spends Sundays alone. His friends Irving Coffin and Charlie Wilsey never have visitors, either. Edna and Caroline LeRoy have a mother who never once bothers to visit. Betty Lappeus and her older sister, Ethel, consider themselves lucky if their mother visits once a year.

Like all days, Sundays begin at 6:30 A.M. with a wake-up call from Mr. Scott. He leads each bedroom of boys into the bathroom for Tooth Drill in front of the thirty-five-foot-long basin. First, Mr. Scott places a teaspoon of powder into each boy's left palm—or right palm for the left-handed brushers. All sixteen boys look at him, waiting for the signal to place the powder on the brush: bottom teeth, one, two, three . . . upper right, one, two, three . . . inside upper left. And again . . .

After breakfast and completing their early-morning chores, which includes helping with the laundry and the ironing and cleaning the kitchen, everyone—both boys and girls—changes into their Sunday best. Then they wait by the side entrance, toward the back of each cottage, for the buses to take them off to one of Albany's churches—Episcopal, Methodist, Presbyterian, Congregational, or Baptist. They have no choice in the matter. The children line up and board the bus in front of them, heading off to their religious denomination of the week. Where they go depends on which turn the bus makes on New Scotland Avenue.

After church, 150 children must stay dressed up just in case someone comes to see them.

When Bob asks his houseparents the Scotts why no one ever visits him, they reply that perhaps someday someone will, but Bob must say his prayers every night and be a good boy. So, in the hope of making his fervent wish to meet his mother and father come true, young Bob dutifully says his prayers as he kneels by his bed each night, and he does all of the right things. And he waits and waits for that Someday Sunday.

Red Light, Green Light

While we sleep, corn-on-the-cob leaves start growing out of Jimmy's and my belly buttons. My mother said that whenever you ate too much, the food becomes like a garden plant inside your stomach and pushes your belly out. She once told us, That's how you get fat and can't run fast. My mother really loved her scale in the bathroom.

Jesus, Mary, and Joseph—John, she would holler to my father if the scale ever went about 2 pounds over 119 pounds. When we heard her say God's relatives' names on the scale we knew what that meant: We would not be able to have the mayonnaise and ketchup all-stirred-together dressing on our salads. Nor would we be able to pour croutons all over the top of our salads so that you couldn't even see the lettuce, cucumbers, and carrots buried down below in our plastic bowls. Instead of Mrs. Paul's Fish Sticks, we have to eat horrible food like broiled cod and steamed vegetables without butter. Butter would not return to the daily menu my mother posted on the refrigerator until she and her scale fell back in love.

Whenever we were on our family diet plan, I put Barbie and her friends on one, too. In her Dream House bathroom, I would stand, hold Barbie on her scale, and then make her holler out, *Jesus, Mary, and Joseph—Ken. Tell Midge and GI Joe, I said, no more fried fish sticks.*

The second night in our new house, long after we go to bed, I hear fire trucks. The horns grow louder as they race faster up the hill from the other end of Academy Road and turn into the entrance of the Home. They go to the immediate right and to the back side of the cottages. They have come to our backyard, and it is just after we move in. Are we now living in a dangerous place? If the cottages burn down, the children will die, including soon-to-be-best-friend Jodie. If there aren't any children left, will we have to move again?

I bolt from my bed when I see the truck's swirling lights, flashing their colors through the white chiffon curtain hanging from my bedroom window. My entire room lights up and blinks red, then white. I run to my parents' room. My mother is up and staring through an open window. She is wearing her light cotton pink nightgown with spaghetti-strap sleeves. It comes down to her knees and keeps her cool all through the summer. We have never had an air conditioner in the same way we have never owned a Cadillac, which is what Jimmy wants. And we don't get to go to Hoffman's Playland to ride the roller coaster and smash each other around in bumper cars every day of the week, which is what I want. My mother says that you have to be rich for all those things and because we don't have them I guess it means we are poor and have to keep our windows open during the summer. When I once asked my mother if we would ever be rich, she said no because my father loved working with children.

After crawling onto my parents' bed, I push myself up and stand on my mother's pillow. I am now beside her, my head about an inch higher than hers. The window next to her side of the bed has the best view of the cottages from our house. While she stands tall and calm, my knees wobble and teeth start chattering in the same way the kids from the cottages had when they got out of the pool and screamed at us.

Where's Dad? I ask. He isn't in their bathroom because the door is wide open and it is all dark inside except for the night-light.

He's inside the cottages, she says calmly. She can be calm because she is a nurse. Sometimes back when we lived in the red house she had to go to the Home with my father when the other nurse called in sick. She was so calm she could even give shots to kids and to Brad and Cammy's mother. None would cry, which is some kind of nurse. But sometimes you can't tell with my calm mother whether things are okay or if you are about to die. Jimmy and I let everyone know exactly what we are feeling.

I don't see smoke, she says. That's a good sign.

Wait, Daddy's *inside* the cottages? I ask in disbelief.

Smoke or no smoke, my father being inside the cottages does not sound like good news. The fire trucks are lined up in the driveway and out onto the street. I can't even count them all because most are hidden from my view.

The fire bell at the Home can still be heard clanging by anyone who lives on Academy Road—except my siblings, who sleep through the entire time our new backyard is about to burn up and all the children and my father are about to die from falling beams and the roaring red and orange flames.

My mother was right about the fire not being a fire-fire. Not long after all the fire trucks came, I spotted my father talking to one of the firemen as he walked back toward his truck. It was impressive to see my father shuffling along the backyard driveway with a fireman, even though he was wearing his light brown leather slippers that Jimmy and I picked out for him for Christmas last year at Macy's. I can see only a little bit of his burgundy-colored pajama bottoms, though, because he had his dark blue robe on and it was tied tightly around his stomach, although he never tied it when he was inside the house. I guess you tie your robe when you speak to firemen out of respect, just like my father wore a tie to church so he could shake the priest's holy hand. When my father headed up the small hill right outside our window, he turned around and waved good-bye to the one fireman as he made his way back to his truck like all the other firemen. They left and drove their big noisy trucks away. It was like a scene out of a scary movie that Jimmy and I weren't supposed to watch because my mother said it would give us nightmares—or give me nightmares, to be precise. Hopefully the firemen wouldn't ever come back again unless they were coming over for a picnic as my father's new best friends.

But a pattern began that night. The firemen came back the very next night and many nights to follow. Sometimes there would be two nights when they wouldn't come and sometimes there would be four. Once in a while, all the fire trucks in Albany would come even twice in one night. It got to the point that I would wake up whenever I heard sirens sounding far off in the distance. I knew they were headed to my backyard.

Every time the fire trucks came, the Home children left their cottages' back doors and stood outside while the adults huddled nearby. The firemen went in to turn off the alarm and check out whether or not there was a real fire. During that first month and then even into the fall, I noticed how the children seemed happy to be outside in their pajamas and slippers. I could hear them laughing and yelling at one another from my window.

I didn't pull it! You pulled it, idiot.

I didn't pull it. You pulled it, moron.

I didn't pull it. You pulled it, shit head.

Asshole.

I hadn't ever before heard some of the words they used. You learn new words every day when you're growing up. When I asked my father what an asshole was he said, Oh, never mind. After I heard another kid say Fuck you one night to a counselor and I asked my father what that word meant, he said, Oh, for Christ's sake, don't say that ever again. And then after I heard one older boy tease a younger boy by saying, *Sod-o-me, Sod-o-me, Sod-o-me,* singing it like it was a song, I asked my mother what that meant. As soon as I said it, replaying the sentence exactly like I thought I had heard it, she shook her head and walked away.

That night when my father came home from work my mother immediately led him to the back bedroom without even talking. I heard her push in the button on the doorknob, locking their door. My parents locked their bedroom door only at 7 A.M. every Sunday morning for almost half an hour and that was it. But on that day after I made my mother sad because of what I said, my heart hurt so bad. As they talked behind the locked door, I stood on the Oriental rug in our hallway, trying to make sure that my mother would be okay and that she wouldn't die from a heart attack. That's how people died on TV all the time. At one point I could hear my father raise his voice like he was really mad.

I'm so sorry, Elaine, but there's nothing I can do. If you want me to, I'll lock our windows.

And so he did. My father nailed the windows so that they could only be opened less than half a foot. It was a new security system, he explained, to keep away burglars.

I didn't even know our beautiful new neighborhood had burglars.

While the nails may have prevented anyone from stealing me and my family, they failed to stop the tormented and distinct sounds that came nightly from the cottages. Nor did they protect me from learning a new variety of words. Even though our windows were partially locked, I could still hear crying howls. Slowly, these eerie night cries seeped into my bones.

Do you know how your teacher tells you to pull the fire alarm only if you see smoke at school? my father asked me one night after the trucks kept coming. I had been waiting in my seat in the living room until he had safely returned through the sliding glass door after putting all the children next door back to sleep.

Yes, I replied. You pull it only if you see smoke because if you pull it and there isn't smoke you get in trouble and have to go to the principal's office and then you have to wait there until your parents come and pick you up in the car and then you are in big trouble because . . .

Right, my father said.

I think I had said all the things he already knew so sometimes he just said Right. With my father, Jimmy and I didn't have to finish our sentences because he knew exactly what else we might say and he wanted to keep it short.

My father continued. The children next door also go to school and they have also heard the teacher say what you learned in your school about the fire alarm. But unlike you and most kids, they pull the alarm.

I was shocked.

Don't they know the rules? I asked. Don't they know their parents will have to leave work and pick them up and they'll be in so much trouble and they won't get dinner and dessert and they'll never get to go to Hoffman's?

They do, my father said. That's why they pull it. And when they can't pull it, they throw their shoe toward the ceiling because there are alarms up there, too.

But why would they pull it or why would they throw their shoe at it?

They want extra attention. Or they just pull it because it's a naughty thing to do. If everything was normal with them, these children wouldn't be living in our backyard.

What about Jodie? Isn't she well behaved?

My father shook his head, looking into the fireplace area in our living room and resting his chin in his hand as he thought about Jodie.

Very troubled, he finally said softly. Jodie may be about your age, but she has been through an awful lot.

Why can't she live with her mother and father? I asked.

She never will, was his reply.

Is she an orphan?

Oh, Susan, he said, shaking his head. That's not a term used today when you're treating disturbed and sick children. You watch too much TV.

But if she needs a new mom and a new dad, doesn't that make her an orphan?

We treat troubled children, he replied. We don't treat normal orphans. A normal orphan wouldn't need to be treated *here*.

But wouldn't an orphan be sad? Mom said we lived here because the children were sad.

Your mother is right. But you don't understand what goes on in your backyard. You're too young. Life is easier for you, trust me. I'm going to bed.

Why can't we love her? I asked.

Who? he asked, somewhat bewildered.

Jodie. Why can't we adopt Jodie? I asked. I would get a new best friend and a new sister—two for the price of one, like the sale sign at Woolworth's.

No.

But, Dad, Jodie would never pull the fire alarm, because she looks just like Mandy.

Sue, he said, Jodie pulls the alarm more than any other child at the Home.

Well, maybe Jodie's scared, I said, trailing him as he headed down the hallway to his room. And then I added, Can I get a fire alarm for my bedroom for my birthday?

I stared into my backyard that first and second month of living on the grounds of the Albany Home for Children and realized that something was strange about a lot of the Home's children. I guess that was why they were there. While my brothers and sisters and I often got our clothes dirty playing outdoors, our socks matched and some sort of color sense seemed to be going on with the clothes my mother either bought or made on her Singer sewing machine. The Home children's socks never matched. No one bothered to tell them that they couldn't go outside if they had on one white sock and one red sock.

Besides the clothing confusion, something else was kind of strange about a couple of the kids in our backyard. Some bobbed their heads up and down like my windup toys. A couple had heads that drooped to their shoulders and looked like they were glued there. It's like they were sound asleep on one side even as they walked.

One named Benjamin was a singing, or rather a humming, dancer.

My father explained that children who were autistic lived in their own world. It's like they're here, but not really.

Out of all the children who lived on the ground, Benjamin—tall with blond hair and blue eyes, looking like an older version of Billy—seemed to break my mother's heart the most because he was autistic. Oftentimes when he danced over in his helmet onto our immediate backyard where I often sat in my father's blue director's chair like I was the master of the bird perch look- ing out onto my entire backyard, I would turn my head around to our sliding glass door and see my mother watching Benjamin waltz across our lawn.

It was always the same. My mother would stop her dusting with the lemon-fresh Pledge and stare out the window, dabbing her eyes with the clean end of her old cut-up winter nightgown. Then she would stand mesmerized, watching Benjamin twirl around our backyard, wearing his white helmet just in case his dance steps led him right smack into an oak tree or the blue spruce my father had recently planted. Often Benjamin would come right onto our little patio and I could look into his eyes, but it's like his eyes never looked back. It was true: He was there but not there, just like my father said.

As soon as Benjamin began his dance around me, humming his song that had only one range in its tone, my mother would walk out the door and take his left hand with her right and his right with her left. She would lead the way as they danced all the way back to the other side of the backyard. As soon as my mother found an adult who worked at the Home, she would dip Ben- jamin's body, safely holding his helmet with her one hand, and then she would hand him over to his new dance partner, who picked up Benjamin's dance where my mother dropped off. My mother made Benjamin's dancing even more magical, like we were watching *The Lawrence Welk Show* right in my backyard. Whenever my mother danced with Benjamin and brought him back to his cottage, my father would come back home for a brief interruption of his workday and give my mother a kiss.

Then they would smile in that way that I knew was a sign that my parents were in love.

As for Benjamin, one day I tried to help him myself. I had been thinking about how my father said the autistic kids lived in a world of their own. If this was true, perhaps there was a way to get Benjamin to snap out of his trance. I decided to write a letter to the people who understood people who lived on Mars and the other planets. One day after I watched my mother dance with Benjamin yet again, I wrote down what I saw and addressed a letter to NASA asking them to help a boy who lived on earth but thought he lived on another planet. Walking up our street, I opened the blue mailbox with the familiar eagle stenciled on the side and slid my letter on behalf of Benjamin to Cape Canaveral where my mother said the astronauts lived with their wives and children before they put on their gigantic white suits and were blasted off to outer space. Part of me thought that since Benjamin didn't really live here in his head, maybe the astronauts would invite him to come live with them or alongside the Man in the Moon.

Rockets came and went into space over time, but no one from NASA or anywhere else ever headed in the direction of Albany to pick up Benjamin.

Angel Food Cat

On the Saturday before Jimmy and I begin School 19, my mother, pushing Sarah in her stroller, leads us to Frenchie's hair salon, which is kind of kitty-corner to Academy Road and New Scotland Avenue. We are there for new haircuts so Jimmy will look Handsome and I will look Beautiful for the new school year. Mandy and I get matching salad-bowl cuts. Jimmy and Billy are buzzed like junior versions of my father.

Not long after we had moved into our new home, the local newspaper, the *Times Union,* had written an article welcoming my father to his new job as assistant executive director. Jimmy and I just said he owned the Albany Home and its kids. My mother was so proud of the article that she placed it away from our dirty chocolate fingers—behind safety glass—in a beautiful plastic frame that she bought at the dime store up the street. For weeks, right before dinner, she made all of us sit in the living room on the sofa side by side and she read it over and over again. When Aunt Mary and Uncle Ed came for a visit, she read it to them, too. And then she read it over the phone long distance to Mrs. Cordes.

Jimmy said Ma Bell really liked our mother.

When my grandmother visited, she would bring her own wooden-framed copy of the article with her, and sometimes my mother and grandmother would both stand next to each other in the middle of the living room, taking turns reading aloud paragraphs of my father's story. I had starred as the Sun in my kindergarten production of *The Sun*, and it was clear they—my mother and grandmother both—wanted to be star actresses, too. My grandmother tried to pronounce her words like she was starring on her favorite daytime soap. My mother read it in a voice that sounded more like Maria in *The Sound of Music*.

My grandmother would turn to my mother and say, He's *my son*.

My mother would turn to my grandmother and say, He's *my husband*.

Then they both would clear their voices with the cough that actresses sometimes use when they rehearse their lines. I don't think my mother and grandmother were best friends. They were just related.

Sarah didn't have hair yet, so Frenchie, the barber, pretended to comb her scalp, which had this nasty red rash right on the lower part of her neck. My mother said it was Sarah's beauty mark even though it was certainly not a beautiful thing to have attached to her head forever.

Frenchie combed all our hair with the same black comb, which he just dipped in and out of the blue food coloring jar. I don't know why our hair didn't turn blue, seeing as whenever we dipped eggs into food coloring for Easter they turned different colors. I was thankful Frenchie's dipping water was weak, because you never want to start a new school looking like a Freak.

Freak was Jimmy's newest word. He used it when he pointed at anything that didn't look right. One of his sort-of friends who lived a couple of streets over told Jimmy that the kids in our backyard were all freaks and should be living in a circus. When Jimmy pointed at one and said Freak in front of my fa-

ther, that was the end of Jimmy's day. He spent what was left of it in his bedroom, and from then on only said Freak under his breath to me. Never again
did he say it about a Home child.

Gilligan is a Freak, he would say. The Skipper is not a Freak. Mrs. Howell
is a Freak. Mr. Howell is the biggest Freak.

I loved walking up the street with my mother to Frenchie's, or the Trading
Port, where we bought some of our groceries and the Genesee Cream Ale
with the green label. I loved it when we all walked with her to the tailor, the
shoe repair man, and the bank, all of which were next door, next door, and next
door to Frenchie's. I felt proud that our mother belonged to us. When I
walked beside her sometimes, "There She Is, Miss America" started playing in
my head.

Often, on our way home on Saturdays after we went with my mother to do
her errands, we passed groups of children from the Home heading in the opposite direction. If they did their chores for the week, the Home kids were allowed to go to Stewart's Ice Cream Store for an ice cream cone. When we
walked past them my mother always smiled and said hello to each of them by
their first name, making sure that we stepped out of their way and onto the
grass so that the Home kids could stay in their single-file line, one counselor
in front leading the way, and another in the rear to make sure no one decided
to make a fast exit to . . . I guess to freedom, or to being my friend.

Unlike my mother, I didn't know their names. It was strange. When you go
to a playground, you always get to know everybody's names.

The Home kids never walked left at the entrance to the Home. I suppose
they always turned right because the walk to the left was boring. The walk
right meant you might be heading to Stewart's for ice cream. On our street in
general, there weren't a lot of houses on our side of the road. On the other
side, only a few yards separated the houses from one another. Many of our
new grown-up neighbors would come out and wave hello to us, although I
think they were mostly interested in talking to my mother because she was
more their age. We were just a bunch of kids. By now, everyone knew my
mother's name, and they would call out Hello, Mrs. Carswell, or Hello,
Elaine. Sometimes they would even cross the street to speak with her and ask
how everything was going in our new house.

Fine, fine, she would say to our new neighbors.

Lovely, lovely, she would say to others.

Wonderful, wonderful.

Beautiful, beautiful.

John and I just love it here.

The kids are having a ball playing in their new backyard.

Sometimes the neighbors would ask her nosy questions about the troubled children who lived in our backyard. And my mother would always say, Every single one of them is special and darling.

She made our new backyard sound as though we were living in a beautiful picture book. Since I wanted to believe her description of our lives, I gave in, falling under her spell each and every time. She made our backyard sound as if it was more fun than Willy Wonka's Chocolate Factory. Why would a kid pick a chocolate factory when you could live on the grounds of the Albany Home for Children?

Mr. and Mrs. Brown were across the street. I think they lived with one thousand indoor and outdoor cats. Every week Mrs. Brown baked our family an angel food cake. She would ring the doorbell and my mother would stand outside talking to her for the longest time, thanking her repeatedly for being so generous.

Mrs. Brown, I've never had *such* angel food cake.

That's exactly how she said it. She never said *such yummy, such tasty,* or *such delicious cake,* like the way she would compliment Miss Mary Fundis or Aunt Mary. My mother said, Such angel food cake.

When Mrs. Brown walked back to her house, my mother stood outside waving until Mrs. Brown was safely back inside, on account of all the burglars in our neighborhood and our windows now being more than halfway shut with nails. As soon as Mrs. Brown had closed her door, my mother would study the cake, turn to me, and say, Oh my, still cat hairs.

Then she would throw the cake away in one of the big garbage cans in our garage. As she put the lid back on the can she would touch her forehead, her chest, her left shoulder, and then her other shoulder with her right middle finger, just like she did in Sunday church. She would shake her head and say, Lord, forgive me.

My mother never allowed us to eat Mrs. Brown's hairy angel food cake.

And it got to the point when even if my mother wasn't home, Mrs. Brown would hand the cake over to me or Jimmy and remind us to tell our mother that she had made the cake. Then she added, Your mother loves my cake even more than my husband does. After we watched her cross the street, to make sure no one robbed or killed her, Jimmy or I would run quickly to the garage.

We knew what to do with the angel food kitty-cat-cake.

Two houses away from Mrs. Brown's house lived the Mendel family. They had a lot of kids, including Laurie, Debbie, Danny, and Eugene. They also had just about the best girl my age living on my street, but she already had a lot of friends. Lisa Mendel was pretty with blond hair and blue eyes, and every night I dreamed about becoming her best friend—or Jodie becoming my best friend. My mother said that if you hoped for something real hard, it might come true. She also said that wishing on a ladybug got you your dreams even that much quicker.

Lisa Mendel's parents owned Mendel's Restaurant, which was about as famous as you could get in Albany. I also wanted to be Lisa Mendel's friend so that I could eat at her family's restaurant for free because it was too expensive for my entire family to go there. My mother said a roast beef dinner for seven costs like a hundred times more than a Big Mac.

Next door to the famous Mendel's Restaurant family lived this lady named Babs and her mother, Mrs. Henry. We were allowed to call Babs *Babs*—strange because she was my mother's age and you always had to call people that old Mrs.

But Babs wasn't a Mrs.

She was a Babs.

Babs was nice. She was almost too nice. Babs laughed at stupid jokes my father said that I didn't think were all that funny. When Jimmy and I told Babs a story she would laugh and sometimes it wasn't even meant to be funny.

Jimmy would say, We went swimming.

Babs would laugh.

I would say, We had Hungarian goulash for dinner. It was good.

Babs would laugh at that, too.

We didn't have to watch *Laugh-In*. She lived on our street.

. . .

Babs spent her days sitting in the rocking chair on her porch, staring out onto our street. Jimmy called Babs a busybody. And she was. Her body was always very busy because as soon as anyone on the street came out of the house she would run up or down or across the street in order to talk with them. Then she always asked everyone, Where ya going? *Huh? Huh?*

When she asked us where we were going, sometimes my father would invite her to jump in our car if we weren't heading too far away. But my father wouldn't ask her to come if we were going to Cape Cod, or to St. Patrick's Cathedral in New York City where my mother lit candles for her mother once a year in order to feel better because she had died when she was so young. But if Babs was disappointed at the lack of an invite, you never would have known it because all Babs Henry ever did was smile and act all happy and nice.

After the fire trucks were there late at night, if you ran to our front windows in the kitchen you could always spot Babs Henry standing outside in her flowery robe, matching slippers and nighttime curlers under her kerchief, waiting on her side of the street until the last truck pulled away. Then she would rush back home in the dark and up the stairs into her house. I think Babs wished she could sit on her porch throughout the night, but maybe her mother told her that was way too scary.

When I asked my mother why Babs wasn't a Mrs., she paused, thought about it, and finally said, Because she looks after her mother instead.

I knew right then that when I grew up, I would be just like Babs. If you got to pick, I'd rather look after my mother, too. And in the same way Babs was determined to look out onto our street all day, I was just as consumed with staring out at our backyard. I was like a little Babs who wanted to grow up to be a big Babs. I just didn't know if I could laugh as much as she did.

Our side of the street was more about workplaces rather than houses filled with families. At the bottom of the street in the direction where the fire trucks came from, and the way we were to go if we were to drive back to our first or second house, was a temple and then a school for girls. My mother said that it was for rich girls. I wouldn't be going that way for second grade. Across the street was the school for rich boys. My mother said Jimmy and I would be going to a free school.

The Albany Home for Children took up the most space on our street or about as much space as the Junior College of Albany next door to our house, or rather next door to Mr. and Mrs. Millard's house. The Millard house looked like our twin, but we had a beautiful garden out front, so there was no mixing up which house we lived in. Mr. Millard was my father's boss like the way my father was our boss. He had a bunch of sports cars, and Jimmy was always asking if he could sit inside them in order to learn how to drive. Mr. Millard was nice and smart because he let Jimmy drive his car, though he never gave my brother the keys.

Mrs. Millard never seemed to go for car drives with Mr. Millard. She did a lot of things by herself. When we found her doing art projects outside near her patio, Jimmy and I would ask if we could help her paint her large signs. Some days we would spend an entire afternoon writing words like PEACE in purple or WOMEN'S RIGHTS in pink or ERA! ERA! After she had made a bunch of them, she would place her large signs on top of her station wagon, making sure they wouldn't fall off by roping them to ski racks, and then she would drive away. Sometimes we didn't see Mrs. Millard for a few days, a week, or weeks. When I asked my mother where she went, my mother would say, She has gone to the White House again. Jimmy and I couldn't believe Mrs. Millard was friends with the president. We wanted the president to know that we knew her, too, so we asked Mrs. Millard if we could write our names in pencil at the bottom of her posters. She always let us. At night we dreamed about the president seeing JIMMY CARSWELL and SUE CARSWELL below the sign that said STOP WAR.

A couple of kids our age lived on the campus of the Junior College. Ned Kirsch lived in a really big house with a lot of bedrooms that was the same size as Parsons, but it was all for his family. He told me boy orphans used to live in his house a long time ago when it was known as Wasson Cottage. Coach Kirsch ran the basketball team at the college, and he was always walking around the huge grounds just thinking about basketballs, I guess, as he smoked his cigars. Ned Kirsch was my age but he was becoming Jimmy's friend. Then one day Ned Kirsch said to me, I love you. Soon we were kissing and I had a boyfriend. Ned had made plans for our future. He said he wanted to own a pig farm.

I was going to be a Mrs. after all.

Megan Murphy and her family lived in another house about the same size as Parsons Cottage and Ned's house on the grounds of the Junior College, too. She said baby orphans used to live in her house a long time ago. I said real orphans lived in my backyard. When I told her she said, Wow. Megan went to the Catholic school that was the same name as our boring church, so it wasn't like we would be walking to school together. My mother said that was okay, though, because I always had Jimmy. I think moms like to believe that their kids all really love each other and that they would be best friends. I didn't want to break her heart and tell her that I hated Jimmy. He was so annoying and had a small dark brown birthmark right below his bathing suit that really bugged me. Whenever I looked at it, I thought *that's gross* and sometimes when I really stared at it, my appetite for sharing Jimmy swim water would just go away. Anyway, Mr. and Mrs. Murphy became my parents' new best friends and frequently came over to our house, knocking on our door at about 8 P.M. to drink a six-pack of beer with them. But by 9 P.M. my father would walk into his bedroom and come back out minutes later dressed in his pajamas and robe. He would sit and talk for a while longer, but you could always see he was trying to wrap things up because he would start yawning and get all fidgety.

Right. Right, he would say.

As soon as the grandfather clock struck nine thirty, my father said good night and headed off to bed, leaving my mother to talk with Mr. and Mrs. Murphy alone, or rather with me, too. I found grown-up conversation fascinating, even if I wasn't allowed to drink the beer.

By the middle of the school year, I had become Megan Murphy's friend. After first practicing on Mandy's lips, which tasted like Skippy peanut butter, I kissed Megan, too. Before the end of second grade I had Ned Kirsch as my boyfriend and Megan as my girlfriend. By the end of the year my mother finally caught on, and it seems I wasn't supposed to be kissing other people until I was much older. I was single again and on the right track of remaining a Miss.

After my first day of school, when I arrived home I immediately grabbed my favorite after-school snack—a chocolate Ring Ding—took a beach chair from our garage, sat down on the grass near our patio, and waited for my father to come home from work. I had questions that I needed answered.

About an hour later after waiting, waiting, and waiting, as I stared off to the right, my father finally came up the small hill from the Home's driveway, carrying his briefcase. I raced in his direction and, like gunfire battle, pelted him with questions.

Why wasn't Jodie at school today?

Why wasn't Mom's dancing friend Benjamin there?

Where was too-tall Tom?

Where was Sean? I asked. He was a handsome black boy who pretended our backyard was his runway and he was a model as he wore the latest in Albany Home for Children donated clothing turned haute couture from his private collection. I never thought a boy could be your best friend, but after Jodie, Sean was my next pick—on account of the fact that he seemed to play with more Barbie dolls by the sandbox than the amount of Barbies I had in my Barbie beach house.

As my father listened to my rat-tat-tat all the way back to the patio, he started to say something, but I cut him off because I just had this real need to get every question I had out in the open just in case he tried to flee from me.

Why is it that not one of the other kids in our backyard was at my new school on the first day? Dad, you get in trouble if you start school on the second day.

School 19? he asked me as he opened the door. Oh, that would *never* be.

And then he walked back to his bedroom to change his clothes.

That night, as he gets ready to walk around our property, making sure the doors are locked, I ask my father if I can come along with him.

Shockingly, he agrees.

First, we head to the last cottage farthest away from our bedroom windows. He allows me to walk inside with him for the first time, and I see some children I recognize and others I don't eating Jiffy Pop and watching TV. Some of the kids in Wasson Cottage are crying or rather yelling so much that it is like a cry-yell. Night counselors try talking to them in order to calm them down, but whatever the Home kids are thinking about inside their heads just won't go away so they can't seem to stop their cry-yells.

We walk through Rathbone Cottage and pass the little kitchen area where Miss Mary Fundis works during the day. Like my mother's kitchen, Miss

Mary Fundis's kitchen is spotless. The silver mixing bowls are so polished I can see my smile. I am so happy to be inside the cottages rather than always wondering about them from outside.

As the counselors greet my father, and my father introduces me to one named Rezington and another named Sheldon, some children run up to my father like he is their best friend. He picks up a couple of the smaller ones and lifts them into the sky or rather up close toward the ceiling of the cottage. I never imagined my father had kids as friends. He isn't our friend. I imagined him as a stern ruler looking over a children's kingdom.

One night right after that first summer, as the sun began its fall, the telephone in my parents' bedroom rang. The special Code Red phone was used only when the counselors next door were in desperate need of my father's help. My father bolted from our house and ran over to the cottages faster than I had ever seen him move. About ten of the really bad boys, between the ages of eight and twelve, seemed to have made a plan to meet each other on top of the roofs of Wasson, Rathbone, and Lansing Cottages after Miss Mary Fundis's supper. Jimmy and I immediately replaced our impromptu game of badminton with real-life excitement and found a place to watch. Standing next to the bike loop, we had a direct view onto the front of the cottages. We knew our place; to cross the long entranceway and walk onto the children's living side of the backyard right next to their cottages would mean huge trouble for Jimmy and me. Standing side by side, we could see the boys tearing off the shingles from the roof. Using the roof pieces as weapons, the boys hurled them through the air like Frisbees, aiming them at the counselors gathering below.

My father shimmied up onto the roof of the first cottage like he was the fastest rock climber who ever lived. Then, as though he was a real-life GI Joe in a surprise ambush, he hollered at the boys in a voice that sounded like an army general. If anyone could scare those boys, it was my father. As he moved closer, leaping from one roof to the next, swinging his arms like Superman, it was clear the boys were powerless against my father. They laid down their shingles in defeat, started to cry, and jumped like little babies, one by one, down into the waiting arms of the counselors.

. . .

On the night when I walked with my father through the grounds, right before we headed back home, he wanted to check on the gymnasium next to Parsons Cottage.

The gym was getting old; my father said it was built around the time he was born—very old. It always sounded hollow because it was so big. If you said your name out loud, the sound of it would bounce off the walls in an echo that went around and around. The gymnasium was always cold, but we loved playing there. Sometimes when it seemed my mother needed a break from us, my father would bring all of us over to the gym and we would run around and bounce off the padded walls until we were dizzy. It felt like you weren't living on earth. That feeling of being there/not being there in your head was kind of scary, but thrilling.

As we head in through the entrance to Van Alstyne Gym, my father shows me the room the children use for art class. When we walk into the room full of small paint jars, I can see the still-drying pictures that the children from the Home had made earlier that day. Rather than using the colors of the rainbow, most of the children drew with just red or black paint. Some of the images were of fire. One child painted a picture of himself and his family, but the people who look like maybe his mother or father are lying on green grass, red paint coming out of their mouths.

Before I can look at more of the artwork, my father tears them off the easel and rolls them all up and places them in a brown tube. I ask him if we are going back to the cottages so that the children can have their paintings back before they go to sleep. He says no, then adds, This artwork goes off to the doctor.

With that, my father ushers me out of the art room and double-locks the door behind him.

I think to myself, *How can art be sick?*

They don't choose to live here, Sue, my father says as we walk across the grass back home. And I'm sure they would like to go to your new school, but how do I explain to you that a child can be very sick without having a temperature? You're too young to understand the meaning of behavioral problems.

Jimmy and I don't behave. Are we the same?

No.

Well, are you their friend or are you their boss?

I try to make them feel welcome at a new type of home that they have to get adjusted to, he says. I'm an administrator. After thinking a moment as he kicks the grass with his sneakers, he adds, Even though these kids live here now, I just think that they have the right to be kids like you and your brothers and sisters. So sometimes I can be their friend, but I also have a job and have to yell. I'm not saying I like yelling. Sometimes after I do it, I can't sleep.

Is that why you move to the couch a lot of nights?

Yes, he says.

I had never thought my father had feelings. I knew my mother had them. I thought feeling sad was for everyone in the world, except my father.

Over the next few weeks I noticed that when the new children arrived in our backyard, my father was the first adult they met. I could often see him talking to new children as he held their hand and took them on the tour of their new home. At the swimming pool, he would make them laugh as he pretended to do the butterfly stroke with his hands above his head. Then he would turn them in the direction of the gym, and I could see him pretending to be Wilt Chamberlain throwing imaginary basketballs into the sky.

Right by the visitors' parking space, my father would lead the new child to the long bike rack, which held up to fifty bikes. Suddenly he would wrestle a new bike free. The one with a ribbon was meant for the newest member of the Home—a blue bike for the boys and red for the girls. Sometimes I could even see a child cry when my father presented the bike. Some of them had never had one before, let alone a loop.

Right before we get back home, I ask my father about the children's first day living at the Home. He says that there are parts of that first day that make them happier than they have ever been. But many cry because they feel very alone.

My father says that when he leads them back to the cottages, because I could never see this part, he introduces the new kids to the other children and then he shows them their new bedrooms complete with goldfish in each of their rooms. My father says every kid in the world loves a pet. For some of them, a goldfish is the first thing they will ever come to really love and trust.

As we slide open our back door that night at the end of our walk in which my father and I make sure all the locks are checked and our backyard is safe for the night, my father asks me a question that I have never quite considered before.

He says, Did you ever notice that a goldfish's mouth is full of kisses? Goldfish kisses are the best way to begin a new life.

Art Propaganda

I t is a crisp Saturday afternoon in the middle of October, only a couple of months since we have moved here. Jimmy and I are jumping outside on the blue trampoline for the first time. We wear off-white fisherman's sweaters that our grandmother knit us—five new sizes for each year. Jimmy and I are well into our new school year. I am seven, Jimmy is eight. Jimmy likes school and has new friends. I don't.

I want to go to the school in my backyard so I can draw watercolors on an easel just like the children who live there—although they're not sleeping over at my house yet and they're still not my friends. Not my mistake, my dad's. Like the Home children, I want to paint pictures of how I feel inside, just like my father said they did. I don't want to draw in the picture books my teacher Mrs. Kelly hands out to us to see who is best at staying within the lines as we draw scenes from history, including the cracked Liberty Bell in Philadelphia, where my mother says Mike Douglas tapes his talk show. My favorite of Mike's frequent guests is the funny lady, Totie Fields. She's short like a kid, has hair bigger than her size, but she's wicked funny. Totie Fields seems naughty, which I like. She's the type that probably growls at kids and I want to meet her so I can growl back. We can have a contest to see who wins. Everything is a contest in my opinion. I can stay in the lines and complete my crayon pictures without ever crossing the highlighted black border. Still, I have feelings outside of lines and I want to paint all my feelings and thoughts and not draw in coloring books that have been Made in China by little children, age four, Billy and Mandy's age, which is what Jimmy explained to me. Whenever he had a news flash, Jimmy would say, Susie, I got some more information about how the world goes 'round.

When I feel sick, I don't want to be seen by the nurse who doesn't smile and whose cold office smells like rubbing alcohol. I am convinced that my exploding temperature goes down to 98.6 degrees only because her office is as freezing as our weekend ski days. We ski starting in late November and end in early March. During half of that time the temperature goes well below the zero-degree mark on the outdoor thermometer. My father says we must put on our skis no matter if it is icy cold or mushy like when the warm spring sun melts the mountain and we ski part snow and part brown mountain. He has paid for season tickets at Gore Mountain up in the Adirondacks—a boring, boring hour-and-a-half car ride away from our house—and we must, must, *Must-Elaine-Must,* get our money's worth. Sometimes he takes Jimmy and me on the hardest trails, like the one called Hawkeye. I know how scary each trail is based on whether it's marked by a black diamond, which means Dead Kid on the Slopes, or a green circle, which means Bunny Hill—Kids Live. Green means I can let myself give a sigh of relief and ski as fast as I want. A black diamond means I must hold my breath because I fear death and living in a cold coffin in the cemetery. The nurse's office feels as scary to me as when I first look onto Hawkeye's black diamond and see that it goes straight down just like a snow-covered Niagara Falls. Only moguls protect me from falling down the steep slant into the white abyss. The nurse's office feels even colder than our ski days when the temperature gets so icy cold that Jimmy and I develop frostbite on our cheeks. Only then can we rest for half an hour and sip hot chocolate while my father warms the white spots away from our faces with his cold, stocky fingers.

You'll be fine, he says. We'll be back on the slopes in no time.

If I am not feeling well, I want to be comforted by the new nurse at the Albany Home. I want my temperature taken by my mother. She is now the nurse to all the other children during the school day, but not to me.

I am young, but I have developed migraine headaches that Bayer aspirin cannot help. My mother is concerned. Even at seven, I know the difference between a headache and a migraine. Your forehead frowns up and your eyes slant when you have a headache. You want to bury your head and cradle your forehead in the dark when you have a migraine. A headache goes away within a couple of hours. A migraine doesn't.

John, do you think she'll be like Mary? my mother asks my father, referring to her sister.

My aunt has bad migraines that sometimes make her stay inside for days. Once she even missed Easter, which made my mother upset. Everyone is together at Easter.

My father says I cannot go to school at the Albany Home, which means my mother cannot be my school nurse.

Is it about money? I wonder.

I ask my father if the Albany Home is a free school and not a rich school like the one at the end of the street for girls, which my mother says is private. He says that the school at the Albany Home is free and it is also private but that I must continue to go to the school that is public and free and for children like me.

I want to go to the school that is free and private. I want to roll out of bed and go to school wearing mismatched socks. Why should it matter anyway? I want to go to the school that is small and in my backyard and has a pool so that I would have more time slots to swim. I want to jump on the blue trampoline and paint, and I want to play with fun counselors who are much younger than my father. I believe my father's decision is wrong and by the end of the school year, I will convince him to allow me to be a student at the Albany Home the next school year. He'd see.

...

I have taken up painting, just like the Home kids. I bring my watercolors to School 19 to show Mrs. Kelly, my nice and old homeroom teacher. I am convinced that she will help me, that by the end of the school year she will tell my father that I can express my feelings with watercolors just as well as any of the Home children.

I paint watercolors all year long to prove to him—through her—that I belong with the Home children who look and act and feel just like me.

I paint as many ladybugs as I can on one sheet of paper. I draw them flying over a rainbow. A gust of wind pushing them represents my breath in order to show how ladybugs make good on promises of wishes just like my mother has always told me.

My second watercolor is of my mother and father kissing and all my brothers and sisters and me standing next to them. I have arranged us from tallest to shortest. Sarah wears pink because she is a baby. I paint Mandy and Billy in yellow because they are twins, which means double color. Jimmy is black because he bugs me and bugs are oftentimes black. I am purple because it is my favorite color. We are all smiling in my watercolor because all the doors in our station wagon are opened wide, signifying we are headed to Hoffman's Playland. To the far right of my painting, I draw a Ferris wheel. I place it right at the far edge of the paper to show that it is only about twenty minutes away.

The third watercolor I bring to Mrs. Kelly is of my mother, whose hair is the color of dark orange even though she says it is red; I make it touch the sun so that they blend in together nicely. My mother is warm like the sun.

Every night before I go to bed I paint watercolors, and the next morning I give them to Mrs. Kelly as a present, even though my mother says you should never give presents expecting something in return, which I do.

At the same time that we flap our arms and hands on the trampoline and fly high into the air and Jimmy and I imagine that we can jump over even the tallest building in Albany, about twenty Home kids, half black and half white, seem to be having a miniature carnival just a hundred feet away. I didn't know we had small carnivals in our backyard. Jodie and the other children are bobbing for apples, having a watermelon-eating contest, laughing and playing with a clown, and getting their faces painted so that their mouths turn upward into permanent smiles, at least for the carnival.

They look happy.

I recognize some of the counselors, like Rezington, a heavy black woman who can sit on the children if they try and run away. She doesn't squish the children but rather places her rear end right near their feet so if they even think about moving, they know her rear end will come down as quickly as a yo-yo—but without the yo back up—and possibly flatten their bodies or break their thin legs. I see the nice counselor Sheldon, who is seven feet tall, and Brent, Miss Mary Fundis's neighbor in Parsons Cottage with his dachshund Marnie, who also plays at the carnival with the children, or rather tries to steal the dead hot dogs off their paper plates. The counselors are entertaining the group of children. Throughout the day, adults who seem more like happy mother and father types drive into the visitors' parking lot in nice polished cars and some in not-so-nice unpolished cars.

No Cadillacs, Jimmy says. More Fords and Chevys. Not new.

I know Jodie doesn't have parents that she can go home to, so I am glad that the mother and father types have come to visit her at least for the carnival. She hasn't had a Sunday visitor since we moved in.

I sit on the bottom of the trampoline as Jimmy tries to do a scissor kick in the air. I watch the mother and father types arriving by car, and it seems as though they walk into the Home kids' carnival and do that thing with their fingers like *eenie, meenie, minie, mo.* It seems everyone picks Jodie first and then they pick the other kids who are less cute. It goes all the way down the cute chain, until it gets to ugly-not-cute. Even though my mother says there is no such word as *ugly* and there is no such thing as an *ugly child*—and I don't want to disagree with her—there really is such a thing and it seems the visiting mothers and fathers agree with me. The uglier a kid is, the more likely he or she isn't chosen to walk around with the mother and fathers. They are left bobbing for apples.

The black children are chosen to play with the clown only when a black mother and black father type is present. Black children are hardly ever chosen to take a stroll around the bicycle loop with the white parents. It seems to me that the white children get more chances to play with the adults because more white mother and father types drive their cars into the Albany Home driveway on this Saturday afternoon.

•••

This was perhaps our last afternoon on the trampoline before the snow would fall. While Jimmy rests his poor, tired, sore legs, I jump up, my arms pumping, my hands flapping higher and higher into the air, and when I reach that point where you know at least for the moment you can't jump an inch higher because you can't put any more fuel into your launch, I grab my knees and fall back down screaming, Cannonball, until I fall onto the blue tarp and my rear end just bobs up and down until my bounce goes completely flat. I repeat my cannonballs laughing every time because it is so much fun.

When I get tired of perfecting the art of the cannonball, I rest my tired, sore legs and I turn my attention back to yet another carnival with the Home children. Suddenly one of the mother types motions her hand toward me.

No, no, a counselor says, as he shakes his head fervently and then points to my mother and father. Carswell child, he says. Not up for adoption. Let me introduce you to Jodie.

Summer moved into fall and soon late fall, then almost winter. From my favorite vantage point sitting in the director's chair on our patio, I increasingly saw more and more children running away, tearing out of the red cottage doors. Sometimes they flew out of their cottages screaming in horror. What was happening inside there? Why were they screaming? The most upset child seemed to be Jodie. I always immediately recognized her when she fled her cottage because she had a distinct way of leaving.

First, you would hear all these smashing sounds coming from a window right behind Winnie Cottage. I knew it was Jodie's room in the same way I could tell if fire engines were leaving their stations and coming in the direction of our backyard. From the sound of it, whatever was in her bedroom, including lamps and her night table, was being thrown against the wall. I prayed the things she threw didn't include the goldfish. I dreaded the thought of a squished goldfish sticking to a wall. Then I could hear the sound of a piercing crash, which I knew was the window in her room breaking into pieces. It seemed the crashing noise would continue until Jodie had created a large enough hole for her to crawl through and burst away.

She would then head in the direction of our house, screaming like she was possessed by some sort of demon deep inside that needed to get out. Then again, maybe Jodie ran in our direction because she wanted to see my mother,

her nurse. Or to be adopted by us, because she was an orphan. Jodie wanted to be with my family as much as I wanted her to.

When Jodie made her daring escapes, up to five counselors came running after her, exiting from the cottage door that faced the backyard instead of through Jodie's nonwindow. Once she had been tagged in what I thought was her version of capture-the-dragon, usually right next to our barbecue grill, Jodie would be pinned to the ground by the counselors until her screams dissolved into quiet whimpers. Eventually, there was a medical solution to treat Jodie's screams. When her tantrums became unbearable my mother the nurse would cradle Jodie in her arms, kissing her hair and softly singing Jodie a lullaby as the clear-colored juice from a needle made its way inside Jodie's body.

After a few minutes, Jodie was sweet again. She would get up from the grass, wobble slightly, and then reach for the hand of her favorite counselor to lead her past our picnic table, over the small slope in our backyard, and back home to her cottage. Whenever she walked away, Jodie would turn in the direction of my mother and throw her kisses with her free hand and smile.

I love you, Mrs. Carswell. I love you, Mrs. Carswell. Please tell Mr. Carswell I said hi.

Sometimes Jodie had attacks, which my father called Jodie's big temper, several times in one day. I'm not quite sure if a day ever went by when Jodie didn't lose her big temper at least once. Jimmy and I had temper tantrums, too. I had them even more than Jimmy. Clearly, there was a dividing line between our temper tantrums and Jodie's. I just couldn't see the difference. The adults could.

Because Jodie broke her window time and time again, one night while Jimmy and I did our homework subjects, my father did his homework, too.

His folder read SUBJECT: JODIE. I suppose he had folders for everyone; I was dying to get my hand on Jimmy's. I imagined sitting him down and fastening him to a seat with our One Adam-12 plastic handcuffs. Then I would slowly read aloud my father's condemning viewpoint on him, adding a few lines of my own between my father's sentences to scare my brother. I would end it by saying, James, my analysis is, patient needs to get juiced. Elaine to give him a shot.

While Jimmy and I sat comfortably on the sofa figuring out impossible math questions like adding and subtracting, my father looked through a pile of catalogs sent to him from places where he had written letters requesting information on how to stop a window from breaking. My father received catalogs from prisons and banks describing the latest developments in bulletproof glass and plastics.

My father said stopping Jodie from crashing through her cottage window was as difficult a problem as, say, figuring out how Wile E. Coyote could catch the Road Runner.

I remember the day when he finally found a page in one of the catalogs and he said, That's it. That's it.

Then he hollered to my mother in the other room, Elaine, I've figured it out. It's like Bonnie and Clyde.

Whenever my father said, That's it, Jimmy and I knew he had solved at least one of the world's problems. Telling my mother he had figured out something meant they would share the excitement together because you always share when you're married. You laugh together; you become serious parents together when one of your kids acts bad (although my mother always cheated on that and just pretended to be mad); and you figure out problems together. Maybe you even die together because that's for the best.

This time, That's it, That's it, meant my father had solved the problem of Subject Jodie: Bad Temper.

As I moved toward him, my father seemed to be jumping in his chair as he eagerly began reading aloud a letter he was writing to a manufacturer that made nonbreakable sheets of bulletproof plastic meant to stop bank robberies.

> *Dear Sirs, My name is John Watson Carswell and I work at a children's home where some of the most incorrigible children are placed by the county and state. We have one young girl here who is the age of six. I would appreciate any assistance you can afford me in stopping this little girl from running away in the most extreme and dangerous of ways. Daily, we find ourselves placing new windowpanes in her bedroom. We are at our wit's end. I wonder if you could slice a piece of your plastic in the following dimensions . . .*

After my father finished writing his letter, he put it in a white business envelope and slid his tongue along the sticky line until the letter was as secured shut as he hoped Jodie's bedroom window would eventually be.

...

About a month later, Jodie's Lexan window arrived, and Jimmy and I (with our father) watched as the maintenance men from the Home installed it. It seemed the Lexan was working, because from my regular vantage point, I didn't see Jodie make another break for it. I started to miss her.

But then a couple of Sunday mornings later, right before we left for St. Teresa's, Jodie was pounding on our sliding glass door again.

Can I eat breakfast with you, Mrs. Carswell? Are you having scrambled eggs? Are you having bacon? Do you have some ketchup? Can I read the funnies?

My father went back to the Code Red phone and called a counselor to come to our house and retrieve Jodie. Returning from their bedroom, he told my mother he couldn't *believe* Jodie had broken through the Lexan. The counselor who came over to pick up Jodie said she pushed it out by banging the desk chair in her bedroom at it until it eventually caved in and fell onto the lawn.

So much for Lexan, my father said, shaking his head as we pulled out of our driveway to attend St. Teresa's in order to listen to the latest news from God.

Later that day, as I made my way over to the sleigh hill past her cottage, I noticed that Jodie had a nonwindow. Until they could figure out a new type of window appropriate for her rather peculiar strength, the maintenance men put a perfectly sized piece of wood in Jodie's window. Because it was winter now, they didn't know what else to do to protect her from the cold.

I felt bad for Jodie. She no longer had a view, at least for now, of our backyard.

Subject Jodie: Bad Temper. My father's homework started all over again.

As the months go by and my school year nears its end, the day of my dreams finally arrives.

I have drawn hundreds of watercolors for Mrs. Kelly throughout the year. I have told her stories of Jimmy, Billy, Mandy, Sarah, and my parents all through my paintbrush. I have drawn her a picture that I have titled *The Golden Hot Dog Day,* using the background color of yellow, when Brent gave my mother Marnie forever because he was moving away. In my painting, my mother cries because she is so happy to have a dog. She holds Marnie in her arms and she gives her kisses on her poop nose.

Mrs. Kelly has called my parents in for a meeting to discuss my schoolwork the past year. Kathy Cahalan, who lives at the end of the street right before the

Boys Academy, babysits us while they are out. She earns one dollar an hour to watch all five of us whenever my parents go to parties, shopping, PTA meetings, and out to dinner once a year for their anniversary. Jimmy and I think she probably has enough money to buy a go-cart by now and a white protective helmet, which she can probably afford to put cool stickers on, too. Jimmy and I think babysitters are rich.

I am anxious so I sit in front of the television by my parents' closet. I push my feet up into the air and rest them on the closet. My mother says I have a tic. Me and my tic can sit/stand like this for an entire TV show. On the night of their meeting with Mrs. Kelly, my feet rest on the closet for three half-hour shows. Finally, my parents come back home.

My father walks Kathy Cahalan down the street to her house, protected from murderers, burglars, and knife-wielding bogeymen by seven-inch-tall Marnie, who has one nasty-sounding bark and could take on a German shepherd if she felt like it.

My mother calls me into the living room. It is just the two of us. She sits in her dark red upholstered rocking chair and thinks. I sit in the chair just a few feet away on the other side of the fireplace, waiting for her to stop thinking. Her silence is making me nervous. This doesn't seem right. I know that I have not misbehaved in school because Mrs. Kelly always smiles at me and she has never once yelled at me. She even says aloud to the class, Now, class, do you notice that Susan Carswell uses the word *may* when she asks to use the bathroom. Let's all practice.

May I use the bathroom, Mrs. Kelly? May I . . . May I?

Finally, I work up my nerve because I am curious and I want answers right away. May I paint watercolors with the other children? I ask my mother.

She says, Yes. You will have the opportunity to paint watercolors.

My wish has come true. She was right about the power of ladybugs.

Then she adds, You'll be wearing a uniform every day. On Monday it will be a pink one. On Tuesday it will be pale blue. On Wednesday, it will be aqua, and on Thursday it will be yellow. Every Friday, you can pick your favorite color to wear for the day.

This is strange. I want to wear play clothes to school just like the Home kids do. What about mismatched socks? I will look strange wearing dress colors according to the days of the week.

She tells me she doesn't know how we will afford my new school, but we will because we must.

Then she says to me, Mrs. Kelly believes you are a highly creative student. Mrs. Kelly says it is very important that your creativity be allowed to grow much like the way a seed can grow into a beautiful flower.

The following fall, I will not walk out the back door to attend the first day of school at the Albany Home for Children. Nor will I walk with Jimmy, Mandy, and Billy to School 19 where the twins will now be in kindergarten. Instead, for my first day of school I will turn left out our front door and walk down our street to the Albany Academy for Girls.

I will be going to the school for rich girls although my parents pay only half the tuition because the school has agreed to pay the other half. I am on scholarship because Mrs. Kelly has written the Albany Academy for Girls a letter stating my creativity would get lost in the public school system.

Mrs. Kelly has given me outstanding marks. Under art class, I received an E for excellent. Then she wrote:

Susan Carswell . . . Exceeded goals, especially in her heartwarming watercolors . . .

She concluded my report card with the words *Unique storyteller. Will go far.*

Mrs. Kelly has ruined my dreams. I throw my watercolor paints and brushes in the garbage can. They are in the same place meant for Mrs. Brown's angel food kitty-cat-cake.

Going the Wrong Way, Kid

Attending grade school was a painful experience for Bob Wygant and the other Home children. They distinctly stood out among the children from regular families. They wore hand-me-down shoes and shabby clothing. The girls felt particularly out of fashion in their practical heavy stockings and sturdy brown oxfords. Often they felt ostracized, isolated from the main student body. Classmates at School 19 were quick to point to the Kid from the Home whenever the teacher asked who was responsible for any mischief or misbehavior at school.

Young, feeling like disadvantaged outsiders, Home children clung to one another for protection and friendship. All longed to be a regular schoolchild, with parents who would attend the school year's biggest function, Parents'

Night, in June just before school recessed for the summer. For Bob and the children from the Home, this was the single most dreaded night of the school year.

Even Bob's houseparents, Mr. and Mrs. Scott, weren't available to sit in the audience, because they had to look after the older boys in their care—the ones in junior high and high school who no longer went to School 19. Bob figured the Scotts were nice enough, but they had to supervise and discipline almost forty boys and make sure everyone did their chores by the clock, just like little soldiers.

Earlier in the day before Parents' Night in June 1937, Bob's second-grade class had decorated the large gymnasium with construction paper cutouts to highlight the night's theme: Hoedown at 19. When his teacher, Miss Frommer, instructed the class to become artistically inspired by the theme, Bob was stuck. He didn't know what a hoedown was. He looked over at Polly, the class know-it-all, and saw that she was cutting out horses, selecting two or three colors of black, brown, and white construction paper for every one horse. Before taping them onto the gymnasium's yellow walls, Polly would write down the hokey name of each of her horses in red glitter.

While these animals seemed stupid to Bob, he searched for inspiration. Following Polly's animal theme, Bob figured he would be safe with cows. Cows and horses—surely they made a hoedown. So for almost the entire day, Bob cut out and created what looked to him like ten green, blue, and yellow artistically inspired cows, without udders. Miss Frommer had run out of pink paper.

His desire all morning, while designing cows, was to see the hands of the clock on his classroom wall reach two o'clock, when the school bell would sound, a full hour before its usual ring. On Parents' Night, all the classes were allowed to leave early. Bob just wanted the bell to ring out loudly so he could run from class.

And so he closed his eyes and counted sheep—which, of course, was a form of math—until the moment when the bell sounded.

When at home, don't forget to practice, Miss Frommer said in her light, musical voice.

Bob knew all too well what she meant. He and his classmates had been practicing that silly square dance number since March, three months before its premiere performance that evening. Running all the way home, he knew he wasn't going to practice anything. The older boys from Wasson Cottage would just tease him, and he was too proud to put himself in a position of being teased. Even at seven, he knew how to take care of himself.

Later that evening, but much earlier than their usual dinnertime, Mrs. Scott prepared his favorite dinner of liver and onions, but Bob was too nervous to eat. This was a shame because, according to the menu rotations, liver and onions wouldn't be served again for another month. Still, there was already something like a giant bubble of air inside his stomach. It made him feel fuller than if he had devoured a Thanksgiving meal with all its trimmings.

At 6:30 P.M., he and the other fifty or so grade-schoolers left their cottages to walk the half mile back to the school. Usually, Bob walked to school with Joe, Donnie, Charlie, or Irving, but on this night even his best friends walked ahead of or behind him. Tonight, Bob just wanted to be alone.

Then again, they all did.

As he made his way, Bob turned around to see the steady stream of children following in his steps. All walked with their heads down, their heavy shoes dragging along the pavement. It would have been an entirely cheerless walk underneath the pale moon had it not been for the sweet sound of Gail Lewis's voice as she practiced "Greensleeves" for her solo that evening.

Although one of Bob's friends had pointed out to him that Gail was a colored girl, what was foremost on his mind was remembering that Mr. and Mrs. Scott had once said she sang like a nightingale.

And as the nightingale sang her beautiful melody, the light June breeze pushed the children toward the imposing mahogany-and-brass doorway of School 19.

Bob peeked from behind the auditorium's stage curtain. He watched the faces. Looking into the sea of parents, he saw them proudly smiling in anticipation. They weren't waiting for him, though. He was just another face in this silly dance troupe, a face that meant nothing special to anyone in the audience, especially in this packed hall of families.

As Miss Frommer began to play the piano, the children joined hands and entered the stage in a chain. Then they danced around in a circle to the hoedown music. Bob decided not to look into the audience, but rather to the side where the other boys, all of whom had parents, were laughing at Bob's hand-me-down underwear that were now slipping through his shorts.

Even though his pal Joe didn't yet understand what Bob was doing, Bob grabbed his hand with all his might and suddenly dropped his other classmate's hand. Breaking through the center of the dancing circle, the two abruptly exited stage right.

Bob decided it was time to make their escape from school and from the Home. He and Joe would be runaways rather than orphans.

At the playground, Bob headed directly to the bicycle rack. Although he knew that the bicycle he picked wasn't his, he was borrowing it for a good reason. He didn't see it as stealing. If Bob was caught stealing, the superintendent of the Home would have taken a leather razor strap and whipped his bottom raw. Stealing was bad. *Borrowing,* however, was a softer word. And so he climbed onto the seat.

But he couldn't reach the pedals.

Fortunately for their getaway, Joe was taller and he could reach the pedals, so Bob climbed onto the crossbar. Instead of heading to the Home, which was to the left on New Scotland Avenue, he and Joe turned right. The boys had never been this way before.

Once they got to the cornfields on the outskirts of town, Joe said his legs were tired, so they decided they would spend the night sleeping right there among the cornstalks.

Bob and Joe wanted to sleep in these fields of gold for all nights from then on.

But as the night grew longer, the air turned cold, and the boys couldn't get comfortable resting their heads on the young cornstalks they had used as pillows. It wasn't summer yet, and wearing only their shorts and T-shirts with the AHC labels, the boys shivered under the scary pitch-black sky.

As the boys thought about their next move, they began to wonder if their friends had returned home from Parents' Night, and if anyone had missed them. Had Mr. and Mrs. Scott called the superintendent? Was anyone looking for them?

Bob remembered crying so long ago in the rain with the nurse from St. Margaret's, when he left his first house. Now he cried because he missed Wasson Cottage even more. So he and Joe ditched the borrowed bicycle, and they ran through the dark night all the way back to the Albany Home for Children.

Even though their adventure, or misadventure, meant that Joe and Bob had to stand at opposite ends of the hall facing two doors on the second floor of their cottage throughout the night as punishment not only for their abrupt exit from the hoedown but also for Mr. and Mrs. Scott's very worrisome night, Bob felt safe. Sleepy, but safe.

Bob was back home.

"You're going the wrong way, kid," he advised the boy.

"Turn around and look for a truck going the other way. What are you, *from* St. Cloud's?" the driver asked.

Like most people, he assumed that orphans were always running away *from* the orphanage—not running *to* it.

—John Irving, *The Cider House Rules*

An Orphan's Big Heart

As they grew older, the boys took jobs to supplement their allowances mowing the lawns of some of the neighbors along Academy Road. Other boys delivered the daily newspaper to neighbors before heading off for school. Bob and his friends also helped handyman Pop Thompson around the grounds. Many afternoons were spent filling in potholes with ashes from the coal furnaces that supplied heat and hot water to the cottages.

The girls cleaned neighbors' houses and babysat for ten cents an hour. When they weren't busy earning new Girl Scout badges under the guidance of Nurse Werger, the girls liked to bake cookies in the Home's giant kitchen and, on Sundays, churned homemade ice cream. They played dodgeball and jumped rope around the quad. On the rare lazy afternoon, they also lay on the lawn to look at the clouds, daydreaming and making up stories about what they saw.

Bob's good friend Charlie Wilsey was known as the Home's biggest daydreamer. Back when he had been living at St. Margaret's with Bob, Charlie had always been standing up in his crib and staring at the ceiling or out the window to the sky.

Sometimes in the wintertime and on rainy days, the boys played in the large cellars of the cottages, where they held contests to see how far each one could swing on the heating pipes. The challenge was to go as far as possible before the pipes started to burn and blister their young and nimble hands.

At night, all the children prepared for bed under a single low-watt lightbulb dangling from the ceiling by a long wire. At Wasson Cottage, the boys lined up before getting into their beds. Mr. Scott inspected each of them carefully, even looking behind their ears, to make sure each boy had scrubbed himself clean.

After lights-out, Bob and the other boys would play ceiling tag with their flashlights. With sixteen boys all sleeping only a foot apart, the children forged close companionships, and more often than not they traveled in packs.

Every fall as they were growing up, Bob, Irving, Joe Lewis, Bobby Elder, and Charlie Wilsey would race to the far back of the Home's property, past the new Van Alstyne Gymnasium with its canopy-covered entrance, past the playing fields, past the farmland, following the well-worn path—cut by years of preceding boys—through the white birch trees separating the Home from the houses on the far side of Academy Road. Their destination: the Albany Academy at the far end of the street, to watch the private school's football games.

With no money for admission, the boys cut under the fence, one after the other. This crowd of Little Rascals would disperse and then meet up with one another on the top bleacher, closest to the scoreboard. Bob, Joe, Bobby, Irving, and Charlie always rooted for Albany High, the public school rivals—and the school they would one day attend. Some of the older boys from Wasson played on the Albany High team.

Perhaps one day, Bob said to himself as he headed back toward the fence after the last game of the season, staring back at the now torn-up playing field, he would not have to sneak through the gates. He would be there because he held the ball and wore the uniform of the Garnet and Gray. He would become a varsity football player and do his best to make Albany High proud, even if he was just a kid from the Home.

Almost a month before Christmas, Bob and his friends all raced home from school for lunch as they did every day. Mingled with their growing excitement at the approach of Christmas was sadness over news they had recently heard. Walter Pringle, a former Wasson Cottage resident, had been killed in the Japanese attack near Pearl Harbor on December 7, 1941. Even if the boys hadn't known him personally, they knew of him. Pringle had thought of Wasson as his home, and each Christmas the cottage residents could expect a box of toys from him addressed TO THE BOYS, LOVE, WALTER PRINGLE.

After the United States entered World War II, Flying Fortresses and fighters—from a nearby Army Air Corps airfield—filled the sky over the Albany Home as they carried American troops to Greenland and on to England to support the Allied forces against Adolf Hitler. Heavy curtains were hung over the windows of the cottages as the Home observed blackout conditions.

When they heard about Walter, Bob asked Mr. and Mrs. Scott if Pearl Harbor and Hawaii were near Albany. They assured him that it was not and that he and all the other boys in Wasson were safe.

The Children's Committee, made up of representatives from each of the cottages, chosen by their housemates, decided to pool their allowance money and purchase a service flag with a gold star sewn in the middle to honor Walter's memory. The flag was flown at half-staff on the flagpole next to the entrance.

As they raced home to touch Walter's remembrance flag first, the boys started packing up snow from the high snow cliffs lining New Scotland Avenue and firing off snowballs at girls as they walked by, or, better yet, at passing black Studebakers, Packards, Fords, DeSotos, and Chevrolets. Spotting the milkman as he made his way toward the Home in his horse-drawn wagon, several of the more fearless children, including Betty Sherwood, dropped their snowballs to hitch a ride on the back of the yellow-and-red Normanskill milk wagon—a much faster way to travel than trudging through the snow on foot.

Bob didn't join them. That afternoon, he felt like walking, and he waved them along. He could feel the sun breaking through the cold, and he was looking forward to going sledding after his evening chores were complete. He hoped it would be warmer than on the previous freezing nights when he and his friends tobogganed beneath the dark, star-clad sky.

He watched the milk wagon move farther away. Then, suddenly, the kids jumped off. It appeared that someone had been tossed into the sky, landing facedown in the snowbank. Bob ran toward his friends, who by now had surrounded the fallen child.

The other children screamed and begged passing cars to stop. When Bob reached the snowbank, he saw Irving lying there on the side of the road, still as could be. He wondered if Irving had broken both of his legs. That would be the only reason he wouldn't get up. Then again, maybe Irving was playing that stupid dead game of his. He liked to play dead, since his last name was Coffin. When he now tickled Irving, he thought it strange that he couldn't even get his friend to smile, or even to open up his eyes.

Later that evening, long after the police car took Irving down to Albany Hospital, the Scotts gathered the boys into the living room of their cottage. Bob thought maybe Irving had to stay in the hospital for a day, which was too bad, but he would be back home soon. Tomorrow night, surely, Irving would be back where he belonged.

But as Mr. and Mrs. Scott stood near the roaring fireplace, Mr. Scott did something he rarely did in front of the children. He wrapped his arm around Mrs. Scott's small waist. Then he told the Wasson boys that Irving was dead, not because of the fall, but because he had an enlarged heart.

Dropped dead from a large heart, Bob thought in disbelief. *Why was it so bad to have a large heart?*

Not even Mr. and Mrs. Scott could explain that.

"The whereabouts of Irving's father are unknown," said Superintendent McPherson, "and for the last three years his name has not appeared in the Albany City Directory. He and the mother of the boy had been estranged for years. Neither parent ever had visited the boy at the Home during the time he had been located there."

—*Times Union,* evening edition,
January 30, 1942

A Coffin in the Snow

B ob had never felt the bitter cold like he did that day when the orphans buried a friend. Dressed in his Sunday clothes, Bob stood back and let the others go ahead of him. He was not anxious to be the first in line as almost 150 children from the Home walked from their school buses, through the slight snow flurry, to pay their last respects to Irving Coffin.

Earlier in the day, he had seen Irving's open coffin at the First Congregational Church. Irving was laid out in a box and also dressed in his Sunday best. Irving and Bob wore the same outfit. They had always looked similar but for the lightness in Irving's eyes and his stockier build. The organ played somber music, and Bob couldn't help but notice that Irving looked just the same as always. But when Bob touched Irving's hands crossed on his chest, they felt cold. And Irving had never been this quiet.

All the orphans went to the funeral. Irving was part of their family. It was hard to understand how one of them could just leave without warning, and without first packing up his toys.

Bob didn't cry. He was numb. He didn't know what death meant, so he just clutched his heart instead, hoping it wouldn't stop beating as easily as Irving's had.

As he looked around Albany Rural Cemetery, just to the right of St. Agnes Cemetery where the Catholics were buried, Bob became aware that none of the other children was crying. Most of them didn't know what to think, or how to feel. The sea of gray-cloaked children created a secure ring around Irving's grave. After the minister spoke solemnly about heaven and angels he then looked down into the ground where he said Irving now must go. The minister then kissed the simple wooden box where Irving lay. The Home, strictly adhering to its annual budget, had not included the costs of coffins.

This later encouraged the older and bravest of Home boys to exclaim with boyish irreverence: Irving Coffin died without a coffin.

Soon, the box where Irving lay was lowered slowly into the iced-over pit by the gravediggers, who held on to large handles of rope, like a pulley, and who appeared to Bob to be a little wobbly in their stance. He wondered why men would want to take a job like this, dropping boys like Irving into the ground every day. Didn't they have children at home to love them?

When the box hit the bottom of the hole, some ten feet below, Irving made a loud thud that sounded to Bob like a clap.

Ha, I gotcha!

For one brief, hopeful moment, Bob's eyes snapped out of their trance. Irving had been playing his coffin game and now he wanted out of the box. Bob would get Irving good when he was hoisted back out of the pit. He'd be so happy to pound his friend on the back and shyly admit he had been truly terrified by this practical joke.

But there were no more claps, no more sounds, and the children were instructed by the Home's superintendent to throw a handful of dirt onto Irving and say good-bye.

As for the seeds and the cycles of life, Mrs. Dugan, Bob's housemother back when he lived in Lathrop Baby Cottage, was wrong about Irving. Some little-boy seeds do fall by the wayside, never to fully bloom but rather to die, just like flowers.

As the bus made its slow drive through the light snow, down the cemetery's long narrow road to Broadway, back toward the Home, two girls about the age of Bob walked toward the cemetery. They were dressed in heavy wool coats and mufflers, warm woolen stockings and mittens, snow boots, and fur toques. The taller girl carried a basket, while the obviously younger girl, who held her hand, stared into the windows of the passing bus.

To Bob, it looked as if they were headed for a picnic on this Sunday afternoon. But why would they ever want to come here to a frozen, dead garden?

Well, young boy, it sometimes happens . . .

And so it was that Reed and Ella Primmer took their young granddaughters, of their beloved and only daughter, Ora, into their own home, caring for them as best they could. They were poor, but Elaine and Mary were loved. That's the most important thing. Or is remembering your greatest loss a lifelong saga?

Ella worked as a seamstress doing piecework for a pajama manufacturer. Although she had made it only through the sixth grade, she carefully kept track of every seam, sleeve, and waistband she sewed so that her employer wouldn't cheat her out of the money she deserved and earned.

At home, in the evenings after her long days at work, Ella was the personal tailor for my mother and aunt. She sewed all their clothes as they grew. She made their school outfits and Easter dresses; she could even recut a woman's used coat into two smaller warm coats for her granddaughters. On each Christmas night, my great-grandmother put them to bed wearing a new pink satin nightgown she made with such pride especially for them. But it was the clothes she made for Elaine and Mary's Sundays that were closest to her own broken heart.

The two young girls went to St. Agnes Cemetery almost every Sunday, always hoping they would run into their father. To Elaine and Mary, their father was such a handsome man. At six feet tall with sandy blond hair, deep-set light blue eyes, and a spectacular jaw, Francis Xavier Kirby was as handsome as a matinee star. Too young to deal with the loss of his wife, whom he met when he worked as a cook and she a waitress at Jackson's Restaurant in down-town Albany, he became for the most part a jakey-bum, a gravedigger who worked on the grounds of St. Agnes Cemetery, a bottle of rotgut always within his hand's reach, and never too far away from the watchful spirit of his dear love.

Although they could feel in their bones that their father might be there, it seemed he preferred playing hide-and-seek without ever being found. He never came back to visit his girls, except for the times when he knew their grandparents were at work. Then he came to see them after school, to cadge for coins. He would say, Go get the blue box, always so friendly. But they couldn't go to the blue box because inside it were their grandmother's treasures.

When their grandmother once caught him visiting, Elaine and Mary never forgot what she had done. But they loved their grandmother and they thought she was a saint, so they figured it must have been the right thing. As they had learned in church, saints always make the right choices. Their grandmother had said then to their father, Frank, you know who I have to call. And he said, Yes, Ella, I understand. He was so polite. A few minutes later, the police pulled up outside their house and took their father away in handcuffs.

They wouldn't see him again for years. And so they always hoped he would appear when they visited their mother's grave. It began in the summer right after the Christmas of their mother's death. Their grandmother would prepare a picnic basket full of chicken sandwiches, hard-boiled eggs, oatmeal-raisin cookies, and lemonade. Their grandfather would drive them to the grave site in his old black Ford. They would lay fresh-cut flowers around her plot, almost as if they were making a heart-shaped wreath. Elaine and Mary would sing songs, do little dances, and, before they left, they would say their prayers. Pray-ing was so quiet, it was like there was no other noise in the entire cemetery ex-cept for the sound of their voices. Prayers, as their grandmother once said, were what their mother most wanted to hear. And so they prayed because Elaine and Mary wanted to make their young mother smile.

At first, it was hard for them to understand why they were even there, since they had been told that an angel had carried their mother within the soft com-fort of its wing all the way up to heaven. Later, when Elaine was a little older, she would look outside her bedroom window every night because she figured her mother was above, a twinkling star. The star was all she had at night to remember her mother; otherwise she would have to wait until Sundays to imagine her mother's spirit beneath the ground again.

Elaine didn't like the thought that her mother's bones were down below in the dark. She hated to think how cold and lonely she must have felt in the winter. By the time she was ten and Mary was eleven, their grandfather's car couldn't make it up that long hill when snowstorms hit, so they often walked it alone. Once or twice, the two girls saw buses full of kids about their age traveling to and from the cemetery. Elaine never imagined they might be full of orphans. Thank God, they had been saved by their grandparents.

Elaine and Mary Kirby visited their mother on Sundays, all the years as they grew. Perhaps they were there the day Irving Coffin was buried, and perhaps their father was working not on the Catholic side, but on the other side where the Protestants were buried. Perhaps that day he was one of the jakey-bums, digging a new home for Irving Coffin.

In 1943, the year after Irving Coffin's death, with the young deceased orphan in mind, the Home's superintendent petitioned the board of directors for coffins and gravestones for any child who died while in the care of the Albany Home for Children.

My Martinique

It is the summer before I enter the Albany Academy for Girls, and almost the one-year anniversary of living on the grounds of the Home. It dawns on me that an invisible line has been etched in sand between my siblings and me, and the children from my backyard. We didn't draw the line. My father did.

On a warm night during the in-between—as my mother refers to the time when supper has ended and the sun has yet to completely lower itself behind the mostly A-frame houses on my street—we sit outside on the picnic table, just the two of us, my mother on one side, me on the other. We drink decaffeinated iced tea. I am not allowed caffeine after 3 P.M. ever since that night I drank fifteen small cups of green tea at a Chinese restaurant after a day of ski-ing and stayed up for two consecutive nights.

John, is it possible for her to be that affected by caffeine?

Elaine, I've never seen anything quite like it.

Well, she won't have caffeine past noon, from now on. That way there will never be nights like *that*. I was tired all day, John.

Settled. Caffeine is limited for Sue.

My mother and I look toward the cottages, because it's the only thing you do when you sit out in our backyard unless relatives or my parents' friends drop by. (Although even with company, when long pauses occur in a conver-sation, people still look toward the direction of the cottages. There very well might be some big temper tantrum drama the likes of which they have never seen before, and then our company can go home, feeling blessed that they have normal little children.) I can see that four of the older black girls from the Home are making their way over toward our patio. As they approach, the girls take turns looking back to see if a counselor is following. But tonight, at least for now, it appears that they have made the Great Escape from the area they are permitted to roam. Although they have crossed the sand line, my mother is friendly as they approach. She greets each and asks them to have a piece of her deliciously half-tart, half-sweet strawberry-rhubarb pie.

Mrs. Carswell, we would love to have a piece of your pie, says one girl.

Mrs. Carswell, you bake this pie or you buy it at the A&P grocery store? asks another.

You fool, Mrs. Carswell baked that pie, says the third. That pie looks home-made, not made by some factory worker wearing a hairnet.

Oh, yeah? Your *mudha* works in a factory, says the fourth girl.

Girls, sit down, have a piece of pie, my mother says, amicably breaking up any possible fight. Have some iced tea with me and my daughter Sue. You know Sue, right?

It is the first time I am introduced to a group of Home children, and they are introduced back to me. Margie. Monique. Rory, and Beverly. My mother believes children are equal, just like when one plays in a sandbox.

It takes forever for them to sit on the two sides of our picnic table, as they continuously look over their shoulders, making sure nothing will spoil this perfect summer night of sliced pie and iced tea. Once they finally sit, I notice how Rory—the girl next to me—gently puts one of her rear cheeks down, and only when she feels safe does she put down her other. Two of the girls, Margie and her older sister Monique, sit to the left and right of my mother. I am shy and slide my body all the way down to the end of the picnic table in order to give Rory and Beverly more than enough room to feel comfortable. I'm so far down the one side of the picnic table that my bony rear end is only halfway on the seat. I don't want the girls to feel crowded. I want them to feel a sense of belonging at our house, like my mother and I were the Welcome Wagoners. I want them to sit and talk with my mother and me long after the in-between passes. Maybe my mother will pitch the pup tent by night's end, and the girls and I can have a sleepover right beneath the stars.

Do you think we are pretty enough to get married? asks Beverly.

Mrs. Carswell, have you ever been away? asks Rory. Have you ever flown on a plane and did the pilot give you a set of wings like they do on TV?

I want to be a housewife, Mrs. Carswell, Monique says to my mother. How do you get to be a housewife? Do you have to go to do more school?

I want to drive a big truck, Mrs. Carswell, says Margie.

Girlfriend, that is a boy thing, pipes in her sister. You a boy thing? Don't see you got a boy thing for as long as I known ya.

As the girls continue to talk to my mother, often interrupting one another, I notice that occasionally they slap their hands down quickly onto their thighs and start giggling because they're having such a nice time. I think my mother feels the same because she pours each of them a second glass of her presweetened noncaffeine iced tea after they gulp down their first, which leads me to believe that they are never offered iced tea by Miss Mary Fundis.

The way they slap their thighs whenever they laugh is just what my mother does when something she hears is really funny. But the sound of their laugh is audible and big, whereas my mother's laugh is from deep down inside, almost like you can see rather than hear the laugh. It's like she is smoking a Virginia Slims, if she smoked, but she doesn't. She even made my father give up his OPs (swiping Other People's cigarettes, as my Aunt Mary called my father's preferred brand) when they met about a year before Jimmy was born. Virginia

Slims are what I want to smoke when I grow up. The commercials say they are specially designed for a lady's mouth shape. For now, I just practice on the Lucky gum cigarettes that Jimmy and I buy at the candy store up the street and pretend-smoke in our TV room. Each time we take a drag of our candy smokes we feel so much cooler than Mandy or Billy, whom we puff our cigarette smoke out on. They never seem to mind, though, because the smoke tastes like confectioners' sugar and Mandy and Billy love licking the area around their mouths whenever a puff comes their way.

My mother inhales a laugh all the way down inside her lungs just like the way Aunt Mary smokes her Salems. She keeps it inside her for this treasured time, which means whatever she just heard is still awfully funny, and she wants to keep it there just like Aunt Mary keeps her nicotine inside her lungs for a minute or so. Then my mother finally pushes the laughter up out of her lungs and through her mouth and nose, until she is ready to inhale a new laugh.

As she turns to me, Rory asks, Mrs. Carswell, this one your daughter or you get her next door?

Fool, what are you talking about? adds Beverly. Mrs. Carswell don't get her children from the Home. She gets them from Mr. Carswell. Ain't no Carswell child come from the Home.

Right, Mrs. Carswell?

Suddenly, the sliding glass door opens and my father walks outside, his hands nervously searching for keys or some other treasure inside the pockets of the orange tennis shorts he wears every, every, every day because he is in love with them so much.

Elaine, are my shorts clean? Did you put them in the wash today?

Elaine, I've only worn them three days in a row. They don't have to go in the wash yet.

Geesh, Elaine. Could you save money on soap detergent. It's expensive.

As he heads directly toward us, not even stopping to pick up the twins' toys that lie scattered around our little yard area, my father does that nervous cough thing with his throat like he is clearing it, but there isn't anything there. I feel like all of us are about to get caught doing something illegal even though my mother and I are just eating pie and drinking iced tea with our good friends. They're paying a visit like the way Mr. and Mrs. Murphy would. We have asked them to stay, or rather my mother has.

Is this where you belong? my father asks each girl as he stares in their dark-almond-colored eyes, looking around the picnic table, skipping my eyes and my mother's.

Yes, I want them to say. Yes, Mr. Carswell, we can eat pie with Mrs. Carswell and sit next to Sue. Our bumpers can rest on your precious picnic table.

But instead they reply, No, Mr. Carswell. Their heads now turn shamefully downward as if they have been caught committing the biggest offense and should be arrested for murder. My heart feels as though it is being torn apart. God has granted my Sunday wish to have friends from my backyard and now my father is being a big bully.

No, Mr. Carswell, we don't belong here.

After a few moments of just shaking their heads in shame, Monique looks up at my father and asks him a favor.

Just this once, Mr. Carswell, will you let us leave on our own if we promise to walk straight back to our cottages?

Then her sister, Margie, raises her head.

Can we walk back by ourselves without you taking us back like you always did ever since we were young?

Rory and Beverly raise their heads, all now looking proud and feeling hopeful.

We're almost thirteen now, Mr. Carswell. Can you just trust us this once? Please.

My father doesn't take a lot of time thinking about their request. His hands come out of his orange pockets and suddenly Monique's and Margie's hands are clutched in his.

I think it's time I took you girls back to your cottages. The staff will be missing you. Rory and Beverly, grab the other girls' hands.

My father adds, You know the rules.

He *didn't* trust them. I knew that when I turned to my mother, who was now clearing up the pie plates and placing the Tupperware cups inside the matching pitcher. She had tears in her eyes about what had just happened, even though she worked for the Home, too, and knew the same rules about possible runaways. It's just that I think on that night she sensed they weren't running away but rather they wanted to learn more about life outside the perimeter of 60 Academy Road. They were running *to* her.

The only way you knew my mother was really angry at my father was when she didn't talk to him for a day. He hated being ignored by her more than anything else. After the girls visited and he escorted them back to their cottage, she didn't speak to him for two full days. When my mother was angry, she was quiet. And when she was quiet, she refused to laugh and inhale her giggles until they exploded from her lungs, even if we were the ones trying to make her laugh.

When my mother was angry at my father, it meant she disagreed with him or thought he had been overly harsh. That hurt his feelings, which I knew because it was the only time he tried to be our best friend. He then played with us more, because she wouldn't play with him.

He had fewer playmates those two long days and nights following the in-between pie incident, because I decided to ignore him as well. He couldn't be my friend, either. My mother got him back, though. She bleached his orange shorts until they were almost pink.

Here's to your never breaking rules, John Carswell, she said aloud to herself as I watched her pour an entire bottle of Clorox into the washing machine.

Although I had kissed my next-door neighbor Ned Kirsch earlier that year, I didn't love him. I just wanted to know what kisses felt like and I had been interested in being a pig farmer's wife. Kisses felt like little butterflies roaming around in my stomach, but I believe the butterflies were there mostly out of the fear that Ned and I would get caught. After, I wondered when one passes the threshold into feelings of love. I loved my toys, my Barbies. I loved candy. I loved my mother and I loved my father, but if love were a measuring spoon, I loved my mother much more.

Not long after my father's orange shorts turned pink, he came home one day after work and told my mother he had a surprise for her. We all sat around the living room as my father opened up his briefcase. We didn't know what was inside. I assumed it included something for us as well.

As he slowly opened the briefcase, building suspense just like they did on *Dragnet,* he pulled out a brochure with pictures of dark men beating steel drums, women wearing colorful towels above their heads, and fairy-tale ocean water that matched the color of my light blue Easter pocketbook.

Elaine, we're going to Martinique.

My mother screamed like she had won the big prize behind one of the doors on *Let's Make a Deal.* She kissed my father like he was Monty Hall, and then jumped and jumped around our living room.

My parents were going to take a vacation without us.

Adults only, my father said to us. You get your grandmother. She'll make you fudge and serve you chipped beef on toast. You kids will love that.

My mother kept telling my father how much she loved him and how much she loved the thought of going to Martinique. Then she would look inside the brochure: at the floral-patterned bedspread and at the bar with seats so you could sit inside a pool and drink piña coladas, twirling the rum around with miniature paper umbrellas. She expressed love for every single object in the brochure, especially the waterfall.

The color of the water in Martinique didn't look real, not like the dark and green water in Cape Cod, where you had to find seashells by diving down to the bottom and picking up whatever shell you could grab. Sometimes you grabbed ugly ones and sometimes ones full of seaweed. Sometimes you even grabbed a rusty old beer can. It was the luck of the draw in that ocean. In Martinique, you could see seashells and colorful streams of fishes from above the water, because it was clear blue. How could water be so different from one ocean to another?

When I asked my mother about love and how you know you feel it, she told me that love was as clear as the water in Martinique. Then she said, Someday you'll see and you'll know.

There was only one day a year when it seems my backyard was worthy of a visit from the ghost of Martin Luther King Jr. One day a year everyone who lived at 60 Academy Road was equal, even if you lived in my house, or a cottage, or if you were my father, his boss Mr. Millard, or a counselor like Rezington, or Sheldon, or Miss Mary Fundis, or even the pool's latest lifeguard. That one day was the Albany Home for Children's Annual Lawn Festival, which was held each June.

During the summer I asked my mother what love really felt like, it suddenly stood right there in front of me at the best Lawn Festival ever.

I am in the middle of the bike loop. Colorful helium-filled balloons are tied to the branches of the trees surrounding me, seemingly pleading with the tree—like little children—to lift off with them way up into the late-afternoon sky. I am wearing white jeans stamped with yellow happy faces and a light blue polyester shirt that my mother bought for me at Woolworth's earlier that day. I eat a hot dog.

A boy I have never seen escaping from cottages or riding his bicycle on Saturday afternoons holds the hand of one of the young adult girls who always come to work at the Home during their college breaks. As he walks in my direction, the boy—who appears to be my age—pulls his counselor's arm to stop so that he can look at me. He suddenly smiles when he sees that the mustard I have layered on top of my foot-long hot dog has fallen backward onto my new shirt as I attempted to aim the dog upward like a space rocket toward my mouth. When I feel his dark eyes zeroing in on me, I immediately look down to the ground and blush. I am embarrassed that I have been this sloppy. My mother always says there is no need to pile mustard that high: It is supposed to enhance the flavor of a hot dog, not overpower it. The boy who smiles but doesn't laugh at me eventually wanders away, pulled by his counselor into the crowd of the hundreds of others who have come to enjoy the festival.

I look for my mother, all upset inside because my clothes are a mustard painting and this is a big day to celebrate (as my father explained), All the meaning and the history of our backyard.

I find her over by the petting zoo. My mother takes Sarah's hands in hers and they walk around the little gated zoo and touch the fur of a goat, a calf, a sheep, a llama, and a pig—which makes Sarah shriek from the strange feeling of prickly fur mixed in with pink skin, like Marnie's fat belly. I run to my mother's side just as she props Sarah up to take a ride on top of a small horse. As soon as she sees my mustard shirt, she asks her friend Mrs. Allegretti to hold Sarah while she quickly takes me behind one of the bushes near Winnie Cottage. Off goes my shirt; she wipes it with her handkerchief from the pocket of her dress, and turns the shirt inside out. I am not completely clean, but she has magically made me look acceptable.

The Lawn Festival is like having Hoffman's Playland in our own backyard for the day. There is a hayride pulled by a tractor driven by two of the maintenance workers, who dress in blue overalls, checkered red shirts, and cowboy hats, and sport long pretend handlebar mustaches right above the long corn pipes that dangle from their lips. The hayride takes you along the inner perimeter of our backyard, and while you sit on top of the square hay piles you sing farm songs and laugh because sometimes the hayride men drive the tractor so fast and you can feel the hay just whip up from the floor of the open trailer until it gets all tangled up and you wind up with hay hair.

Over in the maintenance garage, right next to Parsons Cottage, a food stand like the kind you would find at a fair or at a Little League ballpark is staffed by volunteers. All about the age of my mother, these women talk about living on these very same grounds many years ago to all those they serve food to with a smile.

Sweetheart, would you care for some popcorn?

How about a basket of fries? Would you like an orange soda? Oh, I can tell you would love to have a grape soda, wouldn't you now? Would you like some cotton candy? Look, our friend is twirling the sugar right now onto a cone. How about a foot-long hot dog; have you tried one yet?

The adults who say they once lived at the Albany Home don't look like grown-up versions of Jodie. I can't imagine that they ever tried to set off fire alarms when they were kids. They are all so nice and friendly. It's a bit comforting to know that they are just older versions of the children who now live in my backyard. And when the children in my backyard grow up they will be just like them. They will come back to serve hot dogs to children who will live in the cottages many years from now.

The food at the concession stand all costs one ticket each, and my father gave me and Jimmy about a yard's worth of tickets so that we would really enjoy ourselves. He was like that, my father. Sometimes he could be your really good friend, and then other times he would act so grown up and in charge you were scared of him—or I was. I suppose in a family of seven some-one had to be the real grown-up. He didn't know things like nursery rhymes, nor could he sing all the songs in *Chitty Chitty Bang Bang*. My mother did. She could be your friend all the time. I was glad she was second in charge, al-though it frightened me to think Jimmy was third. More and more, he was getting on my nerves.

After I stood in line for another foot-long hot dog (on my way to eating two full feet of meat), I decided I would finish it and get back in line for a box of popcorn and all the other food items you could possibly buy with a ticket. When I finished one of each, I would get back in line and repeat the food se-lections all over again. With the tickets left over, Jimmy and I joined forces since stuffing our mouths with food was a strictly solitary thing to do and get-ting in line first with one of our tickets was always a race against each other, to see who could eat everything twice in the fastest amount of time.

Eventually, we headed over to the area that was in the far back of our side of the backyard. Two picnic tables were set next to each other for a watermelon-eating contest. It was the one day a year where we were allowed to sit at a pic-nic table with a Home kid and compete against one another as we locked elbows devouring the melon and spitting out the black seeds on the paper plates in front of us. I could have sat at that picnic table handing over my tick-ets as long as they lasted, but you had to give up your spot after only two rounds. Jimmy and I were quick eaters—we could devour dinner in five min-utes—but when it came to a watermelon-eating contest next to the children from the Home we were about as fast as slow little Sarah. It's like watermelon eating was a road race to them, and every time they downed a slice right to its green edge, they kept their eyes steadily on the finish line: the toy prize given to the fastest eater. I wanted the toy even if it wasn't that big of a deal—some-times they were just stickers or a can of Play-Doh. But I could see the boys and girls from the cottages wanted it more.

To the other side of the watermelon-eating contest was a dunking booth where the Home children had the chance to throw basketballs at a lever. One of their favorite or not-so-favorite counselors, or my father, sat above a vat of water in a chair. If you hit the lever just right, down might splash Brent, Marnie's first owner. He always came back to the festival each year to see the kids and I suppose to say hi and give kisses to Marnie. The best part was hitting the lever and seeing hefty Rezington hit the water and pretty much emptying out the vat. She would laugh so hard and scream out, Help me, Help me. I don't know how to swim.

As the night went on, a group of old men whom my father called the Shriners continued playing patriotic music like "I'm a Yankee Doodle Dandy" on their trombones and other horns, tapping their polished black shoes on the yellow cement lines of the area meant for the visitors' parking lot. The Shriners always wore these superlarge Dixie-Cup-looking black hats on their heads and sported red-wine-colored jackets. It seemed all the men were old and fat, but my father said that was okay because they had once fought in the war. My father thought they were heroes and always would welcome them to our backyard like they were movie stars. Most other people ignored them. The songs they played were just noise.

I didn't know everyone who came to our Lawn Festival. In the weeks leading up to it, my father and I would go up and down the streets next to Academy Road and Scotch-tape flyers to the trees on the street, advertising THE ALBANY HOME FOR CHILDREN'S ANNUAL LAWN FESTIVAL—COME HAVE FUN—EAT—GO FOR A HAYRIDE—PETTING ZOO—COME MEET US. WE'D LIKE TO MEET YOU! One night my father sat at his homework table and designed an ad, which he then sent off to the *Times Union* with a check. You had to pay for things if you wanted to place them in the paper, but if you were a story you got in for free.

People came because everyone loves a carnival and seeing things such as clowns walking on stilts. But some neighbors didn't come because they didn't like the idea of having bad kids living near their street. They didn't understand that the kids weren't bad but that some came from bad parents who had hurt them and that they were now just trying to feel better in their heads, or find new, nice parents who wouldn't beat them up like they were just dolls a dog could chew apart, limb by limb.

When I went to bed that night after the Lawn Festival ended, I thought about the nice boy who didn't laugh at my mustard mistake. There was something special about him. I hoped I would see him tomorrow right before our swim time. I wondered what brought the new boy to live here and whether it was because of his parents not being able to love him in the right way, or because he had more emotions than you were supposed to, or whether it was because he was a real orphan—in my book, the saddest type of kid there.

The next day, I went over to the pool ten minutes before our noontime staff swimming hour.

His name was Ryan.

When he saw me holding on to the fence, peeking through the diamond holes, he immediately ran over to the diving board and did a perfect jackknife into the water. Running to the diving board was a big no at the pool, and a counselor screamed out, Ryan, do that again and you'll be taking a five-minute time-out, as soon as Ryan came up for air and shook his hair into shape so that he could look in my direction.

Throughout the course of that summer, I went to the pool a little earlier each day and night before our appointed swim times. I would stare through the fence at Ryan as he practiced his butterflies and breaststrokes. I kept thinking how much the new boy with his deep olive skin and dark brown, almost black, brooding eyes looked like one of the handsome Roman warriors from a history coloring book.

Then again, Ryan looked like a Roman warrior from his left side only. Looking like a real-life Ken doll did not extend to his right side, because he had scars that tore open his skin making it look all blotchy and bumpy starting at the top of his neck, down through his chest, and even past his kneecaps. After Ryan toweled himself off, before my family and I were allowed to enter the pool, he would turn his body to his left side—I think to shield his scars from my view. Then he would turn around all bundled up in two towels and smile at me. A few weeks later when he finally said hello, he used my name.

Hello, Sue.

My heart fluttered with butterfly feelings of love.

I thought about Ryan before trying to go to sleep. I imagined talking to him about everything—from TV shows to snacks. I hoped to one day have the chance to sit right next to him on the lifeguard stand, even if we didn't say much and just dangled our feet like little swings in the air. I wanted to kiss him with this feeling I felt inside. I even came to think that maybe Ryan was my forever—my Martinique.

···

A couple of months after he arrived, Ryan began writing me letters. My father brought the letters that Ryan had mailed to me home in his locked brief-case. Only he knew the combination to the briefcase even though Jimmy and I were constantly trying to figure it out by rolling the numbers around until we hit the right combination. I don't know what Jimmy and I expected to find in the case—we hoped it was full of treasures, like little books that told the story of all the kids in our backyard that we were never supposed to read. Part of us knew in the back of our minds it was probably just boring paperwork. Maybe he even carried a brochure of Martinique that matched my mother's and that he put out on his office desk every day like she put hers on the windowsill in the morning.

Susan, you have some letters.

That was what my father said the day when he came home from work and placed his briefcase on the formal dining table next to the sliding glass door.

Susan, you have some letters, wasn't like my father saying, Sue, I see Cammy wrote you. He sounded serious. I could see caution in his now stormy blue eyes.

Have you been flirting with a boy from the Home?

Flirting with Ryan? I don't know. I have been smiling at Ryan. Is that the same thing? Why is that wrong?

Because he has written you some letters and you are not to have contact with children who live next door. That is a rule that you can never change.

Nevertheless, my father handed me a couple of envelopes full of crayon-colored red hearts on the outside addressed to me. I didn't have to open the envelopes. My father had already taken the liberty of using his work's letter opener to do just that. When I started to read the first letter, I realized my father had also taken the liberty of using a Magic Marker to black out words and sentences that he didn't want me to read.

I was allowed to read sentences that said Ryan wanted to marry me, that I was beautiful, that I was his Rapunzel and would I let down my long blond hair so that he could **Black Mark** into **Black Mark** one night.

I think my father allowed Ryan to keep those words in because I only had short blond hair and our windows were already secured shut with the nails—plus we had the new security system of Marnie, the dachshund-cop, who barked at any sound at night she found disturbing.

In his letters—or at least the letters left in envelopes; the others my father had taken out and left me just the decorated envelope with my name—Ryan let me know that he was devoted to me. In one, he described how we would one day exchange wedding vows on the lawn near the softball field and swings, underneath a beautiful pale blue tent, and he would wear a tuxedo to match the tent. In another letter, he wondered whether I would be patient and wait for him as he had to save money and find a job first before he could take on a wife.

Dear Sue,
   At night . . .

Then my father would mark out complete lines and paragraphs until he found ones he felt more comfortable with.

> *I would like you to swim with me at* **Black Mark** *with no one* **Black Mark.** *We'll have new towels which will* **Black Mark** *next* **Black Mark.** *Under the water* **Black, Black, Black Mark** . . . *when no one . . .* **Black, Black** . . . *until the sun comes up. . . .* **Black, Black Mark** . . . *then one day into the* **Black Mark.**
>
>   *Love, Ryan*
>   *P.S.* **Black Mark.**

Ryan's letters to me were long and written on lined white paper from a school notebook. The words I was allowed to read were chosen by my father. He gave me only those letters in which he was confident I could not read between the lines. The others, he put the envelopes back into his briefcase and locked up. Then he shook his head and said under his breath that Ryan was a troubled kid.

I asked my father if Ryan was sick, considering he lived here now.

No, Ryan has a different form of illness.

Well then, Mom should go to his cottage and make him feel better, right?

No. No one can help him right now. He just needs a lot of time to let his feelings come out.

I asked my father if Ryan was ill because he loved me. He said no.

I asked if it was because of his scars. I doubted my father would answer a question about the reasons a child was placed at the Home. For that type of information I usually hid in the hallway near the entrance to the living room as my father told my mother the stories of his day.

Surprisingly, he did answer this one. He said Ryan was hurt badly in a fire and that's what gave him the scars.

Is that why he's here? I mean just because you get burned in a fire shouldn't make you a Home kid. If I was burned in a fire, would I live in the cottages instead of our house?

Part of me was hoping my father would say yes. I didn't know exactly what kind of burn allowed you to get a bed in the cottages and I knew I didn't want scars as severe as Ryan's, but I could figure out a way to burn myself on the stove. Then I could move in with Ryan and we could get married beneath the light blue tent even sooner than before we were sixteen, which is what Ryan said was the legal age in one of his letters.

No, you don't come here if you are hurt in a fire, my father said. You go to the hospital. You come here if your mother dies in a fire and you try your hardest to save her.

You come here if, miraculously, you escape and live. That's why Ryan is here.

Even though I knew my father didn't like my frequent barrage of questions about the children in our backyard, I couldn't control my curiosity about them. I think he regretted telling me the truth about anything, because sometimes he would just blurt out the words with a measure of life-is-just-unfair in his voice, and then he would immediately turn red and walk away from me, always saying, Oh, forget what I said. Geesh.

But I never forgot. I just kept adding new stories to my memory bank.

My father was frustrated that I didn't understand the complexities of my backyard and yet I had a strong desire to do just that.

But nothing ever really added up—even when I heard the true stories of why this child or that child had been placed there. I listened in as he told my mother while they sat in their chairs, sipping their bottles of Genesee after my father's workday.

It didn't make sense that the boy named Tom who was a bit hefty—which is what I called Jimmy now because he was fatter than me—lived at the Home because when he was a baby he fell off a chair and hit his head and it made him slow. It didn't make sense that Tom saw his mother in a parking lot one day after she had been Christmas shopping with a friend and he was there in one of the Home's vans. When she pulled away, Tom's mother didn't see him frantically waving both his hands, trying to get her attention. Mommy, Mommy, he screamed to her as she kept her gloves on the steering wheel, inching through the snow, laughing like she was having the best time.

It didn't make sense that Sean lived at the Home because his mother wanted him to act more like a boy. If Sean wanted to put on a fashion show over by the sandbox, should that be a reason why you lived there and not at your own home? My father told my mother that Sheldon was trying really hard to make Sean more of a boy, but something wasn't working. He said they still needed to learn more about Sean's condition. To me, Sean's problem had an easy solution. Sheldon should just take away Sean's Barbie dolls and send him home.

It didn't make sense that a little girl came to live at the home because she was too thin. Why should weight be a reason that you lived there? When my father told my mother the girl often heard gunshots coming from her father's basement, then why didn't the girl's mother take away her father's gun? Her father was the bad one. Why did she need help?

It didn't make sense that children who were orphans lived there. If they were just orphans and they weren't sick, why couldn't they just have a new mother and father right away? The world of the children living in my back-yard had no rhyme or reason.

I once heard my father tell my mother about a little girl named Colleen who lived in the farthest cottage from our house. Her story made sense. I could understand why she needed some help and why she lived in a cottage. Colleen had killed her stepmother after hitting her over the head with a golf club because she was even meaner than the stepmother in *Cinderella*. So if Colleen killed someone, it was a good thing she was getting help instead of going off to some scary jail. What didn't make sense was that my father said the judge didn't blame Colleen. My father even said to my mother, who let out a short shriek when she learned what Colleen had done, Elaine, she really is one of the nicest girls here. She is very well behaved. I think she has a real future.

...

Perhaps it was best that the five-year-old girl named Karen, who burned down her family's garage with matches before taking on her aunt's house, lived in the back cottage with Colleen, the good murderer. That kind of stuff sounded like a kid was sick to me.

But wasn't there a difference between Ryan's illness and Karen's? Karen obviously loved the color of fire so much that she wanted to see the flames regardless of the damage. Ryan didn't want to burn anything. His mother was consumed by fire. And what was so wrong about Ryan loving me? He just wanted someone close to him, maybe to take the place of the love he felt for his dead mother.

Even though I kept waiting for a new pile of censored letters or just empty envelopes, it came to the point that I finally realized my father would never again say, Susan, you have mail. When I realized that, I knew that my first real love, my Martinique, was destined to end. Ryan was told that he couldn't write me letters anymore. Now he was embarrassed whenever he saw me at the pool standing there with my father, because he had never imagined his letters would have been read by anyone other than me, let alone deconstructed. Since I was never allowed to write a letter back but rather just smile and say hi at the pool, Ryan finally gave up on me. Things even deteriorated to the point that he would turn his head whenever I passed him while I walked Marnie as he walked up Academy Road with the other Home children toward Stewart's. Nor would he look my way when his head popped up from the water after he jumped off the diving board.

The next month Ryan turned his love toward my sister, Mandy. He even slipped a Cracker Jack diamond ring into my younger sister's all-too-receptive hands. I may have received the first marriage proposal, but Mandy got the first engagement ring.

It was during their first few weeks when they arrived at the Home—right after the summer of Ryan—that the children who lived in the cottages learned about the Carswell children. It was made clear by someone that they were not to go near us and that they could only look and not try to talk to us. It got to the point that I felt like we were characters in a movie. If my father played the role of the king of our backyard, my mother became its beautiful queen. My siblings and I were the princes and princesses of the royal grounds that made up our backyard.

I didn't want the children from the Home to believe that we thought we were better than them. But although our lives were lived together, we were deemed forever separate.

Or maybe not. What is controllable changes over time—such as the mind of a child, such as the mind of me.

Dress Code and Other Necessities

My mother and I stand patiently in line. Our fashionable Dr. Scholl's sandals with matching red leather bands touch the dark polished brick floor of the hallway eventually leading to a small recreation room. There we will buy my clothes for the new school year. And in a little less than a week's time I will begin learning how to play the chords of a flute with my small fingers, speak French, act in plays, and dance in light beige slippers as one of the newest students attending the Albany Academy for Girls, which, as my father points out in another of his History Lessons, is one of the oldest girls' schools in the country. History surrounds where I live, even where I will be going to school, and yet strangely, it is the most boring class of all. Sometimes I just want to scream to him, Who cares, Daddy? But I know if I do that, I will be spanked. I am the only one of my brothers and sisters who has ever been spanked by my father. It's because I am bad, because I am like Jodie. Sometimes I have a really bad temper, so I am spanked even when my mother tries to protect me. I suppose my father thinks it is the best way to punish me, to make me remember what awaits me if I do it again, but still my temper returns again and again. And how come like Jodie, when my temper flares, I just don't get a medicine shot from my mother? When I ask my father if I can have a shot of juice instead of a spank, he says, You're not a Home kid, silly. Your temper's not the same thing. You're a fully functioning child.

Today is a peaceful day as my mother and I wait our turn to enter the room to buy my four new colorful uniforms and a white sweater to wear once the fall chill begins, as well as other items required on the Dress Code and Other Necessities list. The list had been sent to our house earlier in the summer. My mother has studied the list as hard as she does her crossword puzzles.

She slips on her red-framed eyeglasses with their monogrammed gold *E* at the base of the right lens and reads the piece of paper, now dog-eared around its corners, aloud one final time as we wait. Jimmy said right before we left the house, They're not real clothes if you don't buy them at Sears. No clothing store located on Academy Road, Albany, New York 12208.

Jimmy is always showing off the fact that he knows our zip code, like he's Albert Einstein.

My mother looks down at me through the bifocal blurry part of her glasses and says that we will need to buy a Girls Academy–issued gym tunic and matching blue bloomers, a green AAG tote bag to hold my books, two long-sleeved white blouses to wear underneath my pink, aqua, yellow, and pale blue uniforms, and we will buy two short-sleeved shirts for the warmer weather.

The white socks, she says, we can get at Woolworth's.

She adds, When you get home from school each day, Sue, I want you to hurry to the washing machine so that we can have the shirt nice and clean and ready for the next-next day. You can start the washer, but I'll pour in the Clorox bleach. This is a very proper school, but don't worry, you'll fit right in.

I ask my mother to lower the list so that I can look it over with her. Instead, my eyes dart to the right side of the sheet where the cost of each item does not have the usual red slash marks that I have become accustomed to seeing at Sears—where we buy our clothing. The sign at Sears always reads SALE ITEMS, REDUCED, or 50% OFF. Blowout sale means a big clothing splurge for our family. As my eyes wander down the list, I notice that the prices for the things my mother has marked with the letter X in pencil are expensive, a million times the price of clothing at Sears.

Jimmy and I say anything that is really expensive costs a million dollars. He told me I would never get a guitar for Christmas because it cost a million dollars. I told him that he was eating too much and that it would eventually cost our parents a million dollars.

As we inch forward in the line, sharp biting chills run down my spine every time my mother opens her wallet, counts her money, and then recounts the twenty-dollar bills, the tens, fives, and ones, over and over again. My entire body is popping with cold goose bumps even though the warm sunbeams break through the polished windows of the Girls Academy. I wrap my arms around my shoulders and nervously sway back and forth until my mother tells me to stop.

Please, Sue, not another tic.

I am terrified we will be poorer than we already are even though I don't really notice it. I just feel it, intuitively. I start wondering, what if my mother can't go to lovely Martinique and see the rainbows cascading off the waterfalls with my father just because of me?

I feel like I'm back in Williamsburg, Virginia, which is where we went on vacation last spring to learn more about colonial times. My father said it would be good for us and it would make Jimmy and me smarter.

As he said, Seeing history, kids, with your eyes is far better than reading about history in a textbook.

Jimmy replied right back to him, Well, if you're reading history, at least you can skip the pages. Can't skip a long boring day at Williamsburg with people dressed in freak clothing.

The only part of Historical Williamsburg I liked was staying at the Holiday Inn nearby because we got to put quarters in a machine by our bed and magical fingers in the bedspring vibrated it back and forth. It was about as close as you could get to having a roller-coaster ride in your own mattress.

The high point of Colonial Village was the gift shop where we each got a chunk of rock candy. As for the learning part, I guess seeing how people churned butter was a little interesting only because we got a taste of it when it was ready.

When Jimmy asked the butter churner if he had any Skippy and grape Smucker's to go with the bread, my father did his adult laugh, which meant Jimmy said something really stupid.

What I remember most from our history lesson trip to Williamsburg was that when the colonial types misbehaved—because maybe they stole things like churned butter or rock candy—their heads were locked inside heavy wooden stocks for days until they were really sorry.

Our colonial man guide, who wore tights that made Jimmy feel all icky, asked Jimmy and I if we would like to put our heads in the stock for a minute. Even though we pretended to scream Help me, Mommy, help me, we're gonna die, we were only kidding around. But I remembered the heavy feeling of the weight of the wood against the back of my neck.

I made such a big mistake in the way I tried to convince Mrs. Kelly that I belonged at the Albany Home school. I should have used my head and painted everything blood red and painted dead people. I should have copied the actual images I saw when I went into the Home's art room. The Home school was much more difficult to get into than AAG. And if I had, I could have worn my Blowout Sale clothing from Sears every day if I attended that school. With my start at the Girls Academy, I felt like I had ended up in a place way above my family's heads. I had put my parents' heads in a wooden lock because of what I had done by showing off with my ladybug watercolors that didn't serve the purpose I had wanted them to.

I am not looking forward to the minute when we will be at the front of the line to order the items in the Dress Code and Other Necessities list. Once we get there, my mother will hand over her list to a lady who doesn't look too nice. She should be very nice because my mother is opening up her wallet. My mother is going to hand over so much of the money that she has saved working part-time as a nurse at the Home, and the money my father makes, which should be considered special money because he looks over the care of children who don't have parents and some whose parents don't want them. He takes good care of the Jodies and Ryans of the world. The lady really should have better manners toward my mother because, as my father always says, money doesn't grow on trees. Then again I'm getting the sense that money does grow on the trees of the girls who are soon to be my classmates. Maybe it just doesn't grow on the trees in my backyard.

We have stood in line for well over an hour, and while my mother smiles at the woman and her daughter in front of us and the woman and her two daughters behind us, they just give her a quick smile back. No one asks her to talk, and no one says, Oh, is your daughter new to the Academy? and no one says, I saw you at bingo last Saturday night. Weren't you the one handing out the bingo cards?

People at the grocery store ask my mother that question all the time. She has become a celebrity in bingo land, but no one in the Academy line seems to appreciate how famous she really is. It hurts my feelings.

Jimmy was right.

Once I had received the envelope addressed to me and embossed with official Albany Academy for Girls letterhead, stating that I had been officially admitted to the Academy, Jimmy said, Those kinds of people that go to the rich-girl school or the rich-boy school across the street—they don't *drive* Cadillacs. They get driven *in Cadillacs* by people who work for their daddies. They are all rich and have a million dollars. They have ponies and pools and race cars and big TVs, and they all live in mansions. They also wear fur coats, which is like having a dead Marnie tied across your neck.

Then he meanly said, Good luck, Susie, and walked away.

Suddenly my mother stops counting her money in front of the not-so-nice lady. She turns to me, her face now as red as a really bad sunburn, and says, Oh my, we can't afford two long-sleeved shirts. We need to buy the recorder for flute lessons. It says the word *mandatory* under the Necessities list. It's a specific type of flute that we can't buy anywhere else. I didn't know it was a must. I thought we could get a cheaper one up at Montgomery Ward's. I've made a mistake and there just isn't enough money in my wallet to buy the flute and the shirt. I'll have to wash your one long-sleeved white shirt every night, but it will be there for you warm in the dryer every morning.

Is that okay with you?

I want to cry. I don't care about a flute, the stupid dance shoes, or the oxford Academy sandals we have to buy. Why can't I wear my new Keds? They're nice and I would keep them white even if I have to polish them every night before I go to bed. I want only the one blue dress and I want to wear it every day. I don't need the sweater. I'll only spill mustard on it anyway.

If I'm nervous and I don't have to pay, I can't imagine how my mother is feeling at this point especially after the woman asks my mother why she hadn't prepared her list long ahead of time. I want to scream out, She has, you not-nice lady. She has. But the words don't come out. I have yet another tic. When I feel really agitated, I get this feeling in my throat like it's closing up and I'm going to choke to death. I'm choking right now.

I look at my mother, who apologizes profusely and says how truly sorry she is. I look into her eyes and I see they do not look directly at the woman who sells the Necessities, but rather her eyes and her monogrammed *E* glasses have turned downward like she is ashamed of who she is and how little money she has and that she matters so much less than the lady who sells the all-powerful clothing. I want to run out of the front door of the rich little girls' school. I want to take my mother's hand and bring her with me and run all the way back to our house and into the backyard where we do belong, where she is the queen of our property.

I am frozen in my steps as my mother hands over every dollar she has and her three remaining quarters. I am scared to death at the prospect that my mother might clutch her heart again.

The previous Thanksgiving, as my mother was putting the Only for Holidays bone china into the dishwasher, her heart began to flutter like a bird whose wing was hurt and was flapping desperately to fly up into the trees to join its friends. At first we couldn't hear her as she softly called out to my father, who was reading our favorite book, *A Child's Garden of Verses* by Robert Louis Stevenson, to all of us.

> *At evening when the lamp is lit;*
> *Around the fire my parents sit . . .*

Mr. Stevenson's stories, or rather his book of poems, was one of our favorite books. As we lay around the living room by the fireplace, it was nice hearing my father use his kind-toned voice, so much softer than his work voice or his I'm-in-charge-of-this-house voice. My father used his kind voice every morning when he greeted us, and he used it when he came home from work, asking us about our day and then again at night right before saying good night as we headed off to our beds. While my mother usually read us books or recited from memory her mind's treasure trove of stories, on Thanksgiving and Christmas Eve my father was the appointed storyteller as only she could put the bone china in the dishwasher without worrying one of us might break it.

As he nearly finished one poem, we suddenly heard my mother scream from the kitchen.

John. John.

I didn't even know that my mother had that loud voice inside her. But she needed my father to hear her even if it meant upsetting all of us. She made a sacrifice that night by scaring us with the tone of her voice. If she hadn't, I don't know how it all would have ended.

John, John, my heart, my heart.

Everything was a blur after my father ran to the kitchen: My father helping my mother up from the floor where he found her kneeling next to her china . . . My father putting my mother's warm black coat on her back and not putting her arms through the sleeves . . . My father yelling at Jimmy to go next door and get Mr. and Mrs. Millard . . . Mr. and Mrs. Millard running into our house wearing their slippers . . . Go, John, Go . . . You'll be okay, Elaine . . . We'll make sure the children are fine . . . Mandy and Billy crying as Mr. Millard tried to hold the twins in his arms with all his strength as they both kicked his knees in order to run outside in their pajamas to catch up with my mother.

We didn't know what was happening to my mother's heart, but we knew something was terribly wrong. And so we just banged on the frosted-over windowpane as we stood on the chairs surrounding the kitchen table and screamed out our mother's name and pleaded with our father to save her. In order to watch her every move, Jimmy and I kept breathing on the window to make it warm so that we could see our father holding my mother's arm around his neck as he led her to the car with the snowflakes falling all around them.

My parents made their way to my mother's side of our station wagon, careful that neither would fall. My mother wouldn't take her mittenless hands off her heart. It was like she was still trying to keep it in her chest and not let her heart fall out of her coat and roll onto our driveway. As she headed toward the car and my father helped her into her seat, not once did she turn around and wave to us. She did not turn around and give us the reassuring smile that always comforted us because we knew whatever the problem was, everything would be okay.

When my mother walked out of the house that night with her fast heart beating away, we had no idea whether our safe world was shattered or not. We had no answers as to whether my mother would ever come back with her smile and a fixed-up heart. We could only wonder and hope. To do that, all five of us simply cried our eyes out while Mr. and Mrs. Millard tried to get us to play Charades.

We are ending our shopping spree at the Academy. My mother and I help the woman as she packs up my uniform, flute, shirts, tote bag, dance shoes, and oxford shoes into two brown paper bags. I hold my breath, hoping that my mother's feelings have not been too hurt. I say a prayer in my mind and I promise God I will always behave if my mother doesn't have another panic attack, as she did that last Thanksgiving. I pray that her heart stays calm so that she doesn't have to go to the hospital ever again.

Although I know one of the Calm Down Pills is always in her purse, a simple pill never makes me feel that safe about my mother's prospects of living forever.

Not long after that first Thanksgiving when her heart fluttered, I thought I had lost her for the second time in my life—the first being when she went away for what seemed like forever to give birth to the twins. I became obsessed about predicting my mother's life span. Obsessing over things was becoming my primary activity. At night, I would lie awake in my bed, beneath my yellow blanket, and stare at the glow-in-the-dark stars my mother had plastered on my bedroom ceiling because it added a little light to my room and made me feel I was sleeping right under the stars. She had hoped it would calm my fears of the dark. With Marnie curled down by my toes, I would add and subtract the number of years I figured my mother would or could live. Numbers were complicated; I didn't earn good marks in Mrs. Kelly's math class. The longest time I could draw an imaginary lifeline for my mother across my star-draped ceiling was pretty old. I thought, *What if she lives to the age of ninety?* But then I thought about my grandmother with the beehive hairdo: She was in her sixties and she was old. So what if my mother just lived to be that age? And then my grandfather, he was eleven years older than my grandmother, so maybe she would live to my grandfather's age. Still, it all seemed too short a time.

One thing seemed true. Just as babies will always be born, life will end. There came a time when all goldfish died. Marnie would die. My grandparents would die, as would my father and my siblings. All this made me sad and dark inside, like I was in a black hole that I couldn't get out of. The thought of my mother dying made me cry really hard. But the thing is, I couldn't tell anyone about my fear, especially my father. He would say I was irrational, that I should lighten up and not think so much, it wasn't good for me. If I told my mother, she would read me a story from *Mother Goose* or another fable and somehow assure me, there, there, I'm not going to die.

What I hoped was that if my mother died, she would take me with her and we could be buried in the same coffin. She would have her silk pillowcase, so that her hair wouldn't get messy, and I would have my yellow pillowcase and pillow, which was becoming flatter over the years, and not as puffy. At the age of almost eight, even more than when I turned three, I knew I could not live a happy life without my mother. It would be better to be dead with her than to cry every day through the rest of a sad life.

The truth of life ending wasn't included in the fairy tales my mother read to us every night before we went off to sleep. I learned the possibility of that fate the night she walked into the snowstorm with her heart that was beating too fast. When she came back later that evening, I knew everything would not be all right forever. I knew everything was all right for now. My mother's life was about making it through twenty-four hours, and I prayed the same thing would happen the next day, and then the day after that, too.

My father walks me to school my first day at the Girls Academy in September 1969. But first, we stop off at his office so that he can show his work friends how nice I look in my pink uniform.

Susie, you look so pretty . . . Your father is so proud that he is able to send you to the Academy . . . Your father tells me you have one color uniform for every day of the week—except Friday . . . Did your mother iron your shirt for you this morning? . . . It is starched perfectly . . . Your father says you'll be speaking French by the end of the day . . . Will you be a ballerina? . . . Are you excited?

I can't wait to be back in my real clothes when school is over at 3 P.M. I can't wait to be me again. I don't want anyone to look at my face.

My father takes my hand, and we walk down Academy Road. Babs Henry runs after us screaming, Susie, John, I want to take your picture. Please. We stop to pose in front of the bricks that hide the cottages from the street.

Babs asks my father and me to say Cheese twice so she can give another photo to her mother. We resume our walk once Babs kisses me on the cheek like I'm some sort of four-leaf clover.

As we near the end of the Albany Home property and the brick wall becomes lower, I look back toward the cottages. Between them, I can see kids like my best-friend-but-not Jodie, too-tall Tom, and my good friends for one evening Monique, Margie, Rory, and Beverly wearing their play clothes, walking in the direction of Parsons Cottage for their school day. My neck and eyes stay turned on the view of the children until I can't see them anymore as my father and I pass the long sidewalk in front of the property that belongs to Temple Beth Emeth. My father says we cannot cut across the temple's parking lot the first day of school, but he says that when I walk down the street by myself tomorrow, I can do so if I choose.

Today, for my first day of school, my father wants us to enter the Academy through its official entrance, passing the big green-and-white sign that reads THE ALBANY ACADEMY FOR GIRLS, FOUNDED 1814. As we continue walking down the long entranceway, the lawn cut to perfection and the tree branches so precise and measured, sometimes our shoes touch the grass when my father thinks an oncoming car comes too close to us. I am the only student who walks to the Girls Academy and lives on Academy Road. Everyone else lives in the distant reaches of Albany or in its rich suburbs.

Eventually we pass the small circle driveway where girls dash out of their family cars and greet an older woman who wears a long black skirt and a starched white blouse, and has a very fancy hairdo held together with a tremendous amount of hair spray. She stands in front of the school right be-

fore the three steps leading into the glass doors of the Academy. My new
school is a one-story rectangular building with an open corridor in its middle
and a garden that even my father is jealous of.

We walk up to this woman I have not yet met, and my father introduces
me to Mrs. Rich, the headmistress of the school.

Oh yes, Mr. Carswell, how are you?

Please call me John.

John, I've been waiting for your daughter to arrive. We are so happy she is
joining us this year at AAG. Oh my, Susan, what has happened to your face?
Were you in an accident?

Jimmy was right.

Yikes, Susie, Jimmy said to me right before he left for his new year at
School 19. Susie is not going to make any friends with that big white *X* bandage across your face. And that yellow medicine stuff just looks yucky. You
should have been more careful, like the way Jimmy swims. Those kids gonna
say you have a case of the cooties. You look like a Freak. Gonna be a long day
for Susie.

My brother had no idea how painful and lonely that day really was and all
the days after that.

I walk into my homeroom after being escorted down the hallway by Mrs.
Rich. She introduces me to my new teacher, who is about the same age as Mrs.
Kelly. Mrs. Homan then says, Class, let's all welcome Susan C. Carswell and
give her a round of applause for joining us today.

The room is quiet. I hear whispering leaving the mouths of many of my sixteen classmates and landing into the ears of the others. And I see them point
until I can't take it anymore and just put my head down. Mrs. Homan takes me
on a little tour of my new classroom, which includes our own bathroom. She
says that all I have to do is raise my hand and ask and I will be allowed to go. I
won't ask. I'll wait until I get home. Mrs. Homan leads me to an empty desk
and seats me beside two other girls. She says this will be my desk for the year
and that I must keep it clean. Then Mrs. Homan places a white tag over the top
button of my short-sleeved white shirt. She explains it is my posture tag. If any
teacher or Mrs. Rich should see me slouching in the hallways, I will get a mark
on my tag. If I get five marks, she will have to call my mother. If I get ten
marks, my parents will have to come to the school. If I get . . .

I don't need to hear any more. I'll stand up as straight as a ruler. I don't want to worry my mother, and I certainly don't want my parents to have to come to the school to be embarrassed because I ignored the rules of posture.

Mrs. Homan then addresses my classmates, We are delighted to have three new girls this year in the third grade. Susan C. Carswell, why don't you stand in front of the blackboard first and tell us all about yourself?

I am shy when I don't know anyone. And I don't know anyone in my class, or at this school. I slowly walk to the board and stand before the other girls. I try to look at them, but they are looking too closely at me like they are all telescopes and I am the moon. Saying nothing, I look down at my shiny oxford shoes. I feel like I'm going to fall down.

Mrs. Homan kindly leads me with some questions.

Susan, tell the girls where you live.

I point in the direction of my house. And then I say, I live at the Albany Home for Children.

I have messed up and broken my father's rule, but I do not want to say anything more.

Mrs. Homan clears it up for me as some of the girls cover their mouths and laugh. They say to their friends, Trouble girl, sick girl, bad girl.

Susan's father, Mr. Carswell, is the assistant director at the Albany Home for Children, she explains. Her mother is a nurse there, and she and her siblings—and there are twins in Susan's family, a boy and a girl—live in one of the two identical houses right down the street. Now, Susan, do you want to tell the class what happened to your face?

I touch the long white plastic bandages that cover my face in the shape of the letter *X* and also cover my nose. I feel the yellow glue-like substance that outlines all the bandages on my face, which will remain there for two weeks.

Day one of the two weeks began yesterday.

Mrs. Homan asks me the same question again, and I feel my legs sinking to the floor. I say what I have to say as quickly as I can.

Plastic surgery on my nose. Swimming pool accident in my backyard.

And then I run back to my chair and tuck my stomach as closely as I can get to my desk. I push my back up straight so it touches the back of my chair. I will keep my posture tag absolutely clean.

• • •

I don't know why it was, but whenever I did certain activities, I got lost in the excitement, like I was in a constant race in my little world. If I put myself in that race, I forgot all my worries. When I skied with my father and brothers, I imagined I was a downhill racer but only on the easy slopes and where I could go really fast. Even though I didn't have a helmet or tight racing ski pants like the skiers I watched on TV, I would duck down just like they did, pretend I wore the same outfits they wore, and fly down trails like I was competing in the Olympics and I was chasing after the gold.

Something about pretending to go after great goals struck me at an early age, and I got all goose-bumpy thinking I might one day be one of those racers you saw on ABC's *Wide World of Sports*. Whenever I raced down a trail, I forgot about everything around me. I forgot about the things that consumed me—like the age my mother would die. I forgot about the worries I had of someone stealing my brothers or sisters. Whenever I pretended I was a ski racer, I would concentrate on a song I had heard on the car radio riding up to the mountain. It would play inside my head, pushing me faster and faster. I was fearless when I skied.

Without my skis, though, I was a girl consumed with fear.

When I could no longer ski because the sun had turned the mountain into mush and our skis just wouldn't move but felt like they were caught in quicksand, I would have to wait a few months for the time when the sun grew warmer and the long-anticipated opening day of the swimming pool began. As soon as I waded into the water and put on my Speedo goggles, I imagined—at least for our appointed hour—every single day that I went there, that I was an Olympic swimmer. I would try to do the breaststroke faster than anyone in the pool. I'd even compete against two-year-old Sarah in the shallow end. The pool was a place of competition to me even if no one was really racing against me. It was a place where I tried to swim even that much faster than the day before. The pool was where I dreamed that one day I would grow up to win medals and be considered much more special than just the fearful girl that I was becoming. If I could win medals, everyone around me would think that I was fearless.

That mattered to me.

When I asked my mother on the day before I began my new school if she would watch me dive from the board and swim the whole length of the pool and back without breathing on what was also the last day of the swim year, I knew it was my last chance to go even that much faster and maybe make her feel I was someone to be really proud of having as her daughter.

I dived into our swimming pool, pretending all the Home kids had surrounded the link fence to watch me accomplish my goal, and I quickly went to the bottom of the pool where I felt my nose touch the cement. Then I kept going because that's what you do when you're chasing dreams with glory at their end.

I swam all the way to the front of the pool without breathing and all the way back to the diving board. I went faster than I had ever gone before and it felt so good. When I finally came up to breathe, I imagined all the Home kids would be clapping their hands and my mother would be standing there by the side of the pool ready to put her arm out and pull me onto some imaginary winning block. Instead when my mouth hit the late-afternoon air, all I could hear was my mother's scream when she looked over at me.

Before I even knew what had happened, I was in the emergency room and under anesthesia. In my quest for the gold, I had ripped off the top part of my nose.

And so now I just stood before my class and explained that I have had plastic surgery without giving them any more details, before I ran back to my desk, the only place I now feel safe in my classroom. I am that fearful little girl once again who does not have the pool and the ski hills to show them I am much braver than I appear.

At lunch, we walk into the dining room where my class, all seated at one table, is served warm thin-sliced roast beef with mashed potatoes by women dressed in white uniforms who wear hairnets and long white gloves. As they serve us gravy using a polished silver ladle, they address each of us as Miss. Mrs. Homan sits next to me. No one else wants to. I don't eat, because I feel the stares from sixteen sets of eyes. I don't blame them. I would do the same. But my parents have paid so much money for me to be here and wear the clothing of an Academy girl. I will brave it out for now, but I will figure out a way to convince Mrs. Homan to tell my parents that I belong at the school in my backyard. This is not where I belong. She'll soon see that.

After lunch, we have a short recess, and I go to the swings and push myself back and forth. Three swings are empty beside me, but no one comes over. I

don't want to be their friend, either. I know who the kids are that I want to be
my close friends and have sleepovers with even if my father thinks he has put
his foot down finally crushing that dream. Maybe I've just turned eight in August, but my hopes are real. I feel comfortable and at peace with myself whenever I am left to play in my backyard. I get nervous when I have to leave my
yard. That's when the world starts feeling too big. That's when things became
scary. If my family and I could just stay on the grounds all day long, just like the
Home kids do—except for their walk to Stewart's—then we would be safe, always, protected by the warmth of the Albany Home for Children. We had
moved here because my father said it was our forever home. And if we could
just stay there all day and all night and have no outside disturbances, we would
be together forever. But now, as I think about it more and more in my mind as
I sit in the chair in my new classroom, I realize I am not in control of my own
life. Adults are. They determine where children go, turn left, turn right, even
if it scares them so.

At three o'clock, the bell sounds for us to prepare to go home. Mrs. Homan
hands me a note to give to my mother, which I place in my green tote bag. Outside the Academy entrance, my mother stands holding Sarah's hand. They are
wearing matching yellow sundresses, and my mother smiles when she sees me
exit the front door. She pushes her arms out to me and hugs me, and I just fall
into her embrace. On the way home, she asks how my first day went. I tell her.

Once we are home, she wants me to tell my father the same long story I have
told her of the magnificent day I had at my new school. My parents are delighted that everything has turned out so well. I have learned a great deal from
my mother's fairy tales. They make people smile just like the way the movies on
The Wonderful World of Disney make you feel good inside every Sunday night.

At least it is that way until I hand my mother the note my teacher had
given me.

*Dear Mrs. Carswell, Please cut Susan's bangs. They are crooked and quite
long. It would be nice if she could see us and we could see her. Perhaps a haircut would make her feel more confident about speaking to her fellow classmates. Appearances are very important at the Academy. Thank you for
looking into Susan's interest. Otherwise we welcome her here at AAG.
Sincerely, Mrs. Homan*

...

It takes several months for me to actually drum up the nerve to speak to anyone at the Academy. Although I had made a deal with my bladder that I would never have to raise my hand and ask if I could use the girls' room, one day I just can't hold it in anymore and I have to finally throw my cards down on the table.

So I slowly raise my hand in social studies class, and it takes Mrs. Homan by shock.

Why, yes, Susan. What is it? Is something the matter? Are you sick?

May I use the girls' room?

Of course you can, Susan. Class, let's all give Susan a round of applause for finally asking her first question.

Not long after my steps into public speaking, my class is sitting in a circle in the small recreation room, playing a game with our French teacher, Mademoiselle Tribot Laspiere. We each hold on to a piece of a long string and sing songs in French as a little rabbit is passed along the string until Mademoiselle abruptly stops singing, signifying you had to leave your spot in the circle if you had the rabbit in your hand. It is Musical Chairs, but with a French twist. When my classmate Elizabeth gets caught with the bunny and leaves her spot, there is now a space between me and Cheryl Lang, the most popular and beautiful girl in our class.

Cheryl looks over at me and smiles.

Come sit next to me, Sue, she says with a smile. I want you to always sit next to me.

Cheryl Lang's invitation meant immediate acceptance by my entire class. I was instantly one of the popular girls. It meant a whole new beginning, and it would change the course of my plans of where I wanted to go to school. As the year went on, I felt more and more at home at the Academy. When the school year ended, I would miss some of my friends in an entirely new way because I never had real friends before that time, and because it was the first time I had stayed at a school for more than one year. I wanted to go back to the Academy next year. I would not apply to be a student at the Albany Home for Children. I had made my decision and I was happy with my choice. The children at the Home could still be my friends, but I hadn't made any gains in that direction. It seems they were even harder to befriend than Cheryl Lang.

· · ·

At the end of the school year, my mother attended the Academy's annual card party, where she watched a runway fashion show on the stage of the large auditorium. Models walked across the stage, wearing clothes she could never afford. There at her card table she overheard the stories of what happened at the parties at country clubs to which she had never been invited. I walked past the auditorium that day; the door was slightly ajar and I could see her dressed in her finest brown polyester pantsuit, around her neck her pearls from Sears that my father had bought for her at Christmas. She looked so pretty. My mother shuffled her cards and then dealt them right in front of herself. She was playing solitaire. None of the other mothers had sat down at the table where my mother had taken her seat. But my mother, being my mother, just bit her tongue, and smiled politely to anyone who deigned to engage her in even a brief conversation or at least say hello.

My mother would not love my school as I came to. I felt pulled between two worlds. I lived in one with her and my family at our home on the grounds of the Albany Home, but another world was opening up for me at the Academy. That world was more opulent, yet for some reason I felt just as comfortable in it, too.

One thing would never change: Of all the large houses and mansions that I saw when I started to go to sleepovers with my classmates, I always felt like our home was even that much more beautiful.

Our house reflected the beauty of my mother.

Dixie Cups

Everything inside our house is in its rightful place. The only thing messed up there is me.

Whenever we forget to make our beds in the morning, my mother doesn't punish us by letting them stay unmade until we get home from school. She makes them for us even if we forget. Jimmy forgets every day. He pulls a Jimmy. Lately he's been telling me, Ah, it's Jim. My mother makes the bed much better than Jimmy/Jim—plus Jimmy/Jim thinks making beds is for girls. She makes a bed better than just about anyone. Sometimes, I think my mother could be the best bed maker at the Holiday Inn if the maids had a competition. She could win a trophy and it would be placed right on top of our RCA TV next to the little one she won for bowling on the Albany Home for Children's bowling league.

There's something about crawling into my bed at night knowing that my mother has made the bed. The sheets are crisp and they smell like Niagara Falls, which I think is the picture on the starch can she uses to iron my father's dress shirts as well as our sheets. My mother loves ironing my father's shirts. It's like each push she gives her Sunbeam iron is full of kisses for him. When she makes his lunch each morning, before she places it in a brown paper bag, she draws a red heart on his paper napkin that says, I LOVE YOU.

Once when my father went away on a business trip to meet with other people whose job it was to help sick orphan kids like Ryan, or boys like Sean who want to be girls, or girls like bad-temper Jodie—kids who were similar to the kids who lived in my backyard but lived in other states, too—I watched my mother neatly pack his clothing as though each shirt or pair of pants were being placed on the shelves of a fancy clothing store like JCPenney. For each piece of clothing she packed, my mother pinned a little piece of paper onto the label. His Jockey briefs and matching undershirts each had little messages attached to them that said, JOHN, I MISS YOU. I LOVE YOU, XO, ELAINE. She closed his suitcase with a picture of our entire family sandwiched somewhere in the middle of his socks and underwear so that the glass pane wouldn't break on the trip.

My mother used to pack an I LOVE YOU napkin in my lunch bag before I started going to the Academy. I didn't bring lunch there on account of the fact that we got it for free (although not really free, my father said, because the tuition was so high). I missed her decorated napkins so much that I would have preferred her prepared lunch to the one that was served to us by the Academy cooking ladies, who were extremely careful about not dripping the gravy on us as they leaned over our shoulders with their ladles.

My mother loved drawing pictures and writing words expressing her feelings. Sometimes after school at the Academy, during my first year there, I would head over to this little closet area in Parsons Cottage, which was where the nurses' station at the Albany Home was located. She worked there several days a week and sometimes more when the other nurse, Jean, couldn't. If my mother wasn't tending to a sick Home child, she would sit at her small desk and draw names and pictures on little white Dixie Cups. It seemed like every time I entered the clinic, I saw her leaning over her desk, almost eye level with the cup, completely absorbed in her moment of drawing names and pictures, always smiling and holding it up into the air to look at her creation after she completed one. As she sang songs quietly to herself—Frank Sinatra's "Summer Wind" or Tom Jones's "What's New Pussycat?" or Dionne Warwick's "I Say a Little Prayer"—my mother would draw red hearts and smiley faces on the cups and then the name of each kid, every letter of their first name using a different-colored Crayola crayon, including the color that Jimmy and I liked to use the most: burnt sienna.

When she had completed her mini Dixie masterpieces, she would place the forty-eight cups on two large baking sheets and then drop two, three, four, or five different-colored pills into each cup, depending upon which cup was meant for each child. Then she would place her trays in a medicine cabinet until a counselor came to pick them up right before the Home children went to bed.

I think my mother would have liked to go over to the cottages each night, rock each child to sleep in her arms, or give them kisses on their foreheads and their cheeks. But she had to take care of us, and there wasn't enough time to share all the hugs she had inside her by putting the Home children to bed, too. She loved us. She loved my father; she loved Jimmy, Mandy, Billy, Sarah, Marnie, Aunt Mary, Uncle Ed, my cousin Laurie, and me. She didn't have any other relatives left to love. All dead, Jimmy said.

My mother didn't talk about that kind of stuff. And whenever Aunt Mary tried to bring alive the stories of their childhood, usually when she and my mother talked inside our aunt's enclosed porch—sipping iced tea—with caffeine—from a beige Tupperware pitcher—my mother would slowly shake her head. She remembered the stories my aunt told, but she couldn't talk about them. Instead, my mother would try to get Aunt Mary to stop talking about those things that happened so long ago—not in a way of interrupting her, though, because she would not do that to anyone. Rather, she would simply ask Aunt Mary to play cards. My aunt would look over at my mother's sad wet face, and would immediately exclaim, Yes, let's play. Then my mother's big smile would light up her face once again and she would say, Oh good, Mary, I'll shuffle.

I wanted to know everything about my mother's childhood. Even though I kept trying to put the pieces together, my mother's incessant need to play cards rather than relive her days as a little girl kept the story incomplete in my mind. Then again, I pasted together small pieces of my mother's childhood through Aunt Mary's telling and her distant relatives' infrequent visits.

Except for my aunt, it doesn't seem as though my mother has any childhood friends who still phone regularly or drop by our house to talk about all they remembered, or to stare at the cottages next door. My mother has said little to enrich the story of her childhood. Instead, she puts all her imaginative powers into fictional stories she has made up for my brothers, sisters, and me of other things, just not her. I assume it is like a Halloween mask to her sadness. Her story is locked up inside. The remnants of her childhood are in the back bedroom deep inside a white cedar hope chest that only she has the key to.

I often wonder what is in there. Are there photographs of her mother modeling corsets for the Montgomery Ward catalog? Pictures of my mother dancing with her mother? Are there letters her mother wrote to her daughter before she died? Are her mother's dresses in there?

Perhaps her dance shoes?

My mother has added only one line to her childhood story, Oh, how my mother loved to dance with my father.

That is all she has ever said about my grandmother, the one I would have loved to have known.

Are those pills aspirin? I asked my mother right before she picked up the trays of Dixie Cups to lock them inside the big medicine cabinet.

No, Sue, she said.

Are they Flintstone vitamins?

No.

Are they One-A-Days?

No, Sue.

Are they pills that help your poop come out soft?

When she said no again, I was completely confused. The pills I named were the only ones that I ever saw advertised on TV during commercials for my favorite shows. Those were the only type of pills I knew.

When I asked my mother what kind of pills were inside the cups, she replied they were happy pills to help the children sleep and feel better. And then she would name them for me as I pointed to each of them.

What's that one?

It's a pill in the neuroleptic category.

What's that mean?

It's complicated. You wouldn't understand.

Please.

It helps a child who has schizophrenia.

What's that mean?

It's complicated. Deals with voices inside your head.

We moved on. I knew my window was short when it came to questions about anything being locked up. Especially pills for children.

What's that pill?

It's for depression.

That one?

For fears.

Why would a child get a pill for fears? I have them. Can I have some?

No you cannot.

Why?

The Home children are much sadder and have more fears than you do, she said. It's clinical and complicated. You have no worries. You left your sadness behind when we left our old house. Remember?

How do you know I won't get all scared like that again?

You grew out of that. It was a phase.

What's this pill?

It helps treat attention disorders.

Well, Jimmy doesn't pay attention to me. Can we bring him home some and slip it in his milk?

Let's go, Sue. We have to make supper. How 'bout if I let you Shake'N Bake the pork chops tonight?

By nine o'clock, the forty-eight Home children would be in their beds with their version of pill-happy sugarplums dancing in their heads, their empty Dixie Cups taken away by the night counselors, and we five Carswell children would be safely tucked into our beds. Within minutes, all of the children living on the grounds of the Albany Home would float off to sleep. Well, unless the fire trucks came.

...

During my school days at School 19 and then for my first year at the Academy, I felt relatively safe. Fears did not creep into my mind throughout the school day, nor were they there abnormally at night. It's strange how my bouts with anxiety simply flew away when we moved into our house at the Home.

Yet does a girl who once worried so ever really change for that long, or is she just given respite so that all the strength within can build itself up again? My fears would come and go with the fury of the ocean waves ebbing and flowing. I wished my mind could be more like our tranquil swimming pool. Instead, deep down inside, my fears, which for the past two years had rested in a calm cove, were now being brought to the surface by storm-driven waves.

When my second year began at the Academy, it seems only one child of all those who lived on the same property could not sleep through the entire night—disturbing not only the child, but the Home's administrator and his wife as well. It might have been easier for both of my parents if I could have had a Dixie Cup full of happy, fearless, sleepy pills with hearts and the name SUE written on it in burnt sienna.

If only the twins didn't have to grow up and leave the safety barrier that was the grounds of my backyard, and my mother.

A Matching Blue Blanket

For the first time since he came to live at the Albany Home on his third birthday, Bob Wygant received a visitor. On a Sunday afternoon on a summer day in 1944 when Bob had long given up hope for any visitor, a young man signed his name in the guest book and asked to see his brother. He introduced himself to the receptionist as Elmer Rossman and confided that he had been waiting for this day since he was seven years old. Elmer looked joyous.

While this visitor nervously paced the waiting room, the receptionist rang the superintendent's home on the campus. She had worked at the Home for many years, and while she didn't say anything to the man, she was reasonably certain this was a mistake.

The superintendent quickly scurried across the campus to greet the man.

The young man, perhaps in his early twenties, was tall like Bob and also had brown hair. But he didn't have Bob's composure. This young man was nervous, peculiarly nervous. Elmer Rossman apologized to Mr. Hopkirk explaining that he recently left the army with a disability. Shell-shocked, he said. Almost killed. World War II. Still, if it was okay, he would really like to visit his brother. He wanted to ask Bob if he would like to come live with him, since they were brothers, after all.

But the Albany Home had never had such a boy as Bob—with such a promising future. Living with Elmer might threaten all his endless possibilities.

Besides, there was a loophole.

Bob Wygant's transfer papers were marked NEVER next to the question that put an abrupt end to such requests: *If a suitable family inquires, may your child be put up for adoption?*

It had been firmly stamped and signed by Bob's mother right after his birth. She was the only one who could take him away from the Home.

The superintendent denied Elmer his request for a visit and requested that he never return. Like the good soldier he was, Elmer Rossman walked away. He looked toward the wading pool full of children and saw several boys about his brother's age. One mowed the lawn on a shiny new tractor while the others played ball. Elmer wondered which one was his brother, but his eyes got blurry and so he headed toward the entrance. He had blown his chance. He couldn't be with his brother, and it was all because he had fought in the war, was injured, and no longer looked right to people because of his shakes and the thoughts in his head that he could no longer control.

He cried out loud.

Why, Mother, did you ever give my brother away?

Waiting

I am having a breakdown in our backyard in front of my mother. I am stamping my feet, and my face is turning as red as the color of the spaghetti sauce that we had just eaten for supper. My mother is relaxing after cleaning up the kitchen with me after dinner. All five of us have our nights to help my mother prepare dinner and then pick up afterward, according to our birth order. This is also the day when we control the dial on the TV. Jimmy is Monday. I am Tuesday. Billy is Wednesday. Mandy is Thursday, and Sarah is Friday. It is Tuesday and my mother has just delivered astonishing news as we threw half-eaten meatballs into the garbage can before wetting the dishes down and then placing them into the dishwasher. My tantrum began in the kitchen, and it has now moved outside where Jimmy and my father are playing kickball with the twins as Sarah runs circles around the bases even though it isn't her turn. Usually, I have one nasty-growling pout when I'm upset. But I've got things on my mind, and my mother just looks at me and then turns to watch the kickball game as I pelt her with question after question as I stand only inches from her white plastic patio chair while she sips on a cup of de-caffeinated Maxwell House.

How could you ever trust Jimmy to walk the twins home from first grade after school? How could you?

Do you know what that means?

Do you know that Jimmy will forget about them?

Do you understand that they'll be kidnapped by one of those stranger-danger men you talk about who pull their car over to the side of the road and steal children by offering candy and puppies?

Do you know Mandy and Billy will be killed? Do you know that their throats will be slashed and their heads will fall to the ground?

Enough! my mother says, as she takes another sip of her coffee as though she hasn't a care in the world. I know she is not agreeing with me or my point of view, which just gets me even madder and my face turns red meets blue and purple. I look like a bruised kneecap.

Jim is responsible, my mother says, as if Jimmy were just some racehorse that always wins and you know the horse is going to win so you can go ahead and bet on it. My father had taken all of us to the Saratoga Racetrack for the first time this summer, and Jimmy said to me on our way back home, Now, Jim knows how to pick the ponies. Jim gonna be making some good money from his bookie. Jim gonna be rich even though Susie goes to the rich girls' school. Jim needs a cigar. Susie, go find Jim one from *Cooba.*

My mother adds, Calm down, Sue. Jim is going to be in fifth grade now. He will soon be ten years old and your father and I have gone over this with him. He's even getting a fifty-cent increase in his allowance each week for walking the twins home. I trust Jim. And you, young lady, are at a different school and should not worry. Now get a glass of Kool-Aid. Put some ice cubes in it. And then get out there and kick some home runs for Mommy.

Less than a month later, I see them leave each morning. Will this be their last time?

...

Mandy's brown wavy hair falls right below her chin and then curls up. Now six, unlike me, she loves cute dresses. As she stands ready to depart into the crayon-drawing world of first grade, Mandy asks my mother if she'll put a dab of lipstick around her lips. Instead, my mother hurries into Mandy's room and comes back with my sister's Bonne Bell Lip Smackers and traces her lips to make them pink and smell like watermelon.

Mandy is becoming a dancer. Whenever Mr. and Mrs. Murphy come over to share their six-pack of beer with my parents, Mandy turns on the record player in our living room and dances right in the middle of the Oriental rug, blocking my parents' view of the Murphys. My mother allows Mandy just one dance to entertain the Murphys. Then she gets up from her chair, claps her hands, and turns off the record player. She pats Mandy on her rear and says, Mandy, you are the best dancer. Joan, Ted, isn't she graceful? Now go watch TV with your brothers and sisters.

Mandy always leaves the room with a smile. She does the same dance every single time Mr. and Mrs. Murphy come over. She thinks she is part of the night's entertainment schedule.

Beer, cards, gossip, and the Mandy Dance.

On their first day of school, Mandy stands by the door all ready to go.

She asks my mother, Will I have dance class like Susie?

No, Mandy. 'Member what I told you. Next year you'll start the Academy, and then you'll take dance class and you'll even get to wear a black leotard. Next year, Mandy, not this year.

Eventually Jimmy comes out of his room, dressed for school, his hair patted down with water (although I kind of think the water is probably just Jimmy spit). We all take our baths at night, but Jimmy pats his hair down with water/Jimmy spit in the morning. He thinks he looks cool. His hair must be smelly.

Jimmy is becoming more one-wordy.

Leaving. Now.

My mother calls out to Billy, who is racing his Tonka trucks from the big Oriental rug in the living room, over the small space of barren floor, and then to the smaller Oriental rug placed underneath the dining room table.

No, Mommy. I wanna play with my *carth* and my *truckth*.

Billy has a speech problem and we have to accompany him once a week to

Hackett Junior High School where he is being treated for his *sssssssssssss*—which Jimmy and I are *not* to make fun of—while we all wait for two hours in a waiting room, dying of boredom even more so than when we slowly die in church.

My mother hollers Billy's name again.

Billy. Let's get going. Jim is not going to wait all day. You can play Tonkas when you get home . . . No, Billy, you cannot bring a truck to school . . . Because, Billy, Mommy says so.

Billy is a nice little boy—much unlike his older brother—so he leaves his Tonka wherever he last pushed it and runs to the door, still staring back at his truck. Billy is also a giggler. If you tickle him, he just laughs and giggles. In order to make up for his despair of leaving his Tonka truck behind, my mother bends down and tickles Billy under his arm and hugs him good-bye.

More kisses come flying from her lips in the direction of Mandy and finally Jimmy, who now just sort of offers her his cheek.

Too old for kisses, Mom.

Lunch bags, with the I LOVE YOU napkins tucked down below their chunky peanut butter and grape jelly sandwiches, a polished Granny Smith apple, and a bag of Doritos, are placed in each of their hands by my mother as she walks them outside and down our driveway to the sidewalk. She waits to see them cross the road by the stoplight one house away from Babs and Mrs. Henry's.

Since my siblings have a longer walk to School 19 and I have to walk only down the street, I am the last to leave. But I am outside already. I am standing on the sidewalk, and I watch Jimmy, Mandy, and Billy walk away until they blur from my eyes—just about the time they near the end of Academy Road right before taking a left onto New Scotland Avenue. They will have to cross one more stoplight before passing through the giant mahogany doors of School 19. I don't worry about them making it from one side of the sidewalk to the other side because a school crossing guard is positioned by the light right at the corner of the school. All my trust goes into the old lady with the glow-in-the-dark white stripe that is draped across her chest. She is the protector of children who cross the street.

My worry is Jimmy. In the morning, he is so groggy. What if he falls asleep as he walks, and the twins run away because they get scared? What if they then decide to run back to my mother and forget that the red light means stop and that you can cross only on the green and never on the yellow because the yellow is a fifty–fifty chance of making it across the street alive or getting smashed by an oncoming car and thrown into the air and then landing squished and dead on the sidewalk below?

I'm almost hyperventilating by the time my mother finally says, Time to go, Sue. A whole new school year. Fourth grade. You're growing up.

My mother kisses me good-bye and tells me to have a nice day at school. She says, Don't worry, Sue. I trust Jim. He would never want the twins to be in harm's way. Now enjoy yourself. Work hard. Play hard. That's all I expect you to do. Come give Mommy a big hug.

My first day of fourth grade is wonderful. All my friends are back and I'm so happy to see them, especially Cheryl Lang, Ruthie Brandow, Jenny Hanley, and Kathy Schilp. I forget about Mandy, Billy, and Jimmy and put off my obsessional fear of their long walk home.

This year we will be learning how to put together French sentences with Mademoiselle Tribot Laspiere instead of just playing the little-bunny-caught-in-your-hands game like we did last year. *Parlez-vous français? Je suis Sue.*

In music class, we are moving on to the alto recorder. It is almost a foot longer. As the oldest class in our corridor, we are now the kings of our small library. Little kindergarteners look up to us as the older kids. All year long, Mrs. Cox will read us *The Odyssey,* a long book. Mrs. Cox says she will read us about ten or more pages a day right before we take our fifteen-minute nap on the floor with our assigned roll-up mats. From what I can make of her summary, *The Odyssey* is the story of a man coming back home from Troy. I'm familiar with Troy since Aunt Mary lives there, too. It takes him ten years to get to Troy, so he must visit a lot of people. It takes us only twenty minutes to get home from Aunt Mary's by car. (We have a new one this year. It's a yellow Ford— Ford because we have to buy that brand on account of the fact that Uncle Ed works so hard there and we can't hurt his feelings. That's what my mother told Jimmy when he insisted it was now time for us to have a Cadillac. Our new car has wood paneling that makes it look like a new floor has been put on its sides. It's the latest style, my father explained. Very fancy, added my mother.)

In dance class, which I hate with a passion because it's dumb, we will be broken up into groups and prepare four-minute choreographed dances. Each small group has to agree upon a song. I'm going to do my best to persuade my troupe to dance to the theme song from *Hawaii Five-O.*

By the end of the day, each teacher has given us her plans for the year. My mind has had little time to wander. It's a busy day and my thoughts stay on the words of my teachers and catching up with my friends on what we all did over the summer.

Some have traveled to France and Spain, to Greece and Africa. They have gone places on the globe far away from the red dot marking Albany, which my mother has now put on the globe. She likes to spin the globe around and say, Oh, your father and I want to go to Ireland. Oh, your father and I want to go to Paris. Oh, your father and I . . . We were kids without a passport so we pretty much stayed in Albany, went to the Cape, and placed our hopes on ladybugs that we might one day see the beaches in Florida, or at least a different pool.

For my summer, I tell my friends, I swam in our pool twice a day. Lisa Mendel, from across the street, has finally become my friend, but we have not eaten at her family's restaurant yet. I add, And all the children in my backyard still live there.

Are they retarded? one of my friends asks.

Feeling like I have a complete grasp on the reasons kids live in my back-yard after two years of living there, I reply, No, they aren't retarded because then you would have to live someplace else. They are sad and some don't be-have, just like my brother, Jimmy. Some try to run away, and that is against the rules. Some have really bad tempers. Some hum. One girl killed her step-mother. One likes to burn houses down and one or two are autistic, which means they feel like they are scuba diving all day. They go to a free school but it is private. I tried to get in there before I came here, but even though my fa-ther works there and you might think he had some pull, well, he couldn't help me. Oh, and some—and this is sad—are orphans. That's about it.

That very notion caused the biggest quake in the knees of my classmates. One even said, Can my mother bake the orphans blueberry muffins?

The school bell rings at three o'clock, and it is time to make our way back home.

As we stand in a single-file line to say good-bye, Mrs. Cox asks me, Does your mother ever cut your bangs?

...

I cut across Temple Beth Emeth and walk back to our house.

I don't see them.

My eyes are positioned on the other side of the street at the opposite end as I walk along the grass right next to the curb instead of the sidewalk on my side. It gives me a better view. But as I walk closer to our house, I do not see Mandy, Billy, or Jimmy walking from the direction they are supposed to be coming from as my mother had promised.

I am nervous. I don't see them. My heart goes thump-thump. It thump-thumps fast. Is it going as fast as my mother's the night she headed to the hospital, walking out into the snowflakes? Should I clutch it so that it doesn't fall out? I don't see them. My hands sweat, so does my neck. I still don't see them. Why aren't they heading down Academy Road?

We all get out of school at the same time, yet I am moving in baby steps because I want to see them safely walk down from their direction of the street. I am humming, trying to stop my mind from thinking faster than it already is. I am coughing because I feel like I might just choke to death. I am nearing the wall that signifies the beginning of the Albany Home property. My steps are that of a snail, a turtle, and fat Marnie. Something is wrong. Something is very wrong.

I think about their funeral. Mandy will lie in a little pink casket with pink roses draped over her coffin. Billy and Jimmy will lie in blue ones. Jimmy's will have the drawing of a Cadillac on his; Billy will have a Tonka truck attached to it just like the wood panels are now attached to our station wagon. Monsignor Hart, the most important priest at St. Teresa's, will say, Our Father who also does art in heaven . . . My mother and father will be sitting in the front row hugging each other. Both of them will be crying very hard. Aunt Mary will hold my mother's hand, and my grandmother with the beehive will hold my father's. I will babysit Sarah in the second pew because no one else will be able to do so unless we hire Kathy Cahalan to babysit for one dollar. All the people left in my family will mourn and wear black clothes.

I can't take it. I need to know the answer. Did Jimmy bring them home safely? Are they alive, or are my parents up at the St. Peter's Hospital morgue identifying their bodies because Billy might have run after a real truck thinking it is his Tonka truck? Has Mandy been hit by a car because she sees girls playing with makeup on the other side of New Scotland Avenue and she wants some, too?

I run. I run all the way from the beginning of the cement wall at the Albany Home for Children, not even stopping at the entrance to the Home where the sign clearly reads YIELD, and I make a mad dash into my house. I scream to my mother as soon as I open the door.

Where are they? Where are they?

My mother rushes out from the TV room.

Sue. Please calm down. They're not home from school yet. I told you they have a longer walk than you. Let's go outside. I'm sure they are on their way. Or would you prefer to sit and have a brownie? I put the extra chocolate syrup pack on top and walnuts. Sarah and I already had one. They're yummy.

I tell her I hate brownies, which she knows is a lie. So my mother takes Sarah's hand, and Marnie's leash in her other hand, and we make our way down our driveway past the Millards' house. She tells me to take a deep breath. She tells me tears aren't necessary.

You have nothing to worry about. You must calm down. Pretend you are in the pool and you're not racing, you're just practicing your strokes.

And so we walk together up Academy Road, and I try to do what my mother says. I take my arms and I push one slowly in front of me and then the other, and I turn my head from side to side with each move. I try so hard to practice and not to race, but the pace of my strokes starts quickening even though I'm begging my mind, *Slow down, Sue, slow. This is a practice. This is not a race.* But my mind simply won't listen to my swim instructions. I have never been someone who practices. I have always raced.

Hi, Babs! Hello, Mrs. Henry! Yes, today was the twins' first full day of school. Sue and I are heading up the street to meet them . . . What's that, Babs? Well, Sue misses the swimming pool. She's practicing for next summer. Wants to compete in the Olympics.

I pull my mother's arm with the force of a Clydesdale.

Eileen, how are you? Thank you so much for watching Sarah earlier. I had to go fill up the pill cups. Jean called in sick.

How are the kids? Did Johnny like his first day of kindergarten?

We're going up the street to meet the twins and Jim.

Sue? Oh, Eileen, you know how much she loves the pool. She's pretending we're swimming up the street. Ha!

I want my mother to run with me. I want her to run fast like the way we used to run in our first backyard when we had a dog named Spot who was squished down and killed after he ran onto the highway. But she is too busy talking to our neighbors. She is acting as if we don't have a care in the world. I ask her if I can take Marnie since she's too busy playing the Sunshine Lady of Academy Road to a new couple who have just moved to our street.

Hello. I'm Elaine Carswell. Welcome to our beautiful neighborhood. This is my youngest daughter, Sarah. Oh, and that was my daughter Sue who just ran by. We live . . .

Marnie has little legs and is now ever fatter because my siblings and I feed her all the food we don't like. Jimmy and I hate liver for dinner, so we slip our pieces underneath the table to Marnie. Billy hates mushrooms, so he puts them in his paper dinner napkin and pretends to drop his mushroom-filled napkin onto the floor. Sarah hates the cheese on pizza. Mandy eats everything, so Marnie gets her food only if it falls to the floor by mistake. Marnie gets none of our desserts or candy except at Easter. I give her my little pink Peeps.

I am a fast runner and try to make Marnie run as fast as me. After an initial sprint, she has problems. She tries to stop me so that she can smell something on the sidewalk. But I'm in a hurry to race to the end of the street. So I drag Marnie's thick brown hot dog neck on a leash down the street with me, her tummy almost making skid marks on the still-warm sidewalk as we keep moving.

I don't see them yet and I am now passing Megan Murphy's house, the last big building on the Junior College campus. I am just about a hundred feet from the blue mailbox. Marnie needs to do her business with the grass and starts to bark to get my attention.

You have to wait, Marnie. Hold it in. Don't make me slap you, Marnie.

Of all moments, she chooses to go now. Neither she nor my mother understand the urgency of making sure everyone is safe.

Don't they understand that Mandy, Billy, and Jimmy will be the faces of missing kids on TV tonight?

Finally, I get to the position right next to the mailbox that has a direct view onto New Scotland Avenue. I see about ten Home children walking back from Stewart's celebrating their first day of school, each holding an ice cream cone even though most of the ice cream has already melted onto their shirts, shorts, and even their socks.

Move faster. Move faster, I think but don't say aloud. I can't see anyone behind them because they do not walk in a single-line formation. Some walk on the lawn to the right side, others to the left. Some step right on the cracks of the sidewalk. Don't they know you're not supposed to step on the cracks because they'll hurt their mother's back? Soon the Home children all cross the street and walk right past me. Ryan turns his head away. Jodie is an ice cream cone herself. Her strawberry ice cream is on every piece of her clothing. It's even in her now strawberry-brown hair.

As soon as the Home kids see my mother, who is still trailing behind me talking to neighbors like she was collecting news for the *Times Union,* they start to scream out to her, Mrs. Carswell. Mrs. Carswell, we got ice cream cones. I had chocolate. I had butterscotch. I had orange. I had lemon sherbet. Mrs. Carswell, I had strawberry but then I tripped. Mrs. Carswell, will you buy me a new ice cream cone?

I look to my left to see them run and gather around her and Sarah, but immediately turn my eyes back to stare down New Scotland Avenue with a much clearer view now that they are out of my way.

They are there: Mandy, Billy, and Jimmy are walking together. Jimmy stops at the red light and waits for it to turn green. He holds out his two hands and takes Mandy's hand in one and Billy's in the other. They have made it back safely onto our side of the street.

They have lived another day.

I saw them leave and they came back, just like my mother said they would.

But what will happen tomorrow?

As the World Sleeps

Life is the cycle of our grandfather clock, positioned in the alcove entrance inside our home, not too far away from the light beige sofa placed in front of our windows with the view onto our backyard. The safety of my family comes down to whether the grandfather clock has moved around the Roman numeral XII twice a day. The lives of those I love are measured in a twenty-four-hour circle.

My worries are increasingly a large part of that cycle. For every day that my family passes the twenty-four-hour mark, I am grateful and, for a few moments, I feel a rare peace within. When the clock rings its chimes at midnight, it feels like my whole body is celebrating New Year's Eve. In my mind, I throw pastel-colored confetti toward the bedrooms of the sleeping members of my family. But my celebration is short. The clock must repeat its rotation until noon the next day and then two times again the next day, and the day after that . . .

Not long after the twins and Jimmy made it home from school their first day safely, I can no longer handle the grating period of time when I stand outside our house or by the mailbox at the beginning of Academy Road with Marnie just waiting for them to come into my view again.

I am a mental train wreck.

I am nine.

The only way I can make it through that zone of time when Jimmy, Billy, and Mandy are walking home from school is to ride away from our house on my bicycle and stay there until my time estimation has exceeded my expectation. I cannot sit at the dining table and eat my snack with my mother and tell her about the events of my school day, nor can I calmly watch afternoon TV and feel at ease in my skin just waiting for them to barge in from the outside.

Patience isn't a virtue God created inside of me. God gave my mother that.

I come home only when the cows are home. I know this is true whenever I hear my mother ring the cowbell as she stands on our little patio in the backyard at precisely twenty-five past five every night of the week.

The ringing of the bell is the signal to let us know we have five minutes to get home from wherever we are on Academy Road. At five thirty we are to be sitting in our appointed chairs to choose our salad dressings.

My mother would never have rung the cowbell if my two brothers and Mandy hadn't made it home safely to first enjoy their late-afternoon snack and then play or watch TV. What I feared was the cowbell not ringing one day.

Right after our school day ends at the Academy, I bolt out of its front doors and run all the way home. I want to move my legs and Academy oxford shoes even that much faster. I race into our front door. I take a right down the corridor and then a left and a right into my bedroom. I quickly change into play clothes. I throw my pink, aqua, blue, or yellow uniform and my white short-sleeved blouse on the floor, forgetting that promise made to my mother about the shirt going immediately into the washing machine. That would slow down my routine. She'll walk past my room and pick it up. And she'll pick up my uniform, too. I know she will. She always does.

I run back into the hallway.

No, Mom. I don't want a snack. I know you made it yourself. Yes, I like warm chocolate chip cookies. No, Mom, I don't want hot chocolate. I don't care if you put marshmallows on top. I have to go. Time to talk? No. Mom. No. Bye. I said BYE!

I open the garage door through the entrance from the rear of our kitchen and pull my bike from the rack. Only when I have kicked up the kickstand with one foot, the other foot already pedaling, do I quickly begin my journey anywhere but there.

The speed of my pedals grows faster, propelled by the speed of fear whipping around my mind, like a caffeine drip has been embedded in my arm.

I do not head to the back of our property and the all-too-familiar bicycle loop, but rather I pass the front of our house and the Millards' house and then take a quick right onto the long driveway of the larger property next door. There at the Junior College of Albany, I ride my bike only two feet away from the fence that separates our property from theirs until I get to the back. Sometimes I stick my hand out and wipe my bare knuckles along the chain fence as I stare at the gym, Parsons Cottage, the softball field, and the swings over on our side until my knuckles turn bloody. Scraps of blood on your hands are cool. Picking at scabs is a way to pass the time when Mrs. Cox reads from the pages of *The Odyssey*.

The Junior College and Albany Home's shared fence ends at the gully way in the back of the properties. Jimmy tells me his friends bury cats back there. By the time I reach the gully and turn my bike around, the parking lot meant for the students and teachers has begun to empty. JCA has many parking spots for the students because it is a day college and not a sleep-away college like the one my father went to, or the nursing college my mother went to. I pass the hours from 3:30 P.M. on by making sure I have crisscrossed the lines of every parking spot with my bike, sometimes circling a car that is still parked there as the sun begins to lower its rear over Albany's late-afternoon sky.

When I have finished the circumference of the parking lot and its labyrinth maze of yellow lines, I pedal on to the inner sidewalks of the campus quad and ride past all the cottages that look just like Parsons Cottage on our side.

In another one of my father's confusing stories of the history of our backyard, my father explained how all the property at the JCA and all our backyard were once joined together like it was a large family. It was a giant piece of land, he said. And over time living there were hundreds and hundreds of orphans. Parsons Cottage on our side of the property once housed all the female orphans ages six and up, and the Van Alstyne Gymnasium was where the boys and girls played games.

As I rode my bike through the quad, I thought about what it must have felt like to be a real orphan, instead of the pretend one I played on my bike sometimes, or the sick orphans who needed to feel better who lived in my backyard. It was like orphans were ghosts constantly following me wherever I pedaled. The whole thing was just too sad to think about too hard. But the ghosts of orphans were making more and more forays into my thoughts. When I wasn't worried about my siblings, I had an even bigger fear. Whenever I saw my parents drive away for dinner or go to a dance to have fun, it's like I couldn't breathe until they came back home, sometimes crying away my fears in my closet as I thought about car crashes, blood, my mother lying on a pavement, and police officers knocking on our front door.

Are you the Carswell children? We have bad news. You are now orphans.

At the Junior College, I biked over to the library and around the building, pedaling faster and faster, my bumper no longer resting on my seat. By now, my forehead would be sweating—not out of exhaustion but from the growing fear that the cowbell wouldn't ring, that now was the time.

When would it ring?

I wish I could believe that my mother would always ring the cowbell exactly at 5:25 P.M. I wish I could learn to trust that that reassuring sound would come every night.

When the cowbell eventually sounded, which for some reason always came as a complete surprise to me, I headed back home in the same direction I came and eventually saw our part of my backyard in my view. By this time, Mr. Millard would be outside tinkering with his sports cars, and Mrs. Millard would be creating new signs that read ABORTION RIGHTS for what my mother said was her intention of speaking out in order to make sure our country could control the birth population. She added, Not everyone agrees with Mrs. Millard's point of view.

What does that mean? I later asked my mother. We have five kids. Can you have five kids according to Mrs. Millard? Can you have six? Seven? Ten?

Depends, my mother said.

Depends on what?

Depends on whether you can afford them.

But we're poor. Can you afford us?

It's not like that, Sue. It's about teenagers having babies or third-world countries. We'll talk about third-world countries when you're a bit older. She added, It's complicated.

I finally understood that *it's complicated* really meant too long a story for a kid and too many questions for an adult to answer. My backyard was full of *it's complicated*.

When I then entered our house, they would all be sitting at the kitchen table—Jimmy asking my mother for Russian dressing, Billy asking for French, Mandy wanting Wish-Bone Italian, and Sarah playing with the Heinz ketchup bottle as she attempted to pour it over her iceberg lettuce, tomatoes, shaved carrots—because we didn't like them chunky—and croutons.

I sit at my place, sandwiched between my father and Mandy. Everything is fine. Everyone is in their rightful place. My heart no longer swirls inside with butterflies. It feels good. Our world is perfect.

Every night, my father goes around the table and asks each of us about our school day and what we did after school.

Mandy watched *Mr. Rogers.*

Billy asks when he could get a new Tonka.

Jimmy says, Nothin'.

Sarah just smiles and laughs as she continues trying to sneak the ketchup away from my mother, who ends up placing the bottle on her lap.

I rode my bike. I rode my bike. I rode my bike.

Our conversations never change too much. Perhaps my brothers' and sisters' stories change a bit, but my story remains the same. I wonder if they notice.

I am the star of our family's nightly soap opera production of *As the World Sleeps, Just Not Me.* It's a spin-off of my mother's favorite show. While her soap is on for an hour during the middle of the afternoon, mine runs all night.

The black curtain of the theater inside our house pulls across the stage and opens to the first act of me propped up on my pillow beneath my blanket, staring at my open door. It is about midnight. Shadows cast by the moonlight filter through the trees outside my window and the images of leaves, which look like the faces of a witch, sway across the walls of my bedroom in a frenzy. The stage is silent except for the roaring whisper of the wind, which like the tide crashes up against my windowpane.

From offstage, I hear the sound of my father opening the living room's sliding glass door. He shuffles back into our house, wearing his slippers and the new velour bathrobe my mother bought him for Christmas.

Clothes are now all about velour, my mother told me after reading *Good Housekeeping,* her favorite magazine for helpful household hints and cutting-edge style.

My father and the other night counselors have settled the children next door back to sleep after a late-night fire alarm. Because he is back, I know that he has been able to help put them back to sleep.

He tiptoes past my bedroom, careful not to disturb me. But if he looked, he would see that the glow of the moon illuminates my blond hair, which is almost white in the darkness of night. I am looking at him as I lean forward as far as I can clutching my pillow.

Is everything okay? I whisper.

Yes. *Shhh.* Go back to sleep.

My father always says that same line. I think he knows the last part of the line is ridiculous, but it stays in the play. *Go back to sleep* is never edited out.

Okay, I'm going to go back to sleep.

Me, too.

'Night.

Good night, Sue.

The stage curtain is still open onto my bedroom. As Act One continues, I quietly count out loud up to one hundred and then right in the nick of time, I hear my father snore. His snores grow louder, signifying the beginning of the next scene.

Mom?

I wait a moment for her to respond. Then I wait another minute, because sometimes in the middle of the night people have trouble at the thought of

The Albany Orphan Asylum,
my backyard at the
turn of the twentieth century.
(Parsons Child and Family Center)

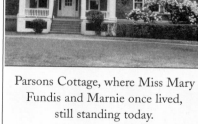

Parsons Cottage, where Miss Mary
Fundis and Marnie once lived,
still standing today.
(Ann Marie Carswell)

**BILL OF FARE FOR CHILDREN OF THE ALBANY
ORPHAN ASYLUM**

Monday
Breakfast — Bread, Apple-butter and Coffee.
Dinner — Bean Soup, Bread, Pork and Chopped Onions.
Supper — Bread or Rice Pudding and Bread and Milk.

Tuesday
Breakfast — Bread, Coffee and Oat Meal.
Dinner — Mutton or Irish Stew, Green Corn or String Beans, Pickles and Bread.
Supper — Bread, Mush and Milk.

Wednesday
Breakfast — Bread, Molasses and Coffee.
Dinner — Corned Beef, Cabbage and Bread.
Supper — Milk, Bread, Butter and Apple Sauce.

Thursday
Breakfast — Bread, Shredded Wheat Biscuit and Coffee.
Dinner — Vegetable Soup, Beets or Green Corn, Bread and Fruit.
Supper — Bread, Apple Sauce, Buns, Milk.

Friday
Breakfast — Bread, Apple-butter and Coffee.
Dinner — Baked Beans, Pork, Chopped Onions or Cabbage and Bread.
Supper — Boiled Rice, Bread and Milk.

Saturday
Breakfast — Bread, Coffee and Oat Meal.
Dinner — Hamburger Steak, Squash, Pickles, Potatoes and Bread.
Supper — Bread, Hominy, Ginger Bread, Buns and Milk.

Sunday
Breakfast — Bread, Doughnuts and Chocolate.
Dinner — Roast Beef, Potatoes, Gravy, Peas or String Beans, Bread and Fruit.
Supper — Bread and Butter, Cup Cakes, Prunes and Milk.

NOTE.— This bill of fare is subject to many extras — such as Bananas, Cakes, Apples and Vegetables in their season.

25

Mary and Elaine Kirby before the death of their young mother.
(Mary Schuh)

House parents supervising nighttime prayers in Lathrop Cottage in the late 1940s.
(Parsons Child and Family Center)

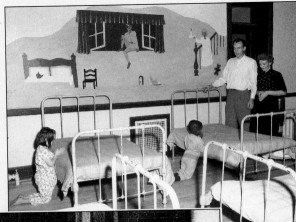

The orphans of Lathrop Baby Cottage on Easter Day 1935.
Bob Wygant is in the second row, fifth from right.
(Parsons Child and Family Center)

Bob "Wiggles" Wygant, all-star four-letter man
from the Albany Home for Children.
(The Times Union)

Bob Wygant's brother, Elmer.
(Courtesy of the author)

Bob Wygant and his wife, Sally.
(Roger Moore)

My maternal great-grandparents, Reed and
Ella Primmer, who raised my mother
and her sister. December 1950.
(Mary Schuh)

My paternal grandparents, Mary and
Watson Carswell. Her beehive hairdo
would only get bigger.
(John W. Carswell)

My maternal grandparents,
Ora and Frank Kirby, on their
wedding day in the late 1920s.
(Mary Schuh)

My beautiful mother on her
wedding day, December 26, 1959.
(Courtesy of the author)

My newlywed parents outside the church where they were married.
(Courtesy of the author)

Orphans from the Home circa 1940, playing in the wading pool.
(Parsons Child and Family Center)

Me, holding my mother's favorite book of nursery rhymes, 1963.
(Courtesy of the author)

Jimmy and me in our Sunday finest.
(John W. Carswell)

Jimmy and me with our mother
in Cape Cod.
(John W. Carswell)

The Carswells and our best friends,
the Cordes kids, on vacation in
Cape Cod in the later 1960s.
(Courtesy of the author)

My father and I carve the
Thanksgiving turkey next to the
sliding glass door in our formal
dining room in 1974. In the background is the old Wasson Cottage.
(Courtesy of the author)

My family outside church in the late
1960s (Sarah was not born yet).
(Courtesy of the author)

My mother in her favorite rocker
holding her first grandchild,
MaryBeth Carswell, in 1992.
(Courtesy of the author)

My parents' last happy
Christmas together, 1995.
(Courtesy of the author)

The Carswell kids, Mother's Day, 2004.
(From left: me, Sarah, Bill, Amanda, and Jim.)
(MaryBeth Carswell)

Completing the second day of the breast cancer fund-raising
walk, exhausted and out of shape. I'm on the left,
my sister-in-law Kathie (Jim's wife) is in
the center, and Sarah is on the right.
(Ann Marie Carswell)

One of the cottages on the
grounds of the Albany Home
for Children, where kids still
live today, now known as the
Parsons Child and Family Center.
(Ann Marie Carswell)

My nieces' and nephews' hands
encircle my mother's plaque
beneath the dogwood tree
planted in her memory.
(Ann Marie Carswell)

IN MEMORY OF
ELAINE CARSWELL
WHO, IN THIS HOUSE, RAISED HER
FAMILY, WELCOMED HUNDREDS
OF VISITORS AND STAFF, AND
EXEMPLIFIED THE MISSION AND
VALUES OF PARSONS CHILD
AND FAMILY CENTER

leaving their pillow. She will eventually say, What? It's there, right there in the script.

Mom? I say again. I say it louder.

Finally my mother utters a flat reply echoing back into my room. You can see a smile start growing on my face.

What?

She says it just like that: What? She does not use the tone of her day voice or, as she sometimes says, our indoor voices. In fact, she says *What?* like an actress who has over-rehearsed her line and is bored with it. I wish we could change her line, but we can't. We've now been doing this same play since the beginning of my fourth grade when she made the bad decision to let Jimmy walk the twins home from school. The play will not go dark during the summer months. It's a long-running off-Broadway show right here on Academy Road. Would you think to change the lines in *The Sound of Music*?

May I have a glass of water?

My heart stops after I say this, because I'm going to get to see my mother soon and even though she has refused in the past, hopefully tonight we're going to play cards and we're going to talk about all my friends at the Academy and decide what we'll have for dinner tomorrow. Then I'm going to ask her to make up a story for me. The look on my face is full of hope. Freeze-frame.

Minutes later, the audience and I can hear my parents' bed creak. My mother gets out of her bed, and you see her pass my bedroom door, shuffling off as she drags her fluffy pink slippers down the hallway. In the scene, I tilt my head to the side of my bed and I watch her in the darkened foyer as she crosses into the kitchen. The scene switches from my bedroom and the look of sheer happiness on my face to the kitchen where in the light of the refrigerator, I see the silhouette of her hands and the outline of her body as she tightens the belt of her robe. She yawns, places ice cubes into a glass, and then turns around and walks to the faucet for water.

After passing the night-light in the front hall bathroom, she walks into my bedroom and places the glass of water on the nightstand beside my bed. Then she leans over, her eyes almost shut, and kisses me on my forehead before saying, Good night.

Oh please, Mom. Don't leave. Sit down and tell me a story. Tell me a happy story about a child from the Home. Or tell me a story about you as a little girl. Or . . .

The script at this point has room for improvised dialogue. But my mother doesn't want extra lines, which is truly strange because she is a great storyteller.

I try to engage her in other ways, trying to stall her return to her bed and save myself from feeling all alone in the dark. I sniff my water glass.

Why does ice smell funny?

Ice does not smell funny. Ice smells like ice. My mother's tone of voice is firm. It is quite unlike *Mother Goose.*

No, it doesn't. Ice smells like hamburgers. I sniff the ice again.

Ice smells like frozen peas. Ice smells like pork chops. Ice smells like cod. Ice smells like Mrs. Paul's Frozen Fish Sticks.

I try my hardest to remember everything in the freezer that is placed next to the ice trays. Finally it gets to the point that she leaves me even though I keep asking her to stay.

Good night, Sue.

I scream out, Ice smells like the dead cows that used to be killed in our first backyard.

Sue. She makes another appearance. We don't live there anymore. Like I've said before, you should forget about that. Instead of telling me to count sheep—which may have brought more gory images to my head—she then says, Count Mommy's favorite ladybugs landing in your hand. Count as high as you can and then you'll be asleep.

My mother exits my room and instead of ladybugs, I count in my mind how long it must take for her to fall sound asleep again and then when I figure that she has drifted away, which feels like thirty minutes but is probably closer to three minutes, I call out to my father.

Dad? Marnie needs to pee.

The scene moves to our living room, where my father slides the door open and the cold breeze causes him to place his hands in his robe's front pockets.

Hurry, Marnie. Hurry, he says.

Take your time, Marnie. Take your time, I say to myself quietly.

My father waits for Marnie to walk around in circles as she searches for the most appropriate spot on the snow, in the rain, amid falling leaves, or on the neatly mowed grass to drop her fat bumper. I now stand at the edge of the corner leading into the living room, hoping Marnie will take forever so that my father will be awake forever. Just like me.

When the door shuts and he locks it tight, my father then turns and walks diagonally across the Oriental rug, I assume greatly anticipating getting back under his covers for a peaceful sleep. Just as he makes his way to the hallway, I dash back to my bed and wait for him to pass before I say good night again. He is the costar of my nights, not my days.

From this point on, *As the World Sleeps* proceeds with a variety of improvised scenes, all evolving from my fear of being the only one awake in our house. One cameo—and my personal favorite—has me slipping into Mandy's bed to sleep under her red blanket. Even though she is my younger sister, I always get scared when she realizes I am there and she says her line, which she never changes, either, even though I promise to sneak her things like Snickers candy bars.

I'm telling Mommy on you.

There is just something disturbing to me about my mother thinking I look for protection by sharing the bed of someone younger than me. I am ashamed of myself, so I crawl out of Mandy's bed and move on to Jimmy and Billy's room.

Jimmy, have you seen Marnie?

Of course, Marnie has been sleeping with me all night, but maybe he doesn't know that so it doesn't seem too inappropriate for me to wake up Jimmy to ask him if he has seen Marnie. I don't care what his answer is. I just want to wake him up so that he's awake.

What? You know what time it is? It's late. Marnie probably got squished by some car before we went to bed. Marnie's dead. Leave.

The continuing scenes of my night have me darting in and out of my brothers' and sisters' rooms, asking all of them, even Sarah, if they have seen Marnie. I am a nocturnal Babs Henry.

Billy, have you seen Marnie? Huh? Have you? Have you?

Mandy, have you seen Marnie? Huh, huh?

Sarah, have you seen Marnie? Huh, huh?

Jimmy, can you just check underneath your blanket again? I think Marnie snuck into your bed.

Billy, can you check underneath your blanket? Can you? Can you?

Mandy, Marnie is missing. I think she's down by your toes.

After half an hour or so of Have You Seen Marnie? I head back down the hallway to my parents' bedroom.

Dad, I think I hear someone inside the house.

After my father gets out of bed again and checks the house and, upon my insistence, the basement as well with his flashlight, he heads back to his bed.

Good night. Go to sleep.

Okay, Dad. Good night.

I try.

I do try. I do. I do. Anyone who watches the play can see that I try. I close my eyes and lie there. But I just can't hook up with the sleep train. So I start thinking about other things, really hard, and with each new thought I have, I walk back into my parents' bedroom.

Mom, I can't swallow.

Mom, I can't breathe.

Mom, I can't yawn.

Mom, what are the signs of a heart attack?

My hand *is* tingling . . . I *do* have chest pains.

As predawn breaks, scattering away the remnants of darkness, I begin the final act of my play, at least for that night's performance. By now all of Albany's murderers, prowlers, and predators of the night—who steal children and do bad things to them like they did to the Home children before they came to live on our property—have completed their dirty deeds and have gone back to their homes. The ghosts of the orphans who lived on our property back in the early 1900s and were buried back by the gully have returned to their underground beds, having spent the night swirling around the ground of their former playing fields, where we live, competing against one another in a game of all-night kick-the-can. As early sunlight cuts through the early-morning haze, my mind grows tired. Only then does *As the World Sleeps, Just Not Me* conclude into its final scene.

A little before four o'clock, I clutch my pillow, sniff my Niagara Falls–smelling sheets once again, tuck the corner of my sheets back into the rim of my bedpost, and clutch the top of my blanket like I am holding a lovely bouquet of red roses given to me by the audience for my performance.

I take my bow, nod my head, and go off to sleep.

Hear no evil, see no evil, and speak no evil.

Three wise rosewood monkeys sit side by side in the front of my parents' favorite wooden cupboard, just behind our formal dining table in the living room. Every morning at a quarter to seven, my father opens the curtains and lets the sun spill its golden warmth directly onto the monkeys, one with hands covering both ears, another its eyes, and the third one its mouth. From their perch, they look directly onto our backyard. They do not look at me in the chair I normally sit in as I eat my cereal. My mother positioned them that way. And every morning my parents drink their coffee, emit deep yawns, and wipe their eyes—tired from their long, constantly disturbed nights. And while they don't speak about it in front of me, behind their questioning eyes they are thinking. How can they help their daughter sleep through the long night and get rid of the dark thoughts that seem to envelop her? How does one help an increasingly more troubled child?

Sunday prayers at St. Teresa's seem to be the only solution.

Lots of them.

Another school year passes. I am growing up. In the fifth grade, I have a beautiful teacher new to our school. She has just graduated from college and has long blond hair and clear blue eyes. I want to look like Mrs. Holly Buehl when I grow up. I ask my mother if Mrs. Holly Buehl can babysit us when she and my father travel to Italy for their Adults Only—No Kids vacation this year instead of my grandmother. My classmates surround Mrs. Holly Buehl the first day. She looks like Peggy Lipton from *The Mod Squad.* I stand back. I am quiet around new people, and Mrs. Holly Buehl has an entire school year to get to know me.

By the middle of the year, I begin to experience twenty-minute blackouts while walking down the Academy's corridors, especially when the dark corridor suddenly meets the window. Inside my head, I sense I am going blind. A buzzing noise begins and I ask permission from Mrs. Holly Buehl to go to the girls' room. Sometimes I barely reach a stall before feeling like I am going to fall. Tipsy, I awkwardly land on the toilet seat before sealing the door shut with the lock. I am sweating profusely. I lose my sense of color. I am panicking. I strain to concentrate on the light, praying for the dark to go away. I clutch my head in my hands and I hold it still, silently counting because I know at some point the feeling will disappear. It takes numbers to make it go: One, two . . . twenty . . . fifty . . . one hundred and one . . .

My vision starts to come back, my racing heart beats normally again, and I pray that no one has noticed that I have stayed longer in the stall than it usually takes to pee. I release the lock and walk back out into the corridor to rejoin my class. Everything feels fine. There is no need to talk about this with my mother. It is too scary and I don't understand it. I don't know what is happening to me. I am not normal.

I am becoming my mother when it comes to secrets. I am the three monkeys all rolled into one.

I am sick, but I do not know what I have. I think it might be a brain tumor. If it isn't that, it is some other Terminal Disease. We are now learning all about Terminal Diseases in Mrs. Wheatley's science class. I do not want to hear anything more about them. I have had enough of Terminal Diseases. Are my blackouts illusions or are they terminal? Throughout our hour with Mrs. Wheatley, I lean my head on my forest-green AAG tote bag with all my books, acting as if it is my pillow. I am always tired, but I don't know why.

I do not think that my not sleeping has anything to do with this. I cannot add these things up in my head. And it's not that I'm just tired, I also feel black and blue inside my head instead of feeling happy.

I hum whenever Mrs. Wheatley speaks about death and sickness. I need to drown out the sound of her voice and the words of doom that she speaks. I am convinced that if I hear about one more Terminal Disease, I will get that one, too. I will be a walking Terminal Disease time bomb.

My school days are becoming much like my nights.

My grades plummet. We are graded by three letters, E for excellent, S for Satisfactory, and U for Unsatisfactory. I am an S student with an occasional E. Mrs. Holly Buehl asks to speak with me one day toward late winter. My homework is falling to a U.

Is there something wrong at home, Sue?

No.

I don't get the sense that you like school recently. And you seem so tired. Do you get enough sleep?

Yes.

Mrs. Holly Buehl looks at me. She looks into my eyes like no one ever has before, unsure whether I am telling the truth. She looks for answers inside my blurry red pupils.

I have soon exhausted Mrs. Wheatley's patience as well.

Miss Carswell, she says rather sternly one day when we are learning all about breast cancer, or rather my class learns while I just hum through the lesson when she draws a big breast and a nipple on the chalkboard and places a circle inside of it representing a lump.

Is there something wrong with you? I suggest you see the nurse about all that humming.

Not only does my mother work part-time at the Home, but she now works part time as the nurse at the Girls Academy. I will go see her, and I will take a nap. During the day, I love my naps. And now that my mother is working at my school, I can take my nap as she sits in the nurses' room reading a book by her favorite author, Sidney Sheldon. I sleep peacefully for forty-five wonderful minutes.

The night, however, never goes away. My sleeping problems at home worsen.

Late in the evening, I pull a wooden chair to my mother's side of the bed, cup my cheeks in my hands, and stare at her stomach to make sure it goes up and down as she sleeps. I like sitting next to her. But soon, and it's never much later, my father wakes up and turns over and sees me. He gets out of bed, puts on his slippers, and asks me to join him in our living room. We sit there together beside the unlit fireplace and talk, he in his chair, me in the one my mother normally occupies.

My father is convinced he can solve the mystery of my inability to sleep. He can do that for children. He solves problems for children all day long and works on plans to treat them for whatever it is that makes them suffer. But their problems are more serious than mine, he has always said, because they live at the Home. I live in *a home* and he says there is a big difference. But I wonder about the difference, and sometimes I think I need to live next door at night so that I can get pills that might help me, but then I think, no, because I don't want to leave my mother, but then I think yes, because it would be fun to sleep with so many children, but then I always go back to not wanting to leave my mother. A game of Ping-Pong goes on inside my head whenever I sit across from my father in the middle of the night. I have to be careful about the information I give my father. I cannot give too much away.

Thank God, I have paid attention to all the bedtime stories and books my mother has read to us through the years. I tell him what I consider typical stories for a girl my age, even if they are a bit far-fetched.

I tell him I am scared Mr. McGregor will capture Peter Rabbit and cut his head off. I ask him whether the East Wind Fairies really nip off children's soft fingers and little toes. I ask him whether Frankenstein could take the Greyhound to Albany. I tell him giant snakes the size of anacondas are living under our house. And I ask him whether his students at Coxsackie State Prison, where he teaches psychology once a week, will escape from their cells, hitchhike all the way to our house, and murder us with my mother's Waterford cake knife, if he gives them bad grades and they don't like it?

My father listens to my rambling thoughts and shakes his head with each new piece of information. I have not given him the truth, only nonsensical data, which he tries to absorb so that he can dispense advice and words of encouragement. After I agree with him that my fears are really just nightmares based on fairy tales, he leads me back to my bed and I promise him that I will go to sleep.

Not long afterward, I am back in my parents' bedroom, and I have placed the black wooden chair over by the window, carrying it by tiptoes all the way to the far end of their bedroom. I open the curtain ever so slightly so that the light from the small security floodlight that shines on the back of our house can be let in. I read *Gulliver's Travels* until exhaustion wins the battle over my fears. Eventually, I fall asleep slumped over in my parents' bedroom chair.

Like Gulliver, I don't think my father understood me. A child from his own blood, I am the one persistent riddle he could never solve.

Nor could I.

My mother had taken my situation directly to the attention of the all-powerful St. Jude, patron saint of hopeless causes. I have been learning about the saints in my religion class that I take at St. Teresa's after school on Wednesdays. My school didn't teach Catholic religion and you had to wait until high school to read the Bible, not that I was excited about that. When Jimmy and I were in church we would try to read the Bible together and we would just end up laughing on account of the fact that people said things like Thou and everyone lived until they were like nine hundred years old. As for my mother, I never thought she would have to go and bother a saint about me. They were bigger than life which is why my mother gave them crisp dollar bills whenever we went to visit them at St. Patrick's Cathedral in New York City.

Each week, my mother walked up Academy Road to the mailbox with Marnie's leash in one hand, Sarah's hand in her other, and in the back pocket of her slacks an envelope addressed to St. Jude/Care of the *Times Union*. I noticed her actions one day when I was playing hide-and-seek behind the large elm trees on the front lawn of Megan Murphy's house, which was just about a hundred feet away from the mailbox. As soon as my mother opened up the letter slot, she would peer around to see if anyone was looking at her, and then she would drop the envelope into the box. Inside the envelope was my mother's special prayer, her signature at the bottom, and a crisply ironed one-dollar bill taped on the back of it.

Every single Wednesday without fail, my mother's prayer would be printed in the newspaper.

> *St. Jude, pray for me . . . Make use, I implore you, of that particular privilege given you, to bring visible and speedy help where help is most despaired of. Come to my assistance in this great need that I may receive the consolation and help of heaven in all my necessities . . . particularly,* please help my daughter sleep and erase her fears, *and that I may praise God with you . . . I promise, O blessed St. Jude, to be ever mindful of this great favor, to always honor you as my special and powerful patron, and to gratefully encourage devotion to you. Amen, Elaine C.*

Once she had read her prayer in the paper, while she drank her orange juice in the morning and after we had left for school, she would cut it out of the newspaper like she did coupons, using a ruler to make sure it was the perfect dimension. Then she would tuck it inside her cherry wood jewelry box beneath her growing number of fake pearls and her mother's engagement and wedding rings.

Sometimes I would walk into my mother's bedroom and catch her reading St. Jude's prayer using her softest tone of voice. Even though she held on to the prayer with her fingers, I knew by now she must have known it by heart. She would do this for seven days according to the instructions in the newspaper, and my mother followed directions exactly as they were written, even for recipes. On the eighth day, as promised by the prayer rules and her one-dollar payment, well, maybe that would be the night I slept.

Raising hopes for that rare peaceful night, St. Jude made a pretty penny off my mother.

The farmer, by this time, was convinced I must be a rational creature. He spoke often to me; but the sound of his voice pierced my ears like that of a water-mill, yet his words were articulate enough. I answered as loud as I could in several languages, and he often laid his ear within two yards of me: but all in vain, for we were wholly unintelligible to each other.
—Jonathan Swift, *Gulliver's Travels**

* Soon after Swift was born, his father died.

Breaking News

As the night advanced, a fierce wind arose from the woods, and quickly
dispersed the clouds that had loitered in the heavens: the blast tore along
like a mighty avalanche, and produced a kind of insanity in my spirits,
that burst all bounds of reason and reflection.

—Mary Shelley, *Frankenstein**

I t is Friday, March 3, 1972. I am sitting in the back bedroom watching my
favorite show, *The Brady Bunch*. Marcia Brady is playing Pygmalion to the
ugliest girl in her class, Molly Webber. But then Marcia has to try and beat
Molly in order to be named Banquet Night hostess. The episode is all about
Marcia, and Jimmy hates it because he likes Peter Brady. Jimmy tells my
mother, right in the middle of the show, that his favorite Brady Bunch show
ever was when Peter Brady asked, Mom, can we have pork shops and apple
shause for dinner. He's pretending he's Humphrey Bogart. Jimmy imitates
Peter imitating Humphrey Bogart.

Mom, can we have pork shops and apple *sauc-ee* for dinner.

---

* Just after her birth, Shelley was orphaned upon the death of her mother.

Jimmy is stupid. *Sau-cee* sounds Italian. It's like Grow up, Jimmy. You're eleven years old, and I'm ten going on eleven. We're in the double digits and you're still acting like an annoying kid. I can't take it, so I finally scream it out during a commercial break.

Grow, up Jimmy. No more kid stuff. Life is serious.

When we are back from commercial break, a TV newsman with jet-black hair slicked back so much with hair gel that it wouldn't move even if a tidal wave hit—is suddenly sitting before us at the news desk. He looks serious. He holds his page of notes and looks up to the camera just like Walter Cronkite does when he's serious. Behind him is an orange sign that flashes BREAKING NEWS. This is big because we rarely see that sign. When it comes on the screen, the three adults in the room—my father, mother, and me—all turn quiet.

Jimmy asks my mother, Has the president been killed? Is he dead? Was he shot in the head again? Huh?

Shh, Jim, my mother says.

Billy starts to cry and says, I want to watch *The Brady Bunch.* I hate the new. (Sometimes Billy doesn't even bother with an *s.*)

Mandy asks if she can turn the channel in order to switch to another show without a newsman.

Breaking News is serious to me and my parents. I love the news, watching Mr. Cronkite every night with my father at 6:30 P.M. right after dinner. On Wednesday nights, we watch the local news together at 6 P.M.

On that night, children from the Home are featured on a segment called "Wednesday's Child." The story of a particular child would unfold as a pretty reporter spoke to the child, while the kid attempted to knock down pins at the local bowling alley. I suppose bowling made the Home kids look adoptable even when they threw the ball into the next-door gutter by mistake. I think they must have edited the temper tantrums out. When the segment was over, the reporter would announce the special local hotline number for anyone interested in adopting the Child of the Week from the Home. Although no price tag was shown on the air—my father said they were free—it did make the Home kid come across like this week's Blue Light Special. I hoped they at least got to keep their worn-in rental bowling shoes.

Back in our TV room as the newsman begins to speak, my mother and father tell my brothers and sisters to hush so that they can listen. It is 8:45 P.M. and the man says that a Mohawk Airlines plane bound for Albany from New York City has landed on top of a two-story house a short car ride away from Academy Road, over and then behind St. Teresa's. As the news breaks, I hear fire trucks coming up Academy Road, and they do not stop to take the right into the Home's entrance. They pass our house with an intensity that they never used to come to the Home.

. . . The Federal Aviation Administration says forty-five people were on board the flight. The plane hit a two-family home at 50 Edgewood Avenue . . . It is not known if there are survivors. Camera crews are on their way.

I look over at my mother, and she wipes her eyes on the cuff of her shirt.

My father gets up, puts on his ski sweater and snow boots, and says to me and Jimmy, Come on, kids, let's go to the accident site. Jimmy and I immediately run to our rooms and put on our ski jackets and zip them up.

As we near the front door, my mother calls out, No, John. The news is back on and the police are urging everyone in the neighborhood to stay home. The traffic is getting too crowded, and the ambulances can't get through.

My father looks at the disappointed looks on our faces.

But, Dad, we want to see the plane on the house, we both say.

Please, Dad.

Oh, Elaine, the kids really want to go.

John, now the police are saying anyone making their way to the accident will be fined.

Jimmy and I take off our snow jackets and head back to the TV to wait for camera crews to show us live images of the plane that has squished down the nearby house.

Throughout the night, we learn the dead pilot and copilot had been taken away, as had the fifteen others who died. Twenty-eight people were injured. Most were Albany residents who worked for General Electric and were flying home for the week after a business trip. Their wives and kids had been waiting at the airport. Miraculously, the couple who lived in the house with their two sons—and had been watching TV at the time of the crash—were thrown from the house by the impact and landed in their snow-covered backyard, injured, but alive. The older man who lived above them had been flattened by the plane, and his wife was rushed to the hospital in critical condition.

According to the reporters who stood near the flattened house, less than a few hours after their departure from La Guardia Airport, all the dead people on board had been laid out under blankets on the back lawn until ambulances could take them away.

It is close to midnight and I see an image of a man who seems like a friendly neighbor, making a neat line of the passengers' checked baggage on the front lawn of Mr. and Mrs. Joe Rosen's house.

I didn't get to see the blood in the snow until the next day.

We are in our station wagon riding up New Scotland Avenue in a blinding snowstorm on our way to visit the Rosen family's former house. Soon we are at the accident site where the once A-frame house is surrounded by yellow police tape. I open the door on my side of our car and head to the tape area where I can get the best view. I am smaller than a lot of the adults who stand there holding each other crying, so I am able to sneak right up to the front of the tape. As soon as I see the tangled wreckage of the white plane with the tail section jutting out in the front of the house and the crumpled cockpit resting on the snow-laden and bloodstained backyard, I realize that with a simple twist of fate this could have been our house. We live under the same flight pattern as Mr. and Mrs. Joe Rosen and their two sons when the plane dropped from the skies and crashed into their home.

For about a year after that night—especially on Fridays from 8:30 until 9 P.M.—I hummed louder than I ever had before in Mrs. Wheatley's Terminal Diseases class. And every Friday night, I put on my new white ski helmet and ducked under the big black chair near the TV set. This was my protective bunker against another Flight 405 destroying our house while *The Brady Bunch* was on.

Not long after the Mohawk Airlines accident, my troubles increased. I now threw violent tantrums, screamed, and cried at the thought of even trying to go off to sleep. It was only when my father rolled out his sleeping bag and laid his pillow beside my open bedroom door that my cries slowly subsided. With him just five feet away from me, I finally found sleep in my own sleeping bag, which my mother had rolled out for me on the wooden floor in front of my closet.

She now avoided any smelly-ice complaints by collecting coupons, which she clipped from the back of Kool-Aid packets in order to buy me a plastic

Kool-Aid canteen. She filled the canteen with cold water and left it beside my sleeping bag for what she called my Nightly Camping Trip with my father. It all seemed more fun and outdoorsy than just going to sleep the regular way—not that I really understood that way anyway.

Finally, I slept.

I was a secret my parents kept.

The silence was broken as far as I know only once by my mother, who shared it with Dr. Abbuhl, our family pediatrician. One afternoon, when my father was away on a business trip, my mother arranged for our babysitter, Kathy, to watch my brothers and sisters while she took me to the doctor's office. I thought this was strange since I hadn't complained of a stomachache. The only thing wrong with me was a twitching right eye, but I got new tics every week so it didn't seem like that big of a deal.

As I sat in the waiting room, pretending to read a tired old copy of *Highlights,* I could see into Dr. Abbuhl's office where my mother was seated in a chair, her back to me. She turned around at one point as tears were rolling down her face. I could hear what she said, even if she tried to say it ever so quietly.

What have we done wrong? John and I have tried so hard. Is she sick, Dr. Abbuhl? I just don't think it's normal. Is there a pill that can help?

It was the first time my mother asked for help from a nonsaint.

Do you see any similarities between Sue and any of the children at the Home? she asked. John says for me not to worry and that we can handle her on our own. But I'm so tired.

What will happen as she grows?

Will it get worse?

Will Sue ever be a regular kid?

Shaking his head as he nervously tightened his bow tie, Dr. Abbuhl replied, I don't know, Elaine. You'll just have to wait and see. John knows what he's doing. Have faith.

And after she begged him, Dr. Abbuhl assured her, Of course I won't tell John you came in. Don't worry, Elaine. One day, this will all be forgotten.

As we quietly drove home, in my mind I questioned the dividing line between the children who lived at the Home and a child like me—who lived in a house with a loving family. One day, would my father finally give up and call his boss, Mr. Millard, and ask that I be whisked away from my family—just like the Home kids were taken away from theirs because of the problems? Would I walk across the lawn with my suitcase that had been used only to go to Williamsburg and St. Louis, carrying my belongings over the small slope in our immediate backyard to live in one of the cottages with their familiar red doors?

An Orphan's Splendor

The years moved swiftly for Bob Wygant. Instead of going to nearby Hackett Junior High, with all his friends from the Home, Bob asked the superintendent if he could enroll at Philip Livingston, another public school not too far away. He knew instinctively that he would get into trouble if he was with all his buddies, and it was important for him to earn good grades if he wanted to forge a decent future for himself. Bob worked hard each year and was exuberant each time he saw his name on the honor roll. He was a disciplined orphan.

Bob exhibited a real talent for sports. If he had a special dream, it was to have his own key to the Van Alstyne Gym. Until that happened, he solved the problem by leaving the club room window unlocked or a door slightly ajar from time to time so he could shoot hoops after hours. Even though he always had nightly chores, Bob also volunteered to spot-clean the beautifully kept basketball floor on his knees using a cloth and lemon oil.

At study time each night and before Bob made his way to the gymnasium, his houseparents, the Scotts, made daily announcements, including a list of items that were now considered war rations. The Scotts also tried to keep the boys informed on matters going on in the world, as reported by the local newspaper. Often the Scotts and the Wasson boys would listen to the phonograph or select radio programs, a favorite being *The Lone Ranger.*

On Friday nights, the boys couldn't wait to listen to the fights. And on Saturday afternoons during baseball season, they listened to Yankee games. They also looked forward to President Franklin Roosevelt's fireside chats. The president's rich, resonant voice enchanted the Scotts.

The former New York governor's surprising death in April 1945 saddened everyone throughout the world, and inside Wasson Cottage, too. In Albany, thousands of citizens headed to the Governor's Mansion to pay their respects to their lost leader. Among this throng were Mr. and Mrs. Scott, accompanied by all the boys from Wasson. At the mansion's gated entrance, each boy added a rose to the growing display of tributes to FDR. They had bought the flowers with their allowances out of respect for the president, and in deep devotion to their devastated houseparents.

After several decades working at the Home, Mr. and Mrs. Scott—now well into their sixties and no longer capable of keeping their steady eyes on some forty growing boys and restless young men—finally retired from their position not long after President Roosevelt's passing. In some respects, Bob felt he lost his parents.

By the time he entered high school, Bob had become more outgoing and fun loving. He was not the shy kid who had entered the Home years earlier. He was the most popular orphan at the Albany Home for Children. True to his boyhood dreams, he was now a star Albany High School athlete, a four-letter man, and a local football hero. Every night after dinner he practiced on the playing fields of the Home, whenever possible working with the Home's athletics and activities director, Coach Ronald J. Huddleston.

Coach Huddleston, a handsome newlywed who lived on campus with his vivacious blond, blue-eyed Norwegian bride, Swannee, was affectionately known by all the children as Coach. Each day after school, everyone—girls as well as boys—gathered in the middle of the quad, near the wading pool, and

Coach led them through calisthenics and the running drills he had learned in the army.

Bob Wygant was clearly Coach's favorite and his protégé.

In fact, every high school sports fan in Albany watched this handsome young man when he ran track and played basketball, baseball, and football—especially football, where his uncanny ability to weave in and out of a football line like lightning earned him the nickname Wiggles.

He also began to catch the eye of many of the girls at school. Bob Wygant was finally beginning to feel like a truly fortunate guy, someone who could make connections in life, despite the fact that he had a secret. Few people knew Wiggles Wygant was an orphan.

By the time they reached high school, none of the Home kids would admit their shared history. Being a teenager was hard enough without the added burden of their lack of a traditional home and family. Of course, their occasionally mismatched clothes and, for the girls, the sturdy brown stockings they wore instead of the more stylish white bobby socks or sheer stockings tended to brand them as residents of the Home. Many of Bob's female friends suffered the Albany cold in the name of fashion, stripping off their heavy stockings on their way to school, drawing lines with eyebrow pencil down the backs of their legs to simulate seams.

During his junior year, while playing for the Garnet and Gray varsity team at the always popular Albany High–Albany Academy game, Bob spotted a beautiful girl rooting for his team sitting in the bleachers whom he had never seen before.

Bob was immediately attracted.

But what would he do?

Dating frequently posed problems for teens who lived at the Home, especially if the object of their affection was not a Home kid. Their lives were just too different and, for many, too difficult to explain.

Compared with their counterparts on the outside, Home children lived sheltered lives—always under the watchful eyes of their houseparents and other child care workers responsible for the care of these growing young wards of the state.

Camaraderie was one thing; cultivating the skills necessary to develop the ability to maintain mature, loving relationships, quite another. Especially for the girls. Well-meaning housemothers taught them that life was going to be

good, so they needed to learn to cook and keep house, to marry a man they
would love, honor, and obey. After all, as they were so often told, someday
Prince Charming would come riding up on his white charger. A girl needed to
be prepared.

Nurse Werger and Swannee Huddleston also had a hand in preparing the
girls for adulthood. When girls turned twelve, they were given a book—*Being
Born*—to read as preparation for menstruation. They knew the basics of how
the body functioned, but they knew only the bare minimum about sex. Some
of the girls thought they would get pregnant simply by kissing a boy.

Bob thought about asking Dorothy to the movies, but he decided that their
time together was far too important to spend in a dark room with a bunch of
strangers. As for kissing Dorothy, even the four-letter man was a bit shy when
it came to that. He had played spin-the-bottle with the other kids from the
Home when he was in junior high school, so he had had the experience of
kissing. Even at the Home, there were places, such as behind the old barn
where Pop Thompson kept his two farm horses, where Home kids played
their love games. When his turn came, Bob spun the milk bottle, and it
stopped by the crossed feet of a rather average-looking girl from Rathbone
Cottage. Although nervous, he figured it would just be a quick kiss. And so he
leaned across the circle, and right there, before everyone playing the game,
their lips locked. That was the end of that *procedure.*

But after that single glimpse of Dorothy in the stands, and later when he
stole glances at her in the crowded hallways at Albany High, he couldn't stop
thinking about her. And he no longer thought about kissing as a quick procedure.

At night, in his dreams, he imagined dancing with Dorothy to the sounds
of George Gershwin's " 'S Wonderful."

> *'S wonderful! 'S marvelous!*
> *That you should care for me!*

He dreamed about her during school and all through athletic practice. No
one before Dorothy had ever distracted him this way. Bob Wygant was a focused young man. Or he had been till now.

He didn't know how to build up the courage to ask her out. Yes, he had talked about Dorothy with Coach and Swannee. He visited them almost every night in the living room of their small apartment, which had been his kindergarten classroom years ago when he first came to live at the Home. And when he started talking about her, slowly at first, and then almost obsessively, the Huddlestons told him to just call her.

Oh, please, Bob, enough already, just call her!

One night, he did. He telephoned Dorothy from the main office building where he was assigned cleaning chores for the month.

It was a nice conversation, a good start. You have to take these things slowly and gradually, even if your heart is pumping with speed. They talked about school and what they liked to do for fun. He told her he liked to go with his friend Coach for rides in his red Oldsmobile convertible, all the way out on New Scotland Avenue way past School 19 to a horse farm where he and Coach took turns riding Coach's show horse. She seemed impressed. And at the end of the conversation, Dorothy asked if she could have his number, too. The question threw Bob. He had not prepared an answer for this. He apologized, saying that she couldn't. His phone, he said, was broken.

As their conversations continued and their relationship grew, Bob worried about bringing Dorothy home. By now, he had gone to her house quite often, and he knew that sooner or later he would be expected to reciprocate. He thought about his future, and somehow he knew even then that one day he would marry her. Bob had life figured out perfectly, even as a young teenager. But first he had to explain his home, or rather the Home situation.

What would Dorothy think about going steady with a boy from the Home? Sometimes, Bob figured, you just have to go with your hunch that everything will turn out just fine.

Bob took a small step and invited her to dinner one night—not to his cottage; too many boys would be ogling Dorothy there. Instead, he asked Coach and Swannee if he could bring her to dinner at their apartment. He struck a deal with Swannee: He would clean her kitchen if she would make a special home-cooked meal for all of them on a Sunday afternoon. He knew Swannee would do it without his cleaning, but it was the least he could do for such a generous favor.

The date was set.

He picked Dorothy up at her house, and as they walked down New Scotland Avenue heading toward the Home, he proceeded to tell his story—minus the stork and the baby bundles from the sky. The stork had vanished with the other fairy tales of his childhood. He told her he was an orphan and that he had lived on the large campus that now loomed in front of them for as long as he could remember.

She expressed sadness, but Bob assured her that his situation was fine because it had always been his home. He told her about his adventures living there, how kind his first housemother, Mrs. Dugan, was, about his friend Irving Coffin dying so young from a heart condition, and how much he still remembered him, and he told her about how he and his friends Charlie and Joe once got caught sneaking bags of grape Kool-Aid in their shorts. They hid in the barn where the cold water was stored—they were going to use it to mix their Kool-Aid—until Mr. Keck, the laundry man, pulled up in his tractor and discovered them beneath a pile of dirty clothes. He got in trouble then—the leather strap came down on his fanny—but he wanted her to know that it was the only time he received that kind of punishment.

As they neared Coach's apartment, Bob pointed to each cottage: Lathrop, where the youngest children lived, and where he once did, too; Rathbone and Parsons, the girls' cottages; and the boys' cottages, Fuller and his own home, Wasson. He promised to show her the boys' garden after dinner.

Somehow he found the courage after their meal to invite her to his cottage. As Bob awkwardly stood in the vestibule introducing her to his new housemother, Dorothy recognized other familiar faces from Albany High. And she spoke sweetly with the younger boys. Bob couldn't believe how comfortable she seemed. He was euphoric that she had responded so well to his home. Perhaps she would even fall in love with him.

Later, when Bob walked her home, Dorothy asked him if he knew anything about his mother or father. He shrugged and said no. In fact, he said, it was so long ago that he no longer cared.

He had told Dorothy a lie.

When does an orphan ever really stop wondering?

The Seasons

"As long as one has a garden one has a future, and as long as one has a future one is alive."

—Frances Hodgson Burnett, *In the Garden**

I love my house through all the seasons of the year.

I love my house in the spring because its start brings the flowers that erase some of my father's sadness, a sadness he rarely shows but I know is there.

I love our front yard. It's full of life.

Our front yard grows more and more beautiful because of my father's grand wizard fingers over his botanical garden and all its many different kinds

---

* Hodgson Burnett (1849–1924) the author of the best-selling book *The Secret Garden*, which tells the story of an orphan girl bringing a garden filled with roses back to life in order to inspire her crippled cousin to walk again, is one of the most influential children's books ever written. Hodgson Burnett's father died when she was four, leaving behind him a widow and five children.

of flowers. If you were a tourist coming to visit the United States from another country, like Russia or Tonga, and you were on a bus tour traveling across the country, you would want the bus driver to ride down Academy Road and stop in front of our house to take photos of our front yard.

But if you were a tourist from Russia or Tonga, you would not be allowed to shoot a photo of our backyard. In fact, if you were a tourist who got off the bus and went running into our backyard without permission from my father or Mr. Millard, you would be arrested by the police and thrown into the jail because you were never, ever allowed to take photos of the children. My father once told my mother that strangers scared the children in the backyard on account of some of them being raped by their uncles or other relatives. I didn't know what that word *raped* meant, but the way my father said it made it sound like a bad word. Those adults or relatives who had raped a kid had to go to jail for almost forever, which my mother thought was proper. Well, that's not true. She actually told my father that they should get the death sentence, but my father hated it when my mother said that and he had to remind her, Oh Jesus, Elaine, death sentence? We are Democrats. We do not vote Republican.

Whatever they were, the *rape* word hurt my mother so much that she always got upset whenever I overheard my father talking about this happening to some of the new children who arrived in our backyard.

Nevertheless, my mother knew a lot about jail and how long you should stay in it, on account of the fact that she watched *Ironside* and *Columbo* on television every week. She felt sorry that Ironside had to live and work in a wheelchair, and I think she watched Columbo because she wanted to wash his trench coat.

Our front yard felt like a plate of warm hors d'oeuvres served by my mother with the warmest of smiles. Our backyard felt like it had a moat around it, with the drawbridge lowered for only the people who belonged inside, whether they lived or worked there. In the winter our backyard was almost completely hidden from view by the snowbanks. During the spring and summer, my father worked hard trying to hide it from people who passed by, or maybe he was just protecting it. His garden extended not only to our front yard but also down the street along the brick wall all the way to the area right before the gully that separated our property from Temple Beth Emeth.

The spring thaw begins. I have lived on the grounds of the Albany Home for several years now. I stand outside our front door and know where I am, finally. I know where I live—although ever since that visit to Dr. Abbuhl's office, I do get confused about whether I am living in the right home on the grounds. I also know that you can find only unhappy stories in my backyard. None of the children I have known through their faces has ever left. Sometimes, like this day, I just want to be out front. I want to smile and I want to forget about the sad children I see each time I open the sliding glass door onto my backyard.

I leave our little cement entrance patio. To my left my father kneels on the ground over by the fence painted barn red. Wearing faded yellow gardener's gloves, he digs through the recently frozen soil with his thick fingers and warms the dirt in the palm of his gloves in order to prepare it before he tucks a seed or a bulb to bed inside it. My father plants more flower beginnings than anyone else on our street or even in our neighborhood.

In a few weeks when a delicate green leaf shoots out from underneath the dirt, he welcomes it in the same way I see him put his arms around a new child who first makes his or her way over the speed bump to come and live at the Home. I know the names of the flowers that my father plants outside our home and around the sign of the Albany Home for Children because if my father is the planter, I am his seed supplier.

I had wanted to deliver newspapers around our neighborhood in order to earn extra money so that I could buy a guitar for the band I had created downstairs in our basement with my siblings and neighborhood friends like Megan Murphy. We would be called the Explosions. I was the lead singer, of course. Mandy and Megan played the tambourines, and Billy was on the drums, or boxes. I put a chair in front of our makeshift stage and made Sarah clap for us after we finished each song. She was our groupie. We had only one song. I had written it and titled it "Billy, Billy Bump-Bump." Billy hated it and cried through the song every time I started to sing. Sarah didn't have a choice when it came to clapping because if she got up from the chair, I slapped her.

The Explosions were going to be bigger than the Jackson or Osmond families. I had already earmarked our wardrobe in the fashion pages of the Montgomery Ward catalog. We would be wearing jean jackets with a rhinestone house stitched onto the back. It was a cute concept, considering we lived on the Home property. We would wear red stretch pants, flared at the bottom. And except for Billy, we would wear buffalo sandals to make us appear taller. Jimmy had been kicked out of the band for attitude problems and his inability to get along with others, or me. I gave him a U for unsatisfactory on his band report card. I made up weekly report cards for my bandmates to give them helpful instructions so we would be ready when we were asked by Ike and Tina Turner to join their world tour.

In order to earn extra money to buy our costumes, I asked my mother to call the *Times Union,* but she was told that I couldn't deliver newspapers because I was a girl. That was a disappointing day for me. I screamed bloody murder about the world not being fair, and then went into the TV room to beat up Jimmy because he was a boy. After I had been sent to my bedroom by my mother for my now frequent Get Your Temper Under Control Time, I banged on the walls. When I eventually got over the crushing news that I couldn't be a papergirl, I answered an ad to sell *Grit,* a newspaper I never actually saw anywhere but in the advertisement in the back of comic books. Again, I received a letter stating I couldn't sell *Grit* because I was a girl.

The letter concluded with the following question:

Perhaps if you have a brother, ask him to write us about an excellent opportunity to earn extra money.

I gave Jimmy a copy of the letter. He looked at it and said, What's this, stupid? He crunched it into a little ball and threw it at me.

Right before I had given it to Jimmy, I took my Magic Marker and drew a long black mark through all the typed lines in the rather brief rejection letter. After, I repented. We had been learning about sins in our Religious and Instructions class up at St. Teresa's on Wednesday afternoons, and it seemed like not showing a letter that the *Grit* people asked me to forward to my brother fell under the sin category. So I showed it to Jimmy, and I asked for God's forgiveness on Sunday.

Dear God. I couldn't restrain myself from giving Jimmy a letter with no words on it, because I didn't want Jimmy to get a job that belonged to me. I know, I'll say three Hail Marys.

Deep down, I knew Jimmy couldn't deliver newspapers the way I could. Jimmy didn't think deeply or obsess about things like I could. Did Jimmy fantasize about laying all the newspapers you get in the morning from the newspaper truck out on our living room by spreading them all over our Oriental rug? Did Jimmy think about rolling the papers and then tucking one end under the other so you had that perfect tube-shaped quality which was essential to throwing a paper from your newspaper bag that you carried around your shoulder? How often did Jimmy fantasize about tossing a paper onto a mat in front of a door with the precision of a pilot landing his plane? Jimmy the boy, who had all the right in the world to be a newspaper boy because of one little difference between us inside our underwear, did not even think about the beauty of a paper being tossed into the blue sky like a perfect Frisbee toss. Jimmy wasn't concerned with newspaper-throwing accuracy. Jimmy couldn't care less if someone's slippers got cold because they had to walk across their freezing front porch to find a newspaper thrown off front steps or on the far side of the porch. That's the kind of newspaper boy you would have gotten with Jimmy!

I got my new dream job when I answered an advertisement to sell flower seeds door-to-door, which I ripped out of my *Archie* comic book. My entrepreneurial prayers were answered. God was finally going to allow me to earn extra money, even if my box of Burpee seed packets was addressed to Sir Carswell.

Eventually, when my father's flowers were in full bloom (half from buying bulbs at Hewitt's Flowers and half from buying my seeds) and the front of our house and the Home's exterior looked like we lived in an open-air greenhouse, my father and I would walk around the vast garden. I would carry the packets I hadn't sold to the neighbors to see how the beautiful real flowers looked against the pretend picture of what they were supposed to look like on the cover of my seed packs. A Burpee flower picture never matched the true beauty of the reality of a flower in its stage of perfect bloom.

The neighbors on our street would often come over and tell my father how lovely his flowers were. When they did, my father seemed glad to not have to talk about our backyard and all the children who continued to grow up there. He got lost in the beauty of his garden. Maybe he forgot about the sadness that sometimes made even him cry inside, especially at Christmas when he thought about the disturbing lives the Home children had lived before they were brought there. My father never shed real tears, on account of the fact that he was a dad. But still, I sensed when the tears fell back from his mouth and down to his stomach.

...

I love my house in the summer because when we aren't swimming out back, we play and work in the front during the long, glowing blue-sky days.

Jimmy and Billy glistened with sweat as they helped my father mow the rich green grass that stretched from our driveway over to the small woods separating our house from the main entrance to the Home. My sisters and I sold Kool-Aid from our three pitchers to anyone passing. Selling Burpee flower packs was my profession; Kool-Aid was a way to add even more income to my savings in my band/bank account. Sarah positioned herself immediately next to the stoplight on the corner, next to the Millards' house and the entrance to the JCA. She wouldn't take no for an answer. She used her cute dimples as propaganda. She turned her head to one side and scrunched up her shoulders as if to say, *Please, buy my Kool-Aid.* When we realized our Kool-Aid profit scale was dismal, we turned our Saturday-afternoon Kool-Aid stand into an impromptu flea market. We waited for our mother to leave for her Saturday-afternoon appointment at Louie the hairdresser's for a cut, color, and blow-dry, or just a blow-dry depending upon her rotating hair cycle. Louie was the Vidal Sassoon of Albany. My mother told my aunt that Louie was gay. It was nice to know someone was happy all the time. I wasn't.

One Sunday afternoon, my grandmother asked my father if Louie was really *gay and why was Elaine spending time with him?* (like feeling gay was a naughty bad thing). My father got up from his lawn chair and yelled at his mother for what I think was the first time in his entire life. My father said he was ashamed of my grandmother. He said it like he was really angry, then added, I'm taking you home right now, Mother. Let's go! Don't you ever be rude like that again. Do you hear me?

After I heard it, I was rather confused as to who the good guy in this story was. Was it my grandmother, who was asking about why a happy-go-lucky guy was spending time with my mother, or was it my father who implied being gay in a certain tone like my grandmother used was rude? I didn't know. And believe me, if I asked, I knew I would get some sort of *it's complicated* runaround. I didn't bother. Besides I liked Louie and I *loved* his pool.

Louie and his best friend had a swimming pool right up the street, so when we weren't swimming at our pool we now went with my mother to Louie's. No one there ever used the pool. We were the only ones doing laps and cannonballs. Louie and his best friend and all their friends, mostly young men in itsy-bitsy Speedos, and my mother in her one-piece, would sit in their lounge chairs, drink frozen margaritas, and gossip. A lot of the talk concerned who in Albany had what haircut. It seemed a bit strange that my mother had friends that were young guys. I was glad Louie was her good friend because unfair swimming time slots were now a thing of the past.

As soon as my mother drove our family car away for her Louie appointment, we pulled out the things we thought she wouldn't miss for our yard sale. We sold her daisy-patterned yellow pantsuit one day for two bucks. She hadn't worn it in two years, so I assumed it was now out of fashion and therefore needed to leave her closet for new clothes.

Besides selling her outdated wardrobe, old issues of *Good Housekeeping* and *National Geographic*—where Jimmy said he liked looking for nudies—we got more money when we sold things like the auburn wig my mother had purchased on a whim on one of her weekly Wednesday-night shopping sprees she enjoyed with her friends, The Girls.

The wig's brownish red color was pretty much the same style and color as my mother's hair, so it wasn't like she even needed a wig. When she first bought it at Macy's, she came home and fixed it up with her comb as she looked into the rectangular antique mirror placed on the wall to the side of the fireplace. She was trying to position the wig over her ears correctly when she said, All the magazines say it's very stylish.

My mother now subscribed to *Redbook*. She also told us that the wig would save on the cost of shampoo. We used Suave floral garden shampoo when it was my week to pick, strawberry when it was Mandy's, green apple when it was Sarah's, and plain Suave when it was Jimmy's and Billy's weeks to pick the family shampoo.

When she first bought her fake hair, my mother wore her wig everywhere. She spent hours making sure it was styled just-so on her Styrofoam head mannequin (whom we named Mommy Head), finishing it off with a few generous squirts from her can of White Rain hair spray. Then she would head out to parent–teacher conferences, bingo, church, or outside to walk Marnie with her other hair.

After about a year with her stylish topper, my mother taped her once treasured wig onto the opposite end of her dust mop. She told me that the stray hairs were helpful when it came to getting to hard-to-reach places.

At our yard sale, Mandy, Sarah, and I were able to get five dollars for our mother's wig—which we had taken off the mop before we tried to sell it. The woman, who pulled her car over from the side of the road and bought it, now had her own stylish wig full of Pledge-smelling dust bunnies and our Mommy Head to put it on.

The seasons change. I love my front yard in the fall when the trees surrounding our house change their colors, baring their branches, the beauty of their leaves gone until the sun shines again. When the crisp autumn chill arrives, out come our new thick Irish sweaters, always hand-knit by our grandmother. On these fine, sun-dappled afternoons, we join the neighborhood kids out front finding pleasure tossing and tumbling in the fallen leaves.

The Home kids played the same games, but that was always in the backyard. Each night after our dinner, my parents, now wearing their warm coats, took their nightly stroll down Academy Road, hand in hand, humming "Misty," their wedding song, and sneaking kisses beneath the whispering leafless trees.

I love our front yard in the winter and the feeling of being all together inside our house even more. The Home's maintenance men plow our driveway whenever the frequent nor'easters hit, leaving us up to twenty feet of glistening snow. We play King of the Hill on the snowplow piles. From the street, it is often hard to see our one-story house except for the fringes of icicles that hang from the eaves. Our house looks so lost amid the piles of snow. You might even wonder if anyone lived there.

But we were always there. Always. And when it was snowing really hard outside, we would all have to stay inside and that felt so good to me. I felt like my family was finally protected as if we lived in a snow globe. You could shake and shake our globe, but our front door would remain locked. Everybody was inside and everybody was safe. The winter wind outside might fly around our house in a furious blast, and the windows to our house might be pelted with its mighty blow, but our snow globe house would never burst. It would stay safe forever. When our snow globe house did open, it was only for our chimney so that the blistering orange sparks of firewood could shoot upward from our fireplace. Outside our protected fortress, the gray ashes from our fire would swirl to the north, south, east, and west, spirited away by the howling winds.

···

Then when the seasons move to the last month of the year, there is Christmas. Our front door looks lovely decorated with its big wreath and red Christmas bow. But as the day unfolds in our backyard with the Home children and inside our house with my family, it becomes the day I learn to hate the most.

It has to do with mothers, or rather, the lack of them.

The Room of Secrets

On the first snow of winter Bob Wygant thinks about all the good things he is grateful for as Christmas approaches—such as his lovely girl-friend, Dorothy, and the brotherly love of his cottagemates, whom he knows will be in his life forever even when he leaves his home. As he makes his way out of Wasson Cottage, Bob puts his hands in his pockets while the wind nips at his neck, pushing him along swiftly. Heavy snow from a recent nor'easter covers the campus grounds. After basketball practice and dinner, the boys of Wasson and Fuller Cottages shoveled the sidewalks and created spotless walk-ways that look like a giant tic-tac-toe board. Yet as he walks along the paths, the snow flurries quietly begin again.

Bob heads to the administration building, where he has been assigned to clean the large office of the social worker, Elizabeth Campbell, this month.

He has never met Miss Campbell, as only those who are having trouble adjusting to the orphanage visit with her. Bob has no problems with where he lives. He mops Miss Campbell's floor, dusts her maple desk, and looks at her framed photographs. He wipes down all the long windows until they squeak with cleanliness. This isn't his favorite chore. Hands down, he, like all the other boys, longs for the coveted duty of sandwich detail. After writing down everyone's names on brown paper bags, the lucky boy of the month makes the sandwiches for the other boys first and then piles his own with extra meat—except when that meat is cow's tongue. In that case, Bob piles the other boys' sandwiches extra full and just slaps some peanut butter and jelly inside his own sandwich bread.

Still, Bob does a good job at his chores, because if not, he will have to do the same chore the following month. So he cleans and shines the social worker's office until everything is spotless. When he walks over to the windows to close the shades, he notices that something is out of place. One of the three long drawers in the confidential file cabinet is not shut and locked, so he walks over to close it. Otherwise, his cleaned room won't be scored perfect.

He stands in front of the open drawer. It is the one marked R–Z. He begins to wonder. Then suddenly, Bob rushes to the door of Miss Campbell's office and locks it. He jumps onto the cast-iron radiator and pulls the shades down. Doing something he had never considered doing before, he pulls the drawer open wider and riffles through the files, passing over Donnie Weber's and Charlie Wilsey's folders until he sees it: his own. It is at the very back of the drawer. He has never even thought about the fact that he has a file.

Inside the heavy folder is his information, his report cards from school, his yearly physicals, dental records with photographs of his teeth over the years, psychological reports stating that he is good-natured and vivacious, annual notes written about him by the different superintendents throughout all these years, and assorted notes written by his houseparents. As he flips through the file, at its very end is a folder marked PERSONAL HISTORY. Bob wonders if he has the right to know that truth. In some way, he knows what he is doing is wrong and that is why the room is off-limits and why folders are marked CONFIDENTIAL. Normally—at least for the others—during the cleaning process Coach stands right outside, but tonight he is wrapping Christmas gifts with Swannee and besides Bob is Coach's good friend. Sure, at any moment Coach could pound on the door to see how Bob is progressing on his cleaning, yet Bob is his protégé, so will he doubt him?

This is Bob Wygant's moment. If he is punished, so be it.

He pulls out his personal history folder and sits on the floor and begins to read. His heart pounds madly. Scrambled thoughts ramble through his usually calm mind as he reads:

There it is—my full name. Robert Rossman Wygant. Is that my middle name? I have one? Rossman . . . Rossman . . . Rossman? Rossman is the name of another housemother. Could we be related? I certainly hope not, because she is one mean lady when put to the test. Wait, there's more. Do I keep going on? Wait, now, there's another name. Helen Wygant. It says right there, Helen Wygant. Who is she? Why do we share the same last name? It can't be. I'm an orphan. I'm a real orphan. No one in this world is related to me. No one. Should I keep going? Do I want to know all of this? Born out of wedlock, it says right there under CIRCUMSTANCES. What does it say under TRANSFER? Adoption, adoption? Was I up for adoption? What does this mean? Wait, it says, NEVER and then it is signed, Helen Wygant—mother. Mother. Mother. Mother. I have a mother? And she has a name? How does this make me feel? Wait, I can't think, because there's more and I need to know everything before I get caught. Who is Elmer Rossman? Is that my father, Elmer, as in the glue? His name is listed under Helen Wygant. No, wait, it says, half-brother. I have a brother? What? There's a note under SUNDAY VISITOR'S CARD: Elmer Rossman, seven years older than Bob, tried to visit his brother Bob today but we decided in the interest of our ward, Elmer is an unfit role model for Robert. Elmer might prove a distraction. A distraction? Visitation denied. 100% disabled. Shell-shocked. Wygant should never be informed of superintendent's decision.

I had a visitor? I've been waiting all these years on Sundays, and I had a visitor? Wait. Where are they now? I have to hurry. 7 Reservoir Street, it says. Who lives there? Oh, Helen Wygant lives there. And where is Elmer? Where is Elmer? Discharged from army. Address unknown. Presumed to be living in New Jersey near his aunt.

I have an aunt, too?

That was all.

He closes his file, and a slip of paper falls out. It had been torn out of the Home's guest book and put into Bob's folder. Now it is in his hands. As Bob looks at it, he smiles, the first of a very long smile that he hopes will last for a lifetime. It is the address of his brother in Poughkeepsie. Of all the toys and presents he has ever received on all Christmases past, this would be the one that mattered more than any other. It is the key to a new beginning.

An aunt? A brother? A mother?

After a lifetime of knowing not even the slightest detail of his origins, everything he ever dreamed of knowing about his life floods over Bob in a matter of minutes. Dumbfounded by his discoveries, he sits on the floor completely still, sweating harder than when he plays sports. He has a family beyond the gates of the Albany Home for Children. A bright ray of sun enters his heart.

Bob Wygant isn't an *orphan*.

Now he just needs to find them. Maybe he and his mother and brother can all live in their own home. He would take care of Elmer, and he would love his mother. He already does. She must have had a good reason to put him in the Home.

His heart is filled with optimism because he has always been taught to think about the good in life, and never the bad.

As he finally rises from the floor, Bob carefully slips the file back in its place and closes the drawer. He turns off the lights, locks the door, slips the key back under the Coach's door, and walks along the marble corridor, toting his cleaning supplies to the closet where they are stored. He makes his way outside.

Bob Wygant hoots and hollers and kicks the fresh-fallen snow as he runs along the path, dancing in the darkened night and bursting with excitement. Outside, all alone, he repeats the details of his discovery quietly in disbelief, although he wants to scream the words from the top of the administration building.

I'm not an orphan! I have a family!

Running back to Wasson, Bob heads directly up the stairs, jumping them three at a time to his bedroom. Beneath the glow of his flashlight, he begins writing a very long letter.

Dear Mom.
It's me, your son, Bob.

The Christmas Walk

It is Christmas Eve and Santa Claus and I are heading over to the cottages. I am my father's elf helping him carry two heavy laundry sacks full of toys for the children next door. My mother has reduced my father's pillow count underneath his red costume around his belly.

Hmm, John. Two pillows . . . I don't think Santa was ever *that* fat. You look like you could sink the sleigh. One is fine.

My mother turns to me and pulls out a fleece thing from a plastic bag after her last-minute shopping spree at the five-and-dime store.

Sue, how about a green elf cap?

No. I'll look stupid.

...

We head down the driveway in the cool winter air and walk toward the cottages through the main entrance to the Home. My father is not wearing black Santa boots. He's wearing his L.L. Bean après-ski boots.

Dad, they're going to know it's you.

Ho, ho, ho. I'm Santa tonight. Don't be negative, Sue. You should have at least put your mother's rouge around your cheeks to look somewhat like an elf. They'll recognize you more than me.

They don't know me, Dad. You never introduced us.

Well, I'm introducing you tonight as my elf. Good enough?

We walk into Wasson Cottage first, where I see boys eating popcorn right off the string on the bauble-draped cheap plastic tree. Spotting my Santa father, they rush toward him.

Ho, ho, ho. It's Christmas Eve. Have my favorite children been good girls and boys this year?

Oh yes, say the mostly young boys who live there and a couple of young girls, all of whom I have never seen before.

We have been very good boys this year, Santa.

Santa, we were good girls, too.

Well, Santa is very proud of you. I'm going to look inside my sack to see if there is a present for each of you to put under your tree. Can you wait until tomorrow to open it up?

No, Santa. No, they say, tugging at his long white beard and poking his fat one-pillow belly.

If you wait until tomorrow, I promise Santa will come back with more gifts while you're asleep.

While my father reads aloud the names of the children that accompany each gift, I wander over to the area the counselors have set aside for his Santa sugar cookies with red and green candy sprinkles. My father is back on Weight Watchers, and so I go ahead and eat them for him, leaving a bite of each cookie behind so that the boys and girls will think Santa touched their cookies with his very own Santa mouth.

I hear a young boy asking my father a question.

Santa, I don't want a gift. I just want my mother to come visit me tomorrow. Where did she go? How come she doesn't like to see me? Santa, will you make sure I get that gift? Will you?

Later, when we walk back home after dropping gifts off at the other cottages, my father is quiet. Santa only brought toys. Santa couldn't make impossible dreams come true. He couldn't change the little boy's past. Nor could my father.

When we walk back into our house, my mother sneaks my father back into their bedroom, as only Sarah now needs to be hidden from the secret of Santa's alias. Eventually, he comes back out in his pajamas and robe to read "The Night Before Christmas," our ritual ever since Jimmy and I could sit on both his knees. Without fail, at the beginning of his reading, my grandmother—who with my grandfather has always stayed overnight on Christmas Eve—begins to blab away on how much she hates various politicians.

This year, it's Nixon who's a crook. The manicurist at Mr. Walt's Beauty Shop in Glens Falls, and the daughter of a gossip columnist for a small-town newspaper in Whitehall, New York, my grandmother exclaims it as if she were the chief Democratic Party pundit.

He's a bum. Vote him out of office. Do you hear me, John?

After a few minutes, my father shouts out, Mother, I am reading " 'Twas." This is not the right time!

Don't you talk to me that way, John Carswell. I am still the captain of the ship.

Mary, my mother says softly, trying to deflect my grandmother's stubborn temper and decreasing attention span, as the Manhattans have now chipped away at my grandmother's tolerance to listen to a children's book about creatures and mice not stirring and sugarplums dancing.

Moments later, my grandmother's tall, gray beehive hairdo droops off to the side as her heads begins to tilt down to her shoulders. As always, each year as I have grown, I see my handsome sweet grandfather Watson lift her up and take her into my parents' bedroom and tuck her into bed for the night.

Say good night to your grandmother, kids, my mother says, ignoring her mother-in-law's annual political protest during the middle of " 'Twas."

As soon as she leaves the room, Jimmy and I push each other until one of us finally wins the sweet-tasting maraschino cherry that remains in her half-empty cocktail glass.

Down the hall, I still hear my grandmother uttering her final thoughts.

I'm telling you, Rose Mary erased those tapes.

...

In the early morning, as the clock rings six chimes, Mandy and Sarah wake me in my sleeping bag, which my mother has rolled out on the floor in the middle of my sisters' beds so that my parents can sleep in my room while my father's parents are in theirs. Even though you get older, you never stop bolting from your bed on Christmas morning to race into the living room to see what surprises have been placed by your piles each year.

It takes self-control for us to open our presents in order—one child, one gift, and on to the next—all of us a lively carousel of varying-sized horses clad in mostly pastel pajamas as we continue to circle the living room, stripping the wrapping off our presents, rolling it into a ball, and then hurling it in the direction of my father. Like a basketball player, he catches our passes and lobs them into the roaring lion's mouth of the crackling fire in our fireplace.

With each gift we open, we cast our eyes in the direction of our mother. She is seated in her rocking chair as she warms herself right by the fire's ruby glow. There she sits as our blue eyes, and Mandy's set of green ones, gaze up at her each time we open a box, waiting to issue her excited *oohs* and *aahs*.

As I strum the chords on my new guitar like I know what I'm doing, now sitting on the floor right next to the grandfather clock, I look at my mother and think to myself how beautiful she is. She sits with her legs daintily crossed beneath her turquoise velour robe with its imitation leopard trim. Her pink slippers touch the Oriental rug for just a second as she slowly rocks back and forth. As she peers across the room through her eyeglasses, now monogrammed with her name ELAINE and not just her initial, she looks so pleased at our excited smiles, and loops her fingers through the handle of her cup filled with coffee and skim milk, and one Sweet'N Low, taking sips, enjoying every moment of the morning. Yet all her smiles, I know this for sure, will soon end. And so then will mine.

In the past couple of years, it has become my Christmas tradition. Our grandfather clock rings out eight chimes. I crawl across the rug away from my gifts and head toward our sofa, propelled by a strange and mighty power that somehow calls for me to come. Climbing onto the couch, I sprawl my body out lengthwise and prop my head up onto the sofa's matching off-white pillow. I turn my head to the side and stare through our long bay windows. I then have an unobstructed view onto our backyard.

And there they are. As they always have been and probably always will be.

Every Christmas, the children of the Albany Home make their way in a procession through cold and sometimes blinding storms toward the cavernous Van Alstyne Gymnasium, where they celebrate their Christmas with punch and cookies and donated presents.

There they walk, heads bowed sorrowfully, as they move in a long, single-file line just like they are members of a chain gang. In their hand-me-down boots, one even wearing my old ski jacket, they drag their feet through the deep, unshoveled snow.

While Jimmy, Billy, Mandy, and Sarah seem oblivious to the Christmas Walk of the Children that takes place not too far away, my father simply stares through the glass door and coughs nervously in an attempt to hide his feelings.

By now, my mother is nowhere to be seen in our living room with the big windows onto our backyard. In the distance, down the hallway and in the far back bathroom, I hear the sounds of the shower washing over the wilted chords of my mother singing "Ave Maria."

I suppose it is best that she does not look out the bay window as I do. I just wish my mother could remain in the shower all day long, so the warm trickling water can wash away her Christmas tears.

But her sadness just moves on.

At nine fifteen, my family piles into our latest Ford Town Car. We head toward St. Teresa of Avila for Christmas Mass. Billy, Mandy, and Sarah hop around me like Mexican jumping beans, high on the excitement of their new toys beneath the tree. Jimmy, the oldest, now sits up front sandwiched in between my parents. In contrast to them, I am quiet and stare intently at my mother's still head and her new hat. She does not budge as we drive closer to the sound of our church's ringing of Christmas bells. My mother, never at a loss for a song, a story, or a rhyme to keep us quiet and entertained so that we won't disturb my father's driving, never speaks a word.

I wonder if this is the way people are expected to behave when they sit in long black cars making their way toward a funeral. I wonder if this was the way that my mother traveled to her own mother's funeral so many years ago, the day after my young grandmother's Christmas wake.

Infant Jesus

Reed, are you feeling okay, my great-grandmother asks my great-grandfather as my mother and her sister lie on their living room floor in awe, staring at their first TV set.

Reed, I asked you if you were all right. Why are you sleeping? You know what today is. And you have not yet done it. Reed? Reed?

Oh, yes, sorry, Ella, I just dozed off for a second. The voices on the TV put me to sleep. But yes. I know. No need to tell me.

Reed Primmer, the quiet and loving grandfather to Mary and Elaine, who has worked all his life as a janitor at an automobile company in Troy fixing cars for other people's journeys, has for all these long years never said a word about his daughter or her untimely death. He and his wife, Ella, never bring up Ora in conversation, because it is simply too heartwrenching.

Still, they remember their daughter every day.

Each night, in a gesture of deep Catholic devotion to her memory, Reed Primmer lights a votive candle beneath the Infant Jesus of Prague figure, where it was first placed above his daughter's viewing coffin so many days, months, and years ago. The only time the Holy Infant is ever touched is when my great-grandmother changes the vestments according to the colors of the canonical year.

And so on the day that Reed Primmer falls asleep in his rocking chair, instead of enjoying the new television set with his granddaughters, he slowly gets out of his chair. His long, thin frame heads to his cigar box, where he stores his beloved special matches for the evening's occasion, and not the ones that he uses for the rolled cigarettes Mary and Elaine faithfully make for him once a week, or for the cigars he buys as his only indulgence after an exhausting six-, sometimes seven-day workweek. As he pulls out a long match appropriately tipped in red, Reed heads to the symbol that he comes to believe is his daughter, if only in memory, and he strikes the match. Right before he begins to recite an accompanying prayer, he falls forward, his heart now clutched in his hand, and instantly dies of a heart attack.

The Infant Jesus of Prague is clothed in red. It is the day after Christmas, the same day he and his wife buried their daughter.

At last, Reed would see her again. And he was happy. Those in the room could never forget his smile as he lay on the floor, while they desperately tried pumping his heart to let it beat again, for their sake. But Reed was on a journey that no automobile he ever fixed could have taken. He was going alone, his spirit outside now flying above in the cooling twilight, toward someone so young and lovely, right there, waiting for him. It had been so lonely all those years in her peaceful heaven, but now Ora Kirby's father would again be by her side, this time forever.

> *Infant Jesus, I adore Thee.*
> *O mighty Infant, I pray to Thee.*
> *So I may enjoy Thee forever*
> *And see Thee with Mary and Joseph*
> *And worship Thee Together with the angels.*

The Carol of Doom

Once inside St. Teresa's, my family files into our pew in the middle of the church. As Monsignor Hart goes through the Gospel, homily, and offertory, I obsessively wait for the countdown to what I have come to think of as the Christmas Carol of Doom.

I imagine my mother's story instead of listening to Christmas Mass. Thinking about her childhood, I get upset and have to do everything in my power not to spring away from my family and run outside, just to get away from her crestfallen heart. I think it is the most dreaded holiday of the year for her. Over the years—because of her—it also has become that way for me. While I know she takes much joy in seeing us full of excitement opening our presents, it is merely a charade and my siblings fall for it. I don't know why I feel her darkness in my bones. Perhaps being able to recognize my mother's inherent sadness, even when she doesn't overtly show it, is something I was just born with, or perhaps cursed with. I obsess over her in a way I don't believe is normal, and certainly not in a way I could ever explain to my father. I know that no matter what—this day through all her life since she was three—is the constant reminder of the fact that she lost her mother so young, and it triggered the reason why her father left his two little girls. He assumed that their grandparents would raise them even if they had little money. But what if they had been unable to? I know my mother doesn't look out onto our backyard throughout Christmas day, and even sits in the dining room seat that places her back to our yard, because she knows how close she was to living next door if she and her sister hadn't been given a home and taken in by her grandparents, or, as she has always referred to them, Our angels. As for the children who celebrate Christmas in our backyard, my mother tries her hardest to avoid it. But our backyard won't go away; nor will her past. It will be there every single Christmas we share.

I imagine her dread of Christmas begins two nights before Christmas Eve, the night her mother died, all through Christmas Day, when her mother's coffin lay by her grandparents' bay window, and then later in life all the way through the day after Christmas, when her beloved grandfather died right at the moment he memorialized his daughter—her mother. She is always so quiet the day after Christmas as she arranges our gifts around the tree, and then rearranges them, and vacuums our house and revacuums it, polishes her silverware, and cleans our holiday china—all alone and deeply removed from us.

Only on the night of December 26 does that blueness inside her seem to evaporate when my father takes my mother out to dinner—always to Jack's Oyster House on State Street in downtown Albany—to celebrate their wedding anniversary with the finest bottle of champagne, and whatever she wants to eat on the fancy menu, even if he has to save extra money for the evening. To my mother, I believe my father is her savior, the one who tries hardest to help her forget her Christmas sadness. Still, not even my father can stop the carol, as it slowly starts to emit its familiar chords on the loud pipes from the great organ in the upstairs balcony at St. Teresa's.

Our family of seven stands with the other members of the congregation. I place my sweaty palms on the curve of the pew in front of me, fiercely digging my fingernails into the freshly polished mahogany. Although I try to keep my eyes shut, I always end up peeking even though I already know what I will see.

Turning my head to the left, I see my mother desperately trying to make it through the words of this song once again. She's been grasping at its words ever since she first sang it with her sister when she was three.

> *Round yon Virgin, Mother and Child.*
> *Holy Infant so tender and mild . . .*

I cannot bear to watch my mother suffer. And so I intercede. I belt out the words to "Silent Night"—the Christmas Carol of Doom—as though I am meant to sing it for both of us. If I sing loud and if my voice carries the weight of another's voice, perhaps no one else around us will notice the inconsolable tears now rolling down my mother's cheeks. No one will see that her new dress, which my father buys her every Christmas in an attempt to make her happy this painful day, is wet from the tears of all her Christmases past.

> *Sleep in heavenly peace.*

If the Christmas Walk of the Home children had made me feel gloomy, the sight of my mother crying helplessly breaks my heart that much more. I wonder sometimes if the blood of the grandmother I never met had been passed down to me to watch over her daughter.

If it was, I will do that. Always.

> *From childhood's hour, I have not been as others were.*
> *I have not seen as others saw.*
> —Edgar Allan Poe, "Alone"*

---

* Poe was orphaned after his mother died of tuberculosis when he was almost three. He remembered seeing his mother vomiting blood and being carried away by sinister men dressed in black. His father later deserted him and died soon after.

Somewhere In Between

I am dying. I will soon meet my other grandmother in heaven. When she hugs me and says, Oh, you're my Elaine's daughter, will she be twenty-five or will she be the age of my other grandmother? Will she have a beehive hairdo? Do you get older in heaven or do you stay the same age as when you die? Does God ask you to pick the age you want to be? If so, when my mother goes to heaven, maybe she will return to the cusp of four years old, so that she can then continue her life with her mother as it was the last time they were together.

I'll know more when I get there. Right now, heaven is on my horizon.

I have two Terminal Diseases. Mrs. Wheatley has discussed one in our science class. I also have a condition that Mrs. Wheatley never discussed, but I read about it in *Ripley's Believe It or Not*. I vow to be brave to the end. Maybe Mandy will perform the Mandy Dance at my funeral to the theme music from *Brian's Song*. Beforehand, I will write a letter to Olivia Newton-John and ask her to sing "I Honestly Love You," which she will do while touching my purple casket. Instead of a flag over my coffin, I want my AAG tote bag to be hanging from the pallbearers' rail. Under the careful instructions I intend to write and leave behind for my funeral, I will tell the mortician that books should not be placed in my schoolbag. It must be empty—symbolic of my death. Jimmy cannot be a pallbearer. *Cannot*. My friends whom I don't know from the Albany Home for Children, can. I will leave everything I own including my Fifth Dimension album, my guitar, my fake lava lamp, my black light, and my flower seed packets to Jodie because she is an orphan.

I am too young to be dying. It seems like it was only yesterday when I longed for tomorrow, and I would be all grown up.

Practicing with red CoverGirl lipstick, extending it far beyond the fine template of my small, heart-shaped mouth, I would fix myself up in my mother's finest double-knit pantsuit, slip her favorite pearls around my neck, and step into her high-heeled Sunday pumps. Then after taking her nicest shiny black patent leather purse from its hiding place deep within her closet and holding it in the crook of my arm, I pretended I was on my way to a fancy cocktail party, where I would not be so little.

Yes, thank you, John. I would love a martini. Extra dry, with olives—*extra* olives. In fact, bring me the jar and a spoon.

As I have grown, the stories, nursery rhymes, and fairy tales my mother spun to explain the world have lost their bewitching hold on my mind. Like the slow Cape Cod tide making its calm retreat, so, too, were her lullabies swept away by time.

I can't recall consciously brushing my mother away as she tried to instill a simplistic virtue one last time. I suppose it was around the same time I began sneaking Judy Blume books under my covers. There with my flashlight, I read about jaw-dropping subjects such as menstruation, boy's body parts, growing up, and, *Jesus, Mary, and Joseph*—masturbation, things that other girls in my class were discussing in whispers.

My mother never explained the birds and the bees to me, at least not in a sexual way—nor had she introduced the complexities of my changing prepubescent body. I believe she didn't want me, or any of us, to become adults and leave her behind. I wonder if she was scared we would forget her.

When I started growing hair under my arms, I was certain I was turning into a boy. According to *Ripley's,* I was becoming a Jimmy. The first time I menstruated, I had no doubt that I was hemorrhaging to death. This was before I learned about Life According to Judy Blume.

Even Mrs. Wheatley didn't take time away from our seventh-grade science class to explain the biological changes our bodies would soon experience. We had moved on from Terminal Diseases to the dissecting of froglets and piglets. Somehow, a frank discussion of how young girls become young women didn't fit into the curriculum of a polite girls' school devoted more to understanding the life of Ovid than ovaries.

Another medical condition heightened my obsession with what was clearly an impending death. A very large pimple was now growing on my right breast sprout. I feared it was breast cancer, and I finally broke down and decided to ask my mother if she would take me to the emergency room at St. Peter's Hospital. It was best that I die at a Catholic hospital. Only nuns could comfort my mother.

It is time I go.

In the living room, my mother slowly pushes herself back and forth on her rocking chair. She is drinking a Molson Light, as my father earns a little more money now, and gone are the days of Genesee Cream Ale and then Genny Light. She is alone because my father is working late.

She stares out into the backyard, at nothing or perhaps everything. I walk up right next to her and take her hand. I need her help, but I equally fear she will drop dead of a heart attack upon hearing the details of my condition times three. After casually asking for a sip of her beer, which she gives me, I tell her that it is time for us to leave for St. Peter's. I have even packed my *Partridge Family* overnight bag with my pajamas, toothbrush, and Crest.

Mom, get your keys, I say to her. I've kissed Marnie good-bye. Perhaps it's best if we not tell the others. They're watching *The Munsters.* Call Dad home and then we'll go.

My mother pauses, takes a sip of her beer, and looks at me with the same face she uses when she can't complete the jumbo word puzzle in the newspaper.

What are you talking about? Where are we going? Why is your bag packed?

I am sick. Very, very, very, very sick.

You went to school today. Were you sick then?

It's been a while . . . And up until now, I didn't want you to worry.

Let me feel your forehead.

This isn't about a fever. I'm dying.

I look at my mother's chest to make sure her heart does not start to pound faster as I finally admit my fate.

Like the way Mrs. Wheatley uses her ruler on a blackboard, I take the straw I have been chomping on out of my mouth in order to point out the two Terminal Diseases and the freak hair growing in my armpits, which I know even St. Jude and a dollar bill can't fix.

Finally, I blurt it all out.

With my makeshift ruler I first point to my underwear.

I am losing blood down here, I say to her. It happened about eight weeks ago and went away but now it's back.

My straw ruler moves upward to my right breast.

I have cancer, here. Right here. The pink Caladryl lotion is not decreasing the size of the bump on my breast. And Mrs. Wheatley said if you have a cyst on your breast, you have cancer and sometimes chemotherapy works, but mostly it doesn't. So you see, I'm dying, although I don't know how soon. But I don't want to worry you, so let's go to the hospital, and you go see the nuns.

My mother looks shocked. Her face is frozen. But I have one more blow to share with her in order to finally be completely honest about my health.

There's one more thing, Mom. You know how Jimmy is a boy and he's getting all hairy now and he has to shave? I'm turning into a Jimmy. I don't wear T-shirts over my bathing suit to hide my breast sprouts like you think I do when I swim. I wear a T-shirt because I'm growing hair under my armpits. My pits smell, just like Jimmy's.

I start to cry.

My mother, with her green beer bottle daintily protruding from her lips, simply smiles back at me like she is glowing. And then she says, Why, Sue. You're becoming a young woman.

Then my mother gets up from her chair and heads down the hallway as I sit in the chair that my father normally sits in, my overnight bag still positioned near my brown loafers. I am dumbfounded. My mother should be crying. I have told her devastating news. This is big, like Breaking News on TV.

Within seconds my mother comes back, and in her arms is a box that reads KOTEX FEMININE NAPKINS. She opens the box and takes out a white pad, which she says I place in my underwear when the blood leaks.

How often will it leak?

Menstruation occurs every twenty-eight days for about five days each cycle. Start marking it on your calendar.

When will it stop?

When you are in your fifties. So, unpack your bag.

But there are still the other matters. Has she forgotten about my breast cancer and the hair that grows and makes me a Jimmy?

But what about my breast? I ask.

My mother tells me to lift my shirt and pull down my training bra.

See, there it is. There's my cancer.

It's a pimple, Sue. Caladryl lotion? Why are you using that? Dab some Clearasil on it.

Our conversation seemingly comes to an end as my mother now walks over and searches for her wallet in her handbag, which is in the front hall closet. I can see she is rummaging for coins. Finally, she takes out fifty cents, walks over to where I sit, and kisses me on my forehead.

I'm so proud of you. Get your bike and ride it up to Stewart's for a make-your-own sundae. Go ahead and put whatever you want on top this time. No limits.

My mother is still beaming when she adds, I just have one question. Can I share this news with your father?

Mom, I just have one more question. What about the hair underneath my arms? Why am I becoming a boy now? Does that happen?

Oh, for God's sake, Sue. Shave it. I do. Go ahead and use my Daisy shaver. It's in the tub in the back bathroom.

Except for the special significance of the sundae, which I smothered with warm butterscotch topping as I sat at the booth at Stewart's all by myself, it was really Judy Blume and not my mother who became my mentor through the maze of my early teenage years. My mother was just too Catholic to talk about some things.

After I finished reading each of Judy Blume's books, I would immediately place it in one of my father's large yellow envelopes, carefully address it, and walk up to the post office on New Scotland Avenue across the street from St. Peter's Hospital. There, I would hand my parcel over to the clerk, with the correct amount of change from my weekly allowance, and send the package on its way from the front yard of 60 Academy Road to the backyard of 60 Academy Road. Each new book went to the attention of my favorite child from the Home.

I don't know what Jodie thought of the books I sent her. And since I had mailed the books anonymously, I couldn't ask my father if she had received them. At least I felt better knowing that Jodie wouldn't tremble in fear at the sight of blood from her Down Under Spot, as she continued to grow up right beside me, still living in my backyard.

Perhaps Judy Blume had the answers to what was bothering Jodie, too.

"Are you there, God? It's me, Margaret. Gretchen, my friend, got her period. I'm so jealous, God. I hate myself for being so jealous, but I am. I wish you'd help me just a little . . . Oh please, God. I just want to be normal."

—Judy Blume, *Are You There God? It's Me, Margaret*

The Great Offal Incident

The trees in our immediate backyard, planted by my parents the first weekend after we moved to Academy Road, inch closer to the vaulted sky. The sapling blue spruce is now over twenty feet tall. The growing row of trees creates a protective fortress that affords us a modicum of privacy, away from the inquisitive eyes of our next-door stepsiblings.

My mother appreciates this separation most, as sunbathing in front of the staff and children at the Home must be awkward, especially when she pulls down the straps to the top of her bathing suit. This summer, my mother and I are really into tanning. We plaster our bodies with baby oil mixed with iodine, just like it was our holy tanning water. While she turns golden brown, I bake into a candy apple red that soon cracks into blister pockets and peels. We have not yet found Hawaiian Tropic tanning oil in the grocery stores of Albany. We have used it only at the Daytona 500. We do not like the word *sunscreen*. Why screen the sun when it can make you look just like Malibu Barbie?

The trees also act as a barrier to Mandy being teased and taunted by the Home boys who—now that we've lived here for almost a decade—are somewhat bad, or naughty. The boys kind of scare me. When they can see her, though, the boys point and giggle at her flag-patterned bathing suit with its translucent, worn-out spot in the rear. Mandy now has an even rounder stomach that my mother refers to as Mandy's Love Handles, and she squeals with delight whenever my mother says, Come let Mommy squeeze Mandy's Love Handles.

Then she kisses my sister's belly button, near a star on Mandy's red, white, and blue Speedo. Mandy's Love Handles are not a seasonal condition. They are her love handles all year long.

One day not long after the first freeze of the year, Mandy runs home from the Academy, slipping and sliding in her plastic winter boots with the fake rabbit-tail-looking fur on top. She bolts into our house, tears frozen like icicles on her bright red cheeks.

My mother and I had been sitting at the kitchen table eating Fig Newtons while she showed me her brochure of Ireland, already marked on the calendar as my parents' next Adults Only vacation.

I'm going to kiss the Blarney Stone in County Cork, my mother tells me with great excitement like she had been invited to the Vatican to kiss the ring of the pope.

I hear the Irish boys pee on the Blarney Stone, I say to her.

How could you ruin your mother's vacation saying things like that? she replies. I believe that is a *myth*.

My mother's enthusiasm immediately returns as she turns the page.

And then your father and I are going to go shopping for Waterford at the Waterford factory in Waterford County. Won't that be fun?

Boring.

Ignoring me, she continues turning the brochure's pages.

We'll find you a new Irish fisherman's sweater in Kerry.

I don't want a new sweater. It's a boring gift. Can you get me a real six-pack of beer at the Guinness factory?

The Guinness factory? You don't drink beer, Sue. You are allowed to taste it and that is it!

Yes, I drink beer. I drink whiskey sours, too.

Who gives you whiskey sours?

Dad does. I try them out for him before he serves a *perfect* one to Aunt Mary.

I'm going to talk to your father. Who serves you beer?

The Lark Tavern. I have a fake ID and I go there with Jenny, Ruth, Dawn, Lisa, Kim, Kathy, and the other Sue. We're fifteen, now, Mom. Last time I was there I drank a pink squirrel. Can you make me one when Aunt Mary comes down this weekend?

Well, I don't know about that, Sue, and I don't want to know anything more.

My mother bites her Fig Newton and then places it daintily by the side of her teacup. She turns the pages of *Eire, Ireland—Tour It by Auto.*

Look at the cliffs of Mohr. Aren't they just breathtaking? Beautiful. Beautiful.

As I look at more of the pictures from the Emerald Isle—where I would not be traveling—my mother suddenly turns to the foyer where Mandy has just entered the house crying hysterically. Mandy stands on the Oriental rug like a defrosting pink snowman in her matching pink ski jacket and pink ski pants. My mother immediately rushes to her, wrapping my middle sister in her arms and kissing her pink ski hat. I finish devouring my mother's three Fig Newtons while she tries to decode the pink Mandy crisis.

It takes some time to get the story out as Mandy sobs away on my mother's nursing uniform. Through a waterfall of tears including coughing bouts and hiccups—Mandy finally tells us what the problem is.

The girls at school called me offal. They laughed at me and then they made it a ditty. *Mandy is an offal. Mandy is an offal. Mandy's a piece of offal.*

Mandy didn't know what the word meant and judging by the cocked position of my mother's head, she doesn't seem to know what it means, either. Whenever we don't understand a word, my mother invariably utters a familiar phrase: Let's visit *Webster.*

I follow my mother and pink Mandy into our TV room. As she opens the giant canvas-bound *Webster's Dictionary*, my mother slips on her glasses.

Watching her move her finger along the O pages, I keep my fingers crossed that offal isn't too horrific because then we will have to deal with real Mandy drama. Even though I know my sister is plump, sometimes you disguise certain facts in your mind so that they seem less cruel. Mandy is a sweet girl, unlike the sarcastic person my mother says I am becoming. Mandy never even hits Billy. Jimmy and I have a rather pulpy past, but now he can't hit me because he is a football player at the Christian Brothers Academy. My father made it clear to Jimmy that even if I tease him (and I do), Jimmy is too grown up to swing back. Jimmy and I have entered a new phase of our relationship. We completely ignore each other and grunt when we have to speak.

Pass ketchup, Jimmy says.

Get self, I reply.

Take hike, he adds.

Mom?

As she continues tracing the sound of the word up and down the pages, my mother says, Oful, Ofel, Offel, until she finally finds it.

Bingo, she says, which was what she always says when she solves a crisis.

Then she pronounces the word once again and reads its description aloud.

Of-fal. noun. 1. Waste parts, especially the viscera or inedible remains of a butchered animal. 2. Refuse or rubbish; garbage. Hmmm.

What does that mean, Mommy? Mandy says, still crying her blessed, blessed little heart out.

Well, I don't understand what those *snotty* girls at your school are talking about, because *offal* means meat *scraps*. It's the piece of the Shake'N Bake pork chop we don't eat but that we give to Marnie. Mandy, you are not a meat scrap.

After discussing the Great Offal Incident with my father later when he came home from work, I overheard my mother say to him, So that's why she goes straight to the TV when she comes home from school. None of those bratty girls will be her friend. She has no one to play with outside. Oh, John, this is terrible. Snacks seem to be the only friend Mandy has, and I've been sneaking her double ones just to make her happy. What should we do?

My mother and middle sister weren't the only ones to feel like they didn't belong at the Albany Academy. They weren't the only ones ostracized by their peers. At about the same time my sisters—which now included a very outgoing Sarah—and I left 60 Academy Road to walk down our side of the sidewalk to the Girls Academy, a young teenage boy named Eric walked the sidewalk across the street and headed to the adjacent Boys Academy. When Sarah, Mandy, and I shut our front door behind us, Eric closed his red cottage door behind him. Often we saw him standing just a little past the entrance sign to the Home, waiting for the cars to pass in order to cross the street. He was a boy from the Home, and the first ever to attend the alma mater of Herman Melville, the elite of Albany and its wealthy suburbs.

When I asked my father why Eric didn't go to school at the Home but rather to the Academy, he explained that the board of directors at the Home decided to send him because he was an extremely outgoing and bright kid, although internally depressed, which was why he was at the Home. They wanted to see if he could be intellectually challenged at a school like the Academy. The board—mostly wealthy and influential members of Albany's social community—paid for his tuition.

As my father said, I suppose it's similar to Nature versus Nurture. Back in 1912, the Home did a study on one class of first-graders. Throughout the entire school year, they kept the windows of their classroom wide open, regardless of the weather. During the brutal winter, the kids wore overcoats, caps, and mittens. Then they wrapped felt around their legs and blankets around their bodies.

Did anyone die? I asked. What happened after they got through the winter and the April rain?

Nothing, he replied. None even got a cold. They did a lot of studies on the children back then.

And then my father just shook his head and said, I don't know if a boy who lives in a cottage belongs at a school like the Academy. We'll just have to wait and see.

So, just like us, Eric woke up every morning, made his bed—well, that wasn't always true with us, but Eric didn't have my mother over there at the cottage with him to help him cheat on the bed-making responsibility—ate his breakfast, brushed his teeth, and practiced his marching skills as he walked toward the imposing entrance to the Boys Academy and its Georgian-style campus. In contrast, his other friends who lived with him in the cottage headed to the new Neil Hellman School that was built way behind the swimming pool and named after a gentleman who owned several of Albany's movie theaters. Eric was the first backyard kid given the golden pass to walk toward the front.

Over time, it came to be that I started to notice Eric missing from the sidewalk across the street. Days went by, and then it seemed more like weeks. When I asked my father where Eric was, he told me it got to the point that Eric didn't want to put on his formal gray trousers with the black piping, or his matching gray shirt and black sweater—the daily uniform for the Boys Academy. Nor did he polish his black oxford dress shoes or shine the school's monogrammed insignia on the sterling-silver buckle of his belt.

So what happened? I asked.

Eric left our backyard, my father replied. He didn't feel like he belonged at the Academy or at the Home anymore. I don't know where he went. It gets to a point that you have to stop looking and wondering. You have to have faith that a kid will find his way.

The Great Offal Incident hurt my mother to her core, and I'm sure many one-dollar prayers to St. Jude were offered up on Mandy's behalf.

The night after it happened, my parents left Jimmy and me in charge, which always brought about a discussion as to who was really in charge, until my parents got so fed up with us that they anointed me the babysitter to Mandy and Sarah, and Jimmy the babysitter to Billy. They went off to Montgomery Ward, and a couple of hours later they returned with a giant cardboard box, which my father hollered for my brothers to help him take through the back door of the garage. Using a switchblade, my father unhinged all the heavy plastic ties attached to the box. When he was finished, he, Jimmy, and Billy put their hands into the box and out came an instantly made twelve-foot circular skating rink.

As we stood by the glass door, my mother yelled to Mandy to leave the TV room and come to her. Making her way slowly to where we all stood, Mandy looked outside and saw my father with a big pail of water in his hands.

When he saw her at the door, he said, Mandy, your mother wanted you to have your very own Ice Palace. Jim and I are going to fill it with water tonight. After school tomorrow you can skate on your rink as much as you want.

My mother took her hands and put Mandy in front of her as she kissed the top of her brown hair. Looking out the opened sliding glass door, she said,

There's Mandy's Ice Palace. If anyone asks if they can skate on your rink, it's up to you, Mandy, to give permission.

The look on Mandy's face was one of awe. Suddenly she was the luckiest girl in the world, even if she had to suffer through an unkind word to become one.

By the time I arrived home from school that following afternoon, the rink was frozen over and full of smooth glistening ice. As I stood by the door, pink Mandy went running out of the house with her white skates on. She ran down the little incline in our backyard with the widest of smiles.

My sister, finally, had a best friend, even if it was just a circle of ice.

Throughout the winter of Mandy's Ice Palace, I watched my sister try out new skating maneuvers as she glided around her small rink, sometimes moving forward on one foot or awkwardly skating backward. I suppose more often than not, I saw her fall over the side of the rink because she misjudged the skating rink's boundaries. Sometimes I think my sister believed the ice rink at Rockefeller Center in New York City was what she had.

By the end of the season, my middle sister was well on her way to becoming someone who mattered because she believed in her newfound achievement. She was well on her way to becoming Dorothy Hamill, especially after Louie, my mother's hairdresser, cut her hair into the style of the Hamill Camel hairdo.

It was spring, not Mandy, who decided it was no longer possible to skate in the rink. By the time winter's thaw softened the ice rink into slush, Mandy's diligent practice inside the protective circle of her Ice Palace had diminished her love handles. By early summer, now taking up the sport of speed walking up and down Academy Road with my mother and Marnie for what my mother explained to Mandy was training for the next ice-skating season, Mandy was well on her way to a flag suit without love handles. And by summer's end, my mother bought Mandy her first bikini.

When school started that following fall, Mandy had resurrected herself into a lean, graceful, and popular girl at a school with a long history of measuring the worth of friendship in terms of your father's occupation, his income, and the majesty of your house.

Perhaps my sisters and I were among the first Girls Academy students who invited our friends home to our not-so-grand house where everyone was made to feel welcome without the pressure of pretense. And pretty soon, all our rooms, Mandy's, Sarah's, and mine, were filled with our classmates by day's end. Although my mother had to serve extra snacks, it came to be that Mandy—because she was so generous—always gave hers away.

A Cottage Good-bye

In June 1948, a few weeks before graduation, Bob Wygant and Dorothy were crowned king and queen of the Albany High School prom.

Not all the orphans were as lucky as Bob, or had such rose-colored views of the world. Most girls at the Home weren't invited to the big prom, and if they were, they couldn't afford a fancy dress so they rarely went. While the girls did have their Christmas perfume, they were resigned to wearing it only to the movies. For them, prom night was almost as lonely as Sunday's visiting hours or, even worse, Parents' Night when they were young.

But shortly after the prom, the (once) little boys and girls Bob had lived with in Lathrop Baby Cottage all graduated from Albany High School. Coach and Swannee yelled out their names as the Home kids took hold of their diplomas and threw their caps as far as they could toward the sky.

More often than not, young men of the Home went right into the police force or the armed services. They knew bravery because they had survived loneliness through the worst of times. And they knew how to live under the strict rules of discipline. But more important, they were anxious to explore the world beyond 140 New Scotland Avenue.

The girls left to take jobs as salesclerks, housekeepers, and waitresses, awaiting the day they would marry. They had learned to cook, clean, and sew, and many accepted the first marriage proposal they received. Leaving the Home meant it was time to find love and never let it go.

Just before his eighteenth birthday, Bob Wygant packed his bag in the same cottage he had lived in for almost twelve years. He put on his new blue suit and a tie. Many of the children couldn't wait until they got out of the Home. Not Bob. This had been the only home he had ever known.

The little guys seemed much bolder and more troublesome than he ever remembered being at their age. It seemed like they all now had regularly scheduled visits with the social worker, Miss Campbell. Now they gathered around him and talked as he neatly arranged his clothing and the mementos of his life at the Albany Home in the new brown suitcase given to him by Coach and Swannee. He would always stay in touch with the Huddlestons, so he had to concentrate on that notion, even if he felt anxious about leaving. As for Dorothy, they had already made plans to marry before he graduated from college.

Bob Wygant had a full War Memorial scholarship to Rutgers University. The Memorial scholarship was awarded yearly to a boy in financial need who also exhibited strength of character and involvement in his community. Bob had been offered admission to fifteen other colleges. The Albany Home never had such a young man with the world at his horizon.

When Bob walked away from Wasson Cottage for the last time, he made his way to catch a bus headed to New Jersey. He was beginning Rutgers football camp in just a few days. As he left, he turned around and stared at the Albany Home for Children and wondered if it would be there forever. He hoped that one day, when he came back, it would look as it always had. You never want your home to change.

Robert Wygant exited the Albany Home for Children in the same direction that he had once entered with a nurse fifteen years before. He slowly walked away from the campus, holding on to an envelope enclosing a seventeen-page letter addressed to a woman he never knew and headed toward a new mailbox placed on the corner of Academy Road and New Scotland Avenue. As he watched the letter fall into the slot, he thought to himself how much he loved happy endings.

> *Though nothing can bring back the hour of splendor in the grass, or glory in the flowers.*
>
> —William Wordsworth*

---

* Wordsworth was orphaned by the death of his mother when he was seven and the death of his father at fourteen.

Days of Wine and Roses

I watch Jimmy closely as he packs up his boxes and bags with all the pieces of his life. It is the night before he leaves for college. He seems upset, although I know that he would never admit it. I help my brother fold his new dark brown-colored bath towels, washcloths, and that in-between hand towel, which I have never understood the use for except to wipe Marnie's now graying belly whenever she gets all wet from the rain or snow. I put his towels into a green Hefty trash bag so that he can just drag them into his dorm room. As I sit on one of the twin beds in his and Billy's basement bedroom, I feel an incredible rush of loss—surprising because it is Jimmy who is leaving and we haven't been particularly close for years.

No one has ever gone away alone in our family for more than two weeks. Mostly, we traveled together on one-week trips to Cape Cod every summer, or

Virginia Beach, and of course boring, butter-churning Colonial Williamsburg. Jimmy and Billy had gone away to Camp Chingacook for two weeks up
in the Adirondacks for the past few years. I was thrown into the holy arms of
nuns who brandished sticks at a Catholic girls' camp for one week. After that
in-depth Jesus experience, I told my mother I never wanted to return; we had
to go to church twice a day, a harsh contrast to Hayley Mills's camp experience
in *The Parent Trap*. I just wanted to swim, drink bug juice, make s'mores
around the campfire, and tell chilly ghost stories. I did not want to hear bibli-
cal words about the Lord while in my bathing suit. Besides, Jimmy and I had
been skipping church and going to St. McDonald's for burgers and fries ever
since he passed his driver's test and got his license.

Even when my father went over to Korea once a year to bring orphans back
to desperate couples looking to adopt baby girls because they couldn't con-
ceive, it was always just a two-week trip. That was all my mother could handle. As we grew older, sometimes it was just better for all of us when my
mother went with my father because she got too weepy when he was gone.

But this was different. I calculated Jimmy's upcoming holiday calendar and
when I would see him again. He would be home for a three-night Columbus
Day weekend, which was over a month and a half away, a five-day Thanksgiving break, and then home for a couple of weeks at Christmas.

While I sat downstairs with Jimmy, my mother was upstairs in her back
bedroom ironing his shirts with her can of starch and her tears. She had closed
the door and, so unlike her, locked the bedroom door so that she might cry in
private. My mother hated separations. My father literally pulled her away
from us at our front door when they went on their Adults Only vacations. I
couldn't imagine her grief at the thought that pretty soon over the course of
the next six years not only would Jimmy be leaving tomorrow, but then me the
following year, a double whammy when Mandy and Billy would leave three
years after that, and finally, Sarah, her baby. As our yearbooks collected into
five new piles each year and pushed aside the youthful adventure books she
once read to us, this must have seemed to my mother like a sad foretelling of
approaching good-byes.

You don't understand, John. You just don't understand.

If my siblings and I, along with my father and Aunt Mary, filled all the
pieces of my mother's heart, with Jimmy's impending leaving her heart began
its initial tear apart.

Something was different about Jimmy now, as I watched him blow off the dust covering his football trophies before he packed them up, as well as his smooth-smelling Aqua Velva, Old Spice cologne, black plastic hair comb, and various other sundries from the top of his drawer. Jimmy was ready to leave.

That year, but mostly toward his graduation, my older brother started introducing me to his friends whenever we ran into each other at Hurley's Bar over on Pearl Street. Sometimes we would pool our money and share a popcorn-sized bowl of Three-Alarm-Hot chicken wings served with carrot sticks and a zingy-tasting blue cheese dressing. Whenever he had a pitcher of beer in his hand, Jimmy would ask me and my friends if we wanted a glass.

A couple of weeks before his senior year ended, on a warm late afternoon, Jimmy spent a lot of time downstairs dressing for his senior prom. Eventually, he came upstairs and asked me if he looked okay.

Yeah. Your tuxedo is a pretty cool blue.

When he left to pick up his date—holding the wrist corsage in a plastic protective box like he would a football—we all stood outside like some corny family from a 1960s TV show and waved good-bye as he drove away. About half an hour later, Jimmy unexpectedly came back with his date, to surprise my mother so that she could take snapshots with her new camera.

Okay, time to go, Jimmy said, pretty much running to the other side of the light blue Delta 88 sedan with the white piping on its sides, which was the exact color of his rented tuxedo and its accompanying white frilly shirt, to make a fast exit from 60 Academy Road. My mother stood at the front of the freshly washed car, holding on to the hood ornament until Jimmy slowly pulled away down the driveway.

My mother would have loved to seize the moment and keep the car with her eldest son in it from leaving. Now it was all about the stages of leaving: the prom, graduation—where Jimmy flew his black cap into the same sky we used to stare at when we were young and looked at it even closer whenever we jumped up high on the trampoline. When summer eventually began, my mother seemed reserved, not herself.

Do you remember when you took my doll on Bohl Avenue that Christmas? I said to Jimmy as I continued helping him pack his shoes and sneakers into a box marked CARSWELL—FRESHMAN.

I took a doll?

Yes. It was wrapped so you didn't know what was inside. Santa Claus had marked it Jimmy when it was supposed to be mine.

Then I must have given it back to you, he said as he started stacking his LPs alphabetically in another box, Bachman-Turner Overdrive, Bee Gees, Cat Stevens, Doobie Brothers . . .

No, you kept it. Why?

I kept it? I don't know. Did we fight back then?

No, not really, I said. I think our fights started when we moved to our second house and then especially when we moved here. But the doll, I've always wondered why you kept the doll. Even though we were young, you must have known it was a mistake.

Jimmy thought about what I said as he moved Lynyrd Skynyrd from L to S.

You know, Sue. There was a time when we believed in all the make-believe things Mom taught us. We believed in fairy tales and pots of gold at the end of the rainbow. And we believed in Santa. Maybe I thought Santa gave me the doll for a reason. And maybe he did.

Wow, deep, I said. Are you going to be a philosophy student?

Nah. I'm going to school to have fun, go to keg parties, and live it up. You've got another year here. But when the time comes, you'll be racing out of here, too.

Won't you miss Mom?

With that simple question, Jimmy just turned his head away from me and said quietly, I can finish this up myself. Thanks for your help.

When I left and started to walk up the stairs, I heard Jimmy latch the door to his bedroom behind me. And then I heard my older brother cry.

It stunned me. And it made me cry for him, and it made me cry for my mother. It made me cry for all the leavings still to come.

Right before he left the next morning, Jimmy walked up to the florist on New Scotland Avenue, and he brought my mother back a dozen red roses and kissed her on the cheek.

We all did that in the coming years. Whenever we left for long periods of time, we gave her red, pink, or yellow roses. I think she knew it was our sign that we loved her so.

Pollock

By the time I was in my mid-to-late-teens, I had mentally moved away from my backyard with all its children. Instead, I daydreamed that we would move to the rich-tony suburb of Slingerlands about twenty minutes away. I wanted us to live in a breathtaking colonial house with a magnificent well-tended lawn, and just my family. I no longer wanted to be a part of a property devoted to the caring of disturbed, troubled, and hard-to-place children. I was embarrassed to be living on the grounds of a place where kids misbehaved, even if they couldn't help it. They had never become my friends. I no longer had the sleeping problems of my youth. I no longer had deep-rooted fears of my siblings dying or, more important, the fear of my mother's death. My parents were right, as was my pediatrician: I had grown out of that phase.

When I was seventeen, I went out back to the Lawn Festival, not because

I wanted to partake in a watermelon-eating contest, or pet an animal that should have been living on a farm or in Africa instead of a zoo that traveled so that kids could tug and pull on its fur or prickly skin. I headed to the concession stand and impatiently waited in line so that I could get some cheap food instead of our usual well-balanced family meal. Billy, Mandy, and Sarah now brought their group of friends to our backyard day of celebration, but I was too embarrassed to have any of my friends from the Girls Academy there. I would just grab a box of food and bring it home and sit at our dining room table by myself in our kitchen. That way I didn't have to look out back or hear the squeals of joy that defined just one day in the year of my backyard.

While I waited for Home kids to decide what they wanted to eat only to change their minds once they got up to the stand, I grew frustrated. It got to the point that I was tapping my foot, my arms crisscrossed tightly in frustration at the delay. I turned around as I waited and caught sight of the girl whom I had once wanted as my best friend.

At the hayride, I spotted Jodie. She still looked like Mandy, just older now. She sat in the back of the ride with a woman I didn't recognize. As the woman went to give Jodie a hug as she took a bite of her hot dog, the mustard grossly went dripping down Jodie's nondescript shirt. As soon as I saw this, I turned my back on Jodie, got out of line, and headed back to our house. As I walked past the dunking booth, I kept thinking, *Don't any of them ever grow up?* When I got to our patio, I picked up a chair, slid open our door and then slammed it shut and headed to our front door, where I put the chair down outside and watched cars go up and down our street.

Not long after, on a spring Friday evening toward my graduation, about seven of my friends were over at my house. My parents were out with their friends for movie night. We had a couple of six-packs of beer, and because it had been such a nice and warm day, I decided we should head out back and get loaded on the swings. I don't know if I was pushing the limits or just finally at the point where I didn't care about rules anymore, but I told my friends to head to the swings to the far right side of my backyard instead of the ones to the left near the old JCA campus where it was dark and quiet. I wanted to drink our Miller Lites and Champale on the swings directly outside the red cottage doors. It was my backyard and we could go anywhere. I don't know how long we were there, but I know it turned darker and finally a counselor headed in our direction and screamed at us to get off the property or he would call the police.

I live here, I said to the male counselor, in a tone that made it my right.

You don't live here, he responded back in a severe tone. I know who lives here. You have five minutes until I call the cops.

Go ahead and call the cops, I yelled back at him. I do live here, I said to him like I was superior. I'm John Carswell's daughter, and I live right over there.

There was a moment of silence. And then I got an apology. And then the counselor offered me a good night and added, Could you please keep your voices down? We're trying to get the children to sleep.

I won, I thought. I just didn't know what it was I won.

Then again, maybe I was just acting snarky and seventeen. And maybe I was scared because in truth I was getting nervous about leaving home that coming fall.

The year after Jimmy left, I chose to go to my father's alma mater, the University of Vermont in Burlington, because, strangely, my application was accepted. Academically, I was ranked smack in the middle of my class. I was student number thirteen of my Albany Academy for Girls graduating class of twenty-six and considered much more of a social student than an academic one.

She'll be a detective, I heard one teacher tell another, who didn't know I was sitting right around the corner.

She'll be a writer, offered another. Her writing is sensitive and she shows tremendous promise.

You've got to be kidding, injected my English teacher. She'll never add up to anything.

It is late August on the day I leave for Burlington. Appropriately, it rains. My father has loaded up our car using math skills that probably involve the symbol pi. He has measured all my belongings, and the trunk of our car, and packed everything as if he worked for a commercial moving line.

I walk around our backyard one last time, clutching my pillow in my arms.

I try to commit every detail of my surroundings to memory. I might be in a tug-of-war over how I feel about the grounds where I lived most of childhood, but I know I am going to miss it. It has been my home for almost twelve years, but I have been visiting its grounds ever since I was a toddler when my father first started working there.

I stare into the copse of trees that separates our house from the cottages and think of what I understood about the children who lived there when we first moved to the property in the late 1960s and what I know now to be the truth as we near 1980.

If you were to ask me to paint a picture of what I saw when I first moved onto the grounds of the Albany Home for Children in the summer of 1968, the backdrop would show a gentle world. I would have painted a vast, impressionistic landscape using rose-colored strokes, full of radiant hues bathed in golden sunlight. I would have omitted all traces of sadness from my painting with happy, smiling children always laughing. My painting would look like a junior Monet, Renoir, or Seurat.

As I grew older, I discovered I lived on the grounds of a world that only Jackson Pollock could adequately capture in its explosive dementia. That was the reality of my backyard, and now, after all those years of wondering, I would leave knowing its truth. We had never lived in Oz.

Back in December 1976, the big black-and-gold sign welcoming a person to the Albany Home for Children was flipped over and jazzed up to read PARSONS CHILD AND FAMILY CENTER. The long-dead John Parsons, one of the orphanage's major benefactors in the early 1900s, now welcomed the new children, who still had to pass over the yellow speed bump, into the initial phase of their recovery from whatever had brought them here. In 1979, my father's boss, Mr. Millard, resigned and moved away to take a job in Chicago. My father was now Parsons' executive director.

With the development of new designer prescriptions in the 1970s, it was becoming less necessary for some of the children to reside in the cottages, although the cottages were always full. Many were immediately sent into foster care or group homes under the auspices of Parsons. Some children even remained in their own homes, where their mothers could put them to bed at night, and attended the Neil Hellman School at Parsons during the day. Those who still lived in the cottages during the late 1970s had been diagnosed with the severest forms of character disorders: schizophrenia and psychological trauma. Discharge planning for those who moved into the cottages was a part of the admissions process. Now, no one grew up in my backyard.

My father has not yet blown the horn signaling it is time for us to leave, so I wander over to the old Van Alstyne Gymnasium. I vividly remember my father taking us there on Sunday afternoons in the fall and the spring. Inside, we climbed the ropes like energetic little monkeys and sometimes played chase with one another or excitedly ran into the thickly padded light blue protective walls.

I continue to my favorite area in my entire backyard: the Olympic-sized pool, where Jimmy and I took our first steps away from our mother. This is where I began to explore the world away from my mother's protective grip; college will be the place that decides whether I have the ability to leave her behind.

As the misty late-summer rain pours down, I step onto the path and remember all the years I watched the Christmas Walk of the Children. Following in their ghost steps, I head in the direction of our old softball field in front of Parsons Cottage and the swings where, as children, we sailed skyward with boundless energy and reckless abandon.

When my mother calls my name from the patio, I turn back toward our house and look to the left for one last glimpse of the single-story brick cottages where the Parsons children live. The Albany Home for Children is no longer a home, nor an orphanage. It is a center, or an institution, now, which will continue to grow in proportion. It will no longer be the special backyard that it once was.

By this time, Jodie, Ryan, fashionable female-dressing Sean, Eric from the Boys Academy, and all the other boys and girls who had shared my backyard as we grew up in uniquely parallel but separate lives have made their departures to points unknown. I wonder whether I will ever see any of them again. Will I even recognize them?

As I near the patio, step in, and close the sliding glass door one last time behind me, I look to our backyard, trying to create an unforgettable photograph in my mind. I know that one day, all of this will fade.

Instead of taking my memories with me to college, perhaps I should have

left them—and all the many nightmares they had once brought—at home behind me.

Only minutes after my father has pulled away from our home for our
three-hour drive north, I become paralyzed by the thought of separation from
my parents. It is my mother I will miss the most. Since it is a rainy day, befit-
ting my despair, my tears echo the steady drops falling from the dark gray
clouds. As we continue our trip to Vermont, I snivel into my pillow the entire
way. For every tear I shed, my mother sheds more as she sits in the front seat,
her head tilted against the window.

Exactly four hours later and after a lunch where I just cry as I try to eat my
eggplant parmigiana, begging my parents not to leave me, my father takes my
mother's hand and leads her away.

It's time, Elaine. We have to go. Sue has to stay.

Forty-five minutes later, I am sitting in the infirmary. A nurse is taking my
temperature. I am dying of loneliness. My temperature is going to burst her
thermometer and all its mercury is going to fall into little balls on the freshly
swabbed floor.

She pulls the little wand that will tell me my fate out of mouth and says,
Normal. Then she asks in astonishment, Do you already have the freshman
blues?

I found little solace living in Buckham Hall, the same dormitory where my
father had lived during his freshman year almost thirty years before. My room
was on the fourth floor, and I was terrified. A day didn't go by my entire freshman year when I didn't think about jumping out the window of my dorm. The
fact that I even entertained the notion of suicide also scared me. I felt like I
was a Home kid now sent to college.

Adding to my discomfort and to my state of mental unrest was my new
backyard. The University of Vermont Medical Center, the biggest hospital in
the state, had ambulances pulling into the emergency entrance with red lights
and sirens blaring into my room at all hours of the day. At night, it disturbed
me the most. It was as if the sirens had followed me all the way from Academy Road.

...

Most of my friends from the Girls Academy couldn't wait to go away to college and be away from their families so that they could be on their own. I couldn't wait to return home and be with my mother. Black clouds engulfed me each August as the time grew near for me to return to Burlington.

As for my mother, it came to be that every fall, after my parents returned home to Albany after dropping us off at our respective schools, my mother frequently found herself wandering around her increasingly empty household, arms folded across her chest, staring blankly into our bedrooms at the sight of our now empty twin beds. She kept our rooms looking exactly as they had the day we left them behind.

In my senior year of college as I was preparing to graduate, I received an unexpected letter from my father. Before it had always been my mother who wrote and whose letters I read with excitement aloud to my friends and then to myself over and over before going off to sleep. In part of his letter, he philosophized about my youth. And he compared me to my mother:

> *Sue, your grandmother's untimely death had a profound effect on your mother. She always had difficulties with separations, whether I went on a business trip, one of you children left for college, or when you were younger and we took some vacation time alone. Her separation anxiety was more than normal or expected. She hurt deeply during these times. I think your own fears, I assume, were picked up from your mother. Love, Dad.*

But what about him? Nothing about my fears came from my father?

That's Life

And so it was that the little boy who, on his third birthday, was transferred from St. Margaret's to the Albany Home for Children on the day that FDR returned to the Governor's Mansion after receiving his party's presidential nomination grew up and went out into the world. The first boy from the Albany Home to receive a full college scholarship, Bob Wygant was compelled by what he considered to be his responsibility to succeed. So, as with everything else he had accomplished, Bob entered Rutgers University with energy and determination.

At football camp, where top high school athletes were inducted into the world of college football and returning players endeavored to keep their places on the varsity team, the Albany High School letterman quickly felt at home. Bob Wygant never told a soul, not even his college roommate, that he had spent his entire life, up to that point, growing up in an orphanage. Bob kept that piece of information to himself.

Following the example set by Coach, the only father figure he had known, Bob plotted his course toward a teaching career and working with children. After graduating from Rutgers with a bachelor's degree in physical education in 1952, Bob first worked as a gym teacher and then became a coach in the Rensselaer County school system, just over the Hudson River Bridge from the Albany Home for Children.

In his first letter to his mother—the one he mailed when he left the Home—Bob had told her right up front that she should never feel guilty or ashamed about placing him in an orphanage. He wanted her to know that he was a happy person and that he was doing well. Whatever had happened in her past was not something he was going to hold against her. He was just glad to know he had a mother and a brother.

Mrs. Wygant had answered Bob's letter in her own time and on her own terms. She told her youngest son about herself. She wrote to him that she was a seamstress, living in California, but she offered nothing more about the circumstances surrounding his birth. In fact, Helen Wygant was rather evasive, even aloof. She obviously didn't feel that the son she had left as a baby to be raised as an orphan needed to know anything more.

Bob eventually made contact with his older brother, Elmer, who subsequently introduced him to other members of his family—an aunt, cousins—but not his mother. Not yet.

I tried, Bob, Elmer had told him in anguish, explaining that, when he was discharged from the service, he had gone to the Albany Home and tried to contact him. I tried my hardest to come get you, but they wouldn't even let me see you.

That's okay, he assured Elmer, who was still obviously tortured by his inability to rescue his only brother and bring him back home. Then Bob added, We're family now.

The first time Bob Wygant saw his mother was at the funeral of his aunt Millie, her sister. By now, he was almost thirty years old and the father of two. As much as he wanted to, he was nervous about meeting this woman whom, since he had first learned she existed, he believed would want more than anything to be close to him. So Elmer suggested that he just look at her this first time. And that's what Bob did. Instead of appearing bereaved as one might at a funeral, he openly stared at the woman who was his mother and envisioned how his life might be with her in it.

The next day, at Elmer's house, mother and son met for the first time since she had given him up at Albany Hospital. Seeing her sitting on a chair, grieving over the loss of her sister, Bob reached out to touch his mother's shoulder. Then he leaned over and gave her a hug, which seemed one-sided. He said what he felt were the most normal words in the world, Hello, Mom.

Mrs. Wygant couldn't look her son in the eye. Guilt was written all over her face, and she brushed him away like an unwanted speck of lint on an expensive suit.

From Elmer and other family members who had welcomed him with open arms, Bob eventually learned the name of his father. After the death of her husband, Elmer's father Mr. Rossman, the young widow had an affair with the scion of one of the most prominent families in Albany. Ironically, in historical papers they are listed as among the most generous benefactors of the Albany Society for the Relief of Orphan and Destitute Children—the original name of the Albany Home for Children—when it was founded in 1829. Bob was born out of this affair.

Although he and Elmer became close, Bob found it impossible to develop a relationship with his mother. Years after their first meeting and knowing that she was in ill health, Bob offered to have his mother come live with him and his family, but she declined his invitation without even a thank-you.

Still, Bob was there for her on her deathbed. When she saw her younger son, Mrs. Wygant simply cried, finally letting him see all that she had kept inside. Bob then said to her, Mother, I'm going to ask you something. I didn't come all this way to find out this answer. I came to be with you—but I do have one question.

Bob took her frail hand in his and bent down to whisper into her ear in the hope that she might finally confirm the name of his father. He said the name he had been given, and his mother nodded yes. She died a short time later, both sons at her bedside.

As for meeting his father, Bob decided it wasn't necessary. His mother was the one he had always wanted to meet. His life was complete.

Well, until it started to break apart.

...

Perhaps he had inherited some of his mother's stubborn nature. Bob, who had married his sweetheart Dorothy while still in college, had his share of problems relating to those he loved most. As skilled as he had become as a teacher, counselor, and school administrator, Bob could not express this love spontaneously with hugs and praise. He taught his only son, Gary, to be a man, but he was never able to teach him how to express affection or any other intimate emotion. Only in his later years did Bob realize how drastic the impact his own unusual childhood, growing up in an institution, had had on his relationship with his own family. He could not remember one time when his son ran to him in excitement for a hug.

Because Bob loved his wife, and thought that she loved him, he was shattered when Dorothy asked for a divorce. They had been high school sweethearts, king and queen of their senior prom. In his eyes, even if there were problems in their marriage, a king would never leave his queen. They went to marriage counseling, and he promised to do whatever it took to make everything right again. Counseling, he had always assumed, was for other people. It was for those who were troubled. And now Bob fell into that category.

But Dorothy had fallen out of love with Bob. This realization was the worst feeling he had ever experienced. He felt really abandoned. He thought he knew this person. He couldn't understand her reasoning.

After twenty-eight years, Bob's marriage to Dorothy ended with a stamp on a piece of paper. For the second time in his life—the first had been when he was three—Bob felt he had transfer papers forcing him to leave home.

And so he did, but it broke his heart.

Landslide

ollege was like four years holding my breath in the deep end of the swimming pool. I just wanted to be home. Graduating on a beautiful day in the middle of May, I smiled the entire car ride back to 60 Academy Road, as did my mother. We were together again. I hadn't even thought about making plans to leave again.

My father oversaw the expansion of Parsons Child and Family Center, with new buildings and a new cottage under varying degrees of construction in our backyard. My mother was now working as a nurse at an allergist's office, behind the grounds of the Girls Academy's soccer field. She now rode her bike to work every day and sometimes walked in the winter, so that Sarah could have the car to drive the extraordinarily long way down Academy Road to go to school.

At Dr. Ball's allergist office, she became many patients' preferred nurse. My mother was quickly becoming a shot-giving legend.

I can never even tell that she pricks me, the patients would say to Dr. Ball. She has a magic touch.

My mother found equal pleasure in talking to four-year-olds and grand-mothers who loved to tell her stories of their children and grandchildren. She treated everyone like they were the most meaningful individuals gracing this earth. However, her favorite patient was anyone who asked after her five children.

By this time, Jimmy had graduated from Oneonta State University and worked as a counselor at a school for troubled boys in Albany. He lived in an apartment with friends from his high school days, just a couple of blocks away from our house. He visited several times a week. The twins were now college sophomores: Mandy at Georgetown majoring in philosophy, and Billy at Notre Dame, majoring in psychology. My mother especially enjoyed hearing out-of-school stories about Sarah, my youngest sister, now a junior at the Girls Academy.

With my degree in political science and a minor in sociology, I quickly found a night job. I was one of Albany's top-selling telephone solicitors. By day, my career was that of a breakfast waitress. My shift started at 5:45 A.M., an ungodly hour for a recent graduate. After I left the restaurant and took a nap, I would eventually head off to convince Albany residents how much they needed solar hot-water systems to heat their freezing-cold houses and trailer homes. Each time a homeowner agreed to schedule a sales call from a Reynolds Aluminum sales representative, my manager would ring a cowbell, signaling that a telephone solicitor had pocketed a twenty-five-dollar bonus. I put aside my growing earnings from both jobs, plus the bonus money I earned from up to ten cowbell rings a night, to pay for law school application fees. My father said I needed to do something meaningful with my life, so I applied to twenty-four law schools, including Pepperdine in Malibu. I imagined going to school near Olivia Newton-John's ranch and getting a part-time job as her ranch hand. Eventually, I was accepted into one law school, far from Malibu, in the heart of the corn-fields of Ohio.

I was peaceful at home. And whatever disturbing thoughts I had had at college were magically gone again. Besides, now I was in my early twenties.

Perhaps having a normal mind had taken me a little longer to achieve than most people. I was late to arrive at this sense of feeling at ease, but I felt I was finally there. I could take a breath in and let the air out with a sense of calmness. I enjoyed having a cocktail with my parents every night before heading out to my second job. I could have stayed home forever. I don't think my mother would have minded, but my father did. Plus, he was so proud that I got into law school, and I thought that maybe for once I could do something that would make him feel like his kids were well on their way to success. I owed him something for a childhood of bothering him every single night. So I went off to law school among the cows in the middle of the cornfields for him because he had slept in a sleeping bag on the floor outside my bedroom all those years ago, in order to make me feel safe—or safer.

A month after arriving in Ohio, I was bored. Instead of becoming a lawyer, I became obsessive-compulsive.

I was abnormally preoccupied by the train track that ran parallel to my law school dorm room. My room was about fifty feet away from the high-speed trains that sped through the small town of Ada, Ohio, in the middle of the night.

The intensity of my obsession became even more distorted after I sat in a torts class one day. The class was focused on a case involving an undergraduate who was too afraid to tell her parents how miserable she felt at school. I hung on every word as my professor continued with a story that gained a bewitching hold on me. Thinking herself a failure and an embarrassment to her parents, the undergraduate walked out of her dorm room one night and spread her blanket and pillow out on the train tracks. I didn't need to hear the rest of the story. I could fill in the blanks. Throughout the rest of the class, I covered my ears and hummed. It was like I was right back in Mrs. Wheatley's Terminal Diseases class at the Girls Academy, but now I was drowning out the more gruesome details about the girl who went to sleep forever on the train tracks.

The next day, I skipped torts class, which I knew would rehash the legalities of the case. Did the school notice the girl was depressed? Did her parents ever have any warning? Who was at fault? I wonder if they ever checked out the story of that girl's backyard.

I skipped torts class again and then again until there were so many again and agains that it was apparent that I had dropped out of the class altogether. Pretty soon, I was skipping nearly every class I was taking. I could no longer handle my fixation. Instead of paying attention to the professors teaching us the different facets of law, the only thing that held my concentration was the notion of how odd it was that your mind made the decision whether your hands and feet move. It was fascinating. I had never thought about the anatomical connection before.

I was losing it.

I holed up in my dorm room and drank Diet Coke or Diet Dr Pepper. I gave up eating food. I was becoming a law school recluse, Ohio's Greta Garbo.

Anything could topple me now. I didn't sleep at night due to the massive amounts of caffeine in my body. I was fixated on how my subconscious mind might force me to take my blanket and my pillow and lay it out on the tracks just like that other girl who had lost her way.

Would I one day be someone else's homework in torts class?

Who was at fault?

After the Thanksgiving break, I tried to put myself together again after a little peaceful reinforcement back home. I didn't want to give up. I had taken out numerous loans to pay for my education and I hadn't a clue what else I might become in life. All my childhood friends were now well into the beginning of their professional careers or in graduate school. Besides, I didn't want my father to think I was a failure as an adult since I had already flunked out of childhood.

One night I decided to join a group of my law school friends, and we headed to a disco in nearby Lima, where we were allowed to drink alcohol other than moonshine. Ada was a dry town, reminiscent of *Mayberry R.F.D.* I'll never forget how on my first day of school the whole town came out for a parade not to welcome the returning and new students to Ohio Northern University but rather to celebrate the arrival of the town's first automatic teller machine. The parade came complete with baton-twirling cheerleaders. I think even Aunt Bee was there walking the parade route with her homemade apple pie.

The disco in Lima was actually the basement dance floor in a VFW bar.

Admittedly, I had a mighty fine time on the dance floor, dancing to the tunes of *Saturday Night Fever* and other Bee Gees songs with my favorite dance partner Dale, a former sheep farmer from Someplace, Indiana.

After drinking way too many margaritas with double shots of tequila, my friends and I headed over to Bob's Big Boy for warm homemade biscuits, crispy bacon, and eggs before our drive back to Ada.

It was there that my friend Kathleen told a truly gripping story about how her grandmother choked to death in her kitchen on a chicken bone while her grandfather was at work.

Within seconds of piling back into the car for the ride back to our dorms, I felt in my throat a piece of the string from the bacon I had been eating. I kept trying to clear it, but the bacon string wouldn't budge. This would seal my fate, too, just as it had for Kathleen's grandmother.

Back in my room, I lay under the covers in my bed, my head sandwiched between the two pillows that I used to muffle the clatter and whistles of the speeding trains and my secret fear I might copy the suicidal fate of the girl we had learned about in torts class. I was right back where I'd started when I was young, but I no longer had my safety blanket. My father wasn't there to roll out his sleeping bag.

Over the next few weeks, my mental state worsened. I couldn't sleep. I was obsessed with the thought that a bacon string would eventually strangle me to death. The tremors of the volcano that lived within me began erupting inside my mind and body. Almost a month into my insomnia, I made an appointment—though I haven't a clue how I even got it together enough to make it, let alone show up. When the time came, sweating like I had completed a lap on a track, I ran across the campus and up the steps into the university's center for emotional counseling.

I met with a behaviorist named George. Through my confused haze, I thought that because I was finally seeing a professional, I would walk back out the door cured. I obviously hadn't paid any attention to the many stories of my backyard. Breakdowns there were normal, and time was always needed for healing—if healing was even possible.

What do you think about when you lie awake at night? George asked, a pencil sharpened to write down my deepest thoughts.

Nothing much, I lied. I just wanted George to hand over some medicine so that I could get better. I didn't understand the concept of counseling. I didn't have the patience to talk about my feelings. I wanted to be fixed.

Within fifteen minutes of my appointment, George decided to hypnotize me. We both closed our eyes and headed up a spiral staircase. When I got to the third step, I cracked my right eye open and peeked at George. He sat in his chair, bobbing his head up and down as he enunciated the number of stairs we were climbing, saying I would soon be relaxed, relaxed . . . He spoke in a sonorous tone, not unlike a bingo caller. When I looked at him, thinking how seriously he took his job, I don't know why I did it, but I started laughing.

I could tell George was angry at me. I was not a good hypnotic subject.

If you want help, you have to concentrate and forget your problems completely and climb the imaginary stairs in your mind. George pointed his thumb at me, which I found odd.

Who points with their thumb? Thinking about that, I kind of tuned out George for a few moments. How fascinating that George's mind told him to point with a thumb whereas most people's minds tell them to point with their index finger. Yet when people pretend to play with guns they use the index and thumb fingers together. I wondered if George ever played cops and robbers as a kid. If he used just a thumb, he would never get a good shot.

Let's try it again, said George. Close your eyes, Susan. Come up the stairs with me. Follow. Follow. One, two, three, four. Concentrate.

I interrupted him.

George, that's my whole problem. I can't concentrate. Don't you have some pills that will help me? I need to stop some thoughts completely and turn my mind in another direction. Don't you have some slow-down-your-mind kind of pills? I know they make them.

What thoughts do you need to stop? he asked, his paper pad and pencil at full attention.

It's personal, I replied.

We don't dispense drugs here. We talk about emotions.

At the end of our appointment, or rather nonappointment, Emotional Counseling Center George loaned me a couple of soothing biorhythm tapes to listen to when I lay in bed at night. He told me that if I listened to them carefully I would soon fall asleep.

Works like a charm, said George. I use them myself. The sounds of the gentle stream washing over rocks and birds chirping will reach deep inside your mind and you will sail off into a deep sleep.

When the tapes didn't work after that first night, I became People's Express Airlines newest frequent flier, traveling home to Albany from Columbus, Ohio, almost every other weekend with my first credit card.

During my second visit home in as many weeks, my mother finally had enough of the latest mystery surrounding my inability to sleep. I was no different at the age of twenty-three than when I was three.

Sue, I want you to take your Blue Cross and Blue Shield card and go to the hospital and get this thing checked out. I honestly believe this is all in your head. If the bacon string you keep talking about wasn't digested five weeks ago when it happened, then you would be dead by now.

It's not about choking me instantly, Mom. It's about the string dislodging and moving from the left side of my throat into that space right below the hanging thing in my throat. That's when I'll die. Do you know what I'm talking about?

I opened up my mouth to show her my throat by sticking a Popsicle stick right into the area where I feared the bacon string might move if I coughed too hard or if I ate any food.

This is just sick. I've got to get back to the office. Go to the emergency room and if there are any problems, call me at Dr. Ball's office.

And who do they call in the event of my death? I yelled out to her as she headed down the driveway on Sarah's bike. My mother and I were in the midst of a rare fight but I was prepared to go the length. I was Ali, Cassius Clay.

Have them call your father. I'll see you at supper.

I called Jimmy and asked him to drive me to the hospital. On our ride up New Scotland Avenue, I explained what had happened.

Uh-huh, he said. Jimmy really wasn't much of a talker.

Do you think I'll be okay? I asked.

Yep.

Thanks for the ride. Can I call you if I need you here?

Yep.

Okay. Hopefully I'll see you but if I have to stay for an operation, you promise you'll come back?

Yep.

And with that final nod of reassurance, Jimmy sped out of my sight, off to help control the restless and disturbed children at the La Salle School for Boys. He had become John W. Carswell Jr.

I walked inside the emergency room at St. Peter's, where I had always felt like royalty because my mother had gone to nursing school there. Eventually, I was seen by a nurse.

So you're one of Elaine's daughters? she said. Then added, I love your mother. What is she up to? Still working bingo? Now tell me what's wrong with you.

Well, I was at the VFW in Lima, Ohio, since Ada is a dry town and you can't drink . . . and then we went to Bob's Big Boy . . .

I told the story that had now taken me on a long journey to St. Peter's Hospital. I knew the skilled nurses and doctors of Albany, not the nurse at Ohio Northern University, or George, the emotional-thumb-pointing-stair-climbing man, would be able to determine exactly where the bacon string was and pull it out with some sort of highly technical medical fishing rod instrument. After hours of tests, in which they had me drink barium and drew blood, a doctor came into the room where I awaited my destiny.

I had a condition known as *globus hystericus*.

I knew it was something, and I couldn't wait for my mother to feel bad that she made me go to the hospital all by myself.

So there we were again, my mother and I standing side by side staring at *Webster* just like we had done many years before when the Great Offal Incident happened.

Do you want to read it aloud, or should I?

No. You go right ahead, Mom. You read.

Fine. *Globus hystericus*. Latin . . . A choking sensation, commonly experienced in hysteria . . .

Interesting, added my mother.

When I returned to law school, my Latin *globus hystericus* came back with me. I dropped out a week before the end of my second trimester, right around Valentine's Day. That was also the day I came close to dropping out of life.

...

I made my way to the Toledo Amtrak station at about 5 A.M. in order to meet my father. He had taken an emergency overnight train from Albany to pick me up and take my shattered and interrupted mind all the way back to the safe house at 60 Academy Road. There was little traffic on the two-lane road leaving town. I passed one milk truck that was driving even slower than I was. I kept my eyes alert for signs directing me to the interstate. I didn't see any signs. Instead I saw a silo here, a silo there. Everywhere a silo . . . and snow-blanketed cornfields. A lone farmer stood by his mailbox, surveying his land. He glanced my way, following my car with his steady gaze as I passed. In my rearview mirror, I watched him turn back toward his land as the corduroy collar of his well-worn beige field jacket blew upward by the winter's still-strong wind.

Eventually I saw the sign I had been looking for: TOLEDO, with an arrow pointing to the right, indicating my turnoff was near.

As I made my way onto the highway, I realized I could easily lose control of my car, either by smashing it into a large snowbank on the right-hand side of the road, or in a bloodier scenario; I imagined ramming my new green Renault into a vehicle full of passengers coming toward me on the other side of the median. Gory visions flashed through my buzzing, dazed head. My mind raced back in an entirely new way.

Realizing I was losing it, I pulled over at a gas station and sat in the parking lot, thinking how much I wanted to ask a truck driver to take me to the train station. I would beg for help. But I kept thinking, once I got to the train station, I wouldn't have a car for my father to get us back home.

I pulled out of the gas station and drove on the emergency lane of the highway meant for broken-down cars. I assumed it was also meant for broken people. Every window in my car was wide open, despite the subzero temperature, in my effort to stay conscious. I hadn't slept even a partial night since late November. Sweat poured from my brow and my quivering hands. Finally, after exiting the Toledo ramp, I headed into the train station and came to a stop. I let go of the steering wheel. I had been clinging to it like a life preserver. My hands left the wheel only when I saw my father standing there. He had ridden fourteen hours by train, bringing only his toothbrush, to immediately turn around and drive us both back home. He now took the wheel for the long and quiet ride home. An even longer road lay ahead for me.

I was suffering through my first nervous breakdown. In hindsight, these troubles probably began with my earliest frightened thoughts at a very young age. It seemed my parents and I had simply kept a blanket over it until the one day the fears could no longer be kept at bay.

I never drove on a highway again. Sometimes, getting places is all about side streets, even if it makes your journey that much longer.

Bridge Over Troubled Waters

Safe at home, I sit sprawled out on the sofa in front of our bay window and stare to the right, onto my backyard. I look out all day long, but see nothing. I don't look at buildings or the staff members I have known ever since I was little. When I get up to go to the bathroom, my parents insist that I do not lock the door. I think they even stand right outside. One of them stays home with me at all times, and when they can't, Jimmy comes over to babysit. When he isn't available, my youngest sister watches over me. At night, my father sleeps outside my bedroom door. This time he is scared that I will leave.

We follow the same routine for months, even though my father is silently grieving the loss of his own father, my grandfather, who died a week shy of turning ninety.

When I seem to start coming out of my spell, my parents gently encourage me to find something to do. To help me build back my sense of worth, they arrange for me to work alongside my cousin Laurel during the day. I suppose this was so that she could also keep an eye on me.

I work at a factory in the nearby town of Cohoes, not too far away from Aunt Mary's house. I pin labels on merchandise on an assembly line, and I clock in every morning at 8 A.M. and clock out when a ringing bell declares our shift is over at 5 P.M.

I drive only on small, less-traveled streets to and from work.

I'm not getting better. I think my mind will eventually sink into complete darkness. One night I pull my car over on the 112th Street Bridge, the same bridge in Troy that my mother and aunt once traveled across on the bus to say their final good-bye to their mother right before Christmas on a snowy afternoon. I get out of my car and look down onto the raging waters of the Hudson River. The ice is now melting and a new spring nears, not that seasons matter to me anymore.

I have two choices. One is to take a final dive into the fierce rapids of the bitter-cold water below for an unknown adventurous ride to heaven.

No. Then again, I have only one choice. If I make the first decision, I will be killing her, too. My mother would not be able to survive the death of one of her children. She must go before us, and only then can we go.

The only choice I have is to not jump, and as I head back to my car, I decide it has to be on my terms. I need to find that right place where I can live and work without ever having to drive again. It should be a place where I can get the right psychiatric help.

In March 1986 I move to New York City. Getting there was something short of a miracle. Maybe St. Jude finally felt he owed my all-too-faithful mother a favor. It was a big one.

My father once said to me casually, like it was just an off-the-cuff remark, Perhaps you should have seen a child psychiatrist. Your mother and I often wondered about that.

He told me this years after I was under the care of my first psychiatrist, whom I visited weekly and sometimes more. During my first visit with Dr. Marianne Horney Eckardt, the daughter of Karen Horney—often described as the female Freud—she asked me the obvious question all psychiatrists ask their patients:

What was it about your childhood?

The Dream Beside Me

Feeling so utterly alone after the breakup of his marriage instinctively reminded Bob Wygant of the sad Sundays of his childhood. Bob couldn't stand the solitude of his new life. Now that his family was torn apart, he wanted to be around friends. Maybe he had gotten so caught up with having a family for the first time that he lost touch with many of the children whom he'd thought of as his brothers and sisters all those years. Someday, he wanted to get them all back together, but right now he needed the immediacy of someone who never judged him, but rather loved him like a son. Bob knew where he belonged. When he reached the point that he knew he had to get out of the quicksand of loneliness, Bob called Coach—now living in Sarasota, Florida. Without a moment's hesitation, Coach instructed Bob to pack a suitcase and come down immediately. Bob had always said to anyone they met, I want you to meet my dad.

Once again, Coach was able to steer the man he had first met at the Albany Home so many years ago through the often choppy waters of life and love.

After a relaxing time with Coach and Swannee, Bob felt like he could get back into the ball game again, and slowly begin a new life. Because he had lived such a structured childhood, he knew staying busy and being optimistic was how one survived.

One spring day in 1980, about three years after his marriage to Dorothy had ended, Bob was patiently waiting for a court to open up at his gym so that he could take his turn playing racquetball. When he sat down courtside to watch a game while waiting for his name to be called, a little girl came over and sat down beside him on the bench. She piped up, Hi, Mr. Wygant.

He looked down and smiled. Then he asked the child who she was.

Lisa, she answered brightly. You're my assistant principal. I'm in the fifth grade.

Where are your parents? Are they out there playing? Bob asked the nice girl with the friendly smile and big eyes.

Yes, my mom is. She's the one over there, Lisa replied as she pointed across the court.

Bob followed her gesture and spotted an attractive blond woman swinging her racket competitively. Sometimes things are just instinctively in your gut, and Bob began to wonder . . .

The next day the first thing he did when he arrived at school was pull Lisa's file. He could do that legally now—he was the assistant principal—unlike that time long ago when he had opened Elizabeth Campbell's file cabinet and read his own records. He had never regretted that act, nor thought of it as mischievous. If anything, Bob wished he could have given all his friends back then their folders, too, so that they might eventually find closure in their life, if they had any questions, spoken or not, about who they were.

Learning that Lisa's mother was divorced, he was pleased to realize that he was attracted to a woman for the second time in his life, in the same over-the-top way he had felt when he first saw Dorothy. Her name was Sally and he desperately wanted to meet her.

Bob Wygant didn't need Coach and Swannee to plead with him to call a lady anymore. A confident and proud man, Bob just picked up the phone.

Soon they were going on dates, all three of them. Each week, either Sally, her daughter, Lisa, or Bob would choose where they would go out to eat or what they would do on Friday nights. He always wore a suit and tie as he courted the second woman he had ever been interested in. Bob was all dressed up the night Lisa chose McDonald's for their Friday-night date because she loved their french fries.

Bob had thought he felt true love when he first saw Dorothy in the bleachers at that Albany High School football game. Decades later, he knew this was something more. When he looked into Sally's eyes, his feelings were of a deeper, richer love.

The following fall, when Sally's elderly parents were visiting, Bob pulled her father aside and asked permission to marry his daughter. Sally and Bob said their I do's right before Christmas and went on their honeymoon to Aruba, where they strolled the white sands all alone but very much together.

It had taken all this time for Bob Wygant to get love right.

Surfing

In the late 1980s, I was living in a fourth-floor apartment on the Upper West Side, in a safe doorman building on a safe block. But with all the security around me, something didn't feel safe. While my psychiatrist had prescribed a potent anti-obsessional drug, my mind was resistant to that drug. I was still plagued with deep-rooted fears of flight or suicide. My days were fearful and I was scared of things that had no obvious origin. No amount of talking about my feelings with my psychiatrist could take away the darkness I felt inside. Clinical depression is not easy to understand for those who don't suffer it. It seems like the world wants to help you, but sometimes nothing can help. Prescription drugs make things a little easier. It's like surfing. Inside your mind, you ride the waves. Depression comes and goes just like the tide. The crashes are high, and when the storm in your whirling mind settles, you are grateful. It's like you're lying in a hammock with no worries, reading a good book and drinking a piña colada. You pray your mind stays that way forever. But it doesn't. Depression, or at least the kind I have, will be with me forever.

My recovery from all that was, all that I felt and all that I could remember, would become a part of my life, along with my little Dixie Cup filled with morning and nightly doses of varying medications.

My only conscious recognizable fear was of losing my mother. The time line of how long she would live, which I had first imagined back when I was a child, had returned with a vengeance in my adult years. And so I called my mother every day from Manhattan, either at work or at home. I sometimes touched base with her three times a day. Usually, my mother and I talked about what was going on back in Albany, my family, and the fun things I did in New York City, which invariably led her to say, Be careful. You know I worry about you living there. We did not speak about my mental condition. I wasn't sure if my parents believed I was as sick as I was, or perhaps they just didn't want to hear about it—which was fine because I didn't have any conclusive answers for them anyway.

Still, I kept moving on with life, using the protective devices of my childhood. The day I moved into the Upper West Side apartment, and as soon as my boxes were unloaded into the living room, I immediately walked a block up to Broadway and went into a hardware store where I bought a box of heavy nails. I then went back to my new home and immediately hammered the nails into a space above the window frames, ten on each side, so that neither of the two large windows in my apartment could ever be opened more than two inches. This had nothing to with a fear of anyone breaking in. It was about keeping me from jumping out.

My life in that apartment mirrored my childhood. I couldn't sleep in my bed or on the sofa bed in my living room. The only place I could find myself drifting off to sleep was on the floor right beside the front door, a glass of water at my side. There I could hear the elevator man carrying passengers up and down throughout the night, and it made me feel secure.

When I couldn't handle my anxiety attacks in the middle of the night, I called paramedics or just took a taxi to the hospital. There, I would be given Valium drips to calm down. I was never hospitalized or institutionalized. I was a girl on the verge, a medicated individual desperately searching for calm coves. One of the two places I always felt safe was at work. I assumed my co-workers would rush to my side if I screamed out in despair. Sometimes when the darkness in my mind felt blacker and blacker, I shut the door to my office and cradled my head as I sat on the floor, and rocked back and forth until I could get my thoughts under a degree of control.

About once a month I went up north to Albany to visit my parents—or, more honestly, to be with my mother and to sleep. I took the train from Grand Central Station to the Albany-Rensselaer train station, where my parents would be parked right outside waiting. Sitting in their biannual newest car, they waited to hear the growing hum of the rails and the eventual blare of the train's horns. Everything had reversed itself: 60 Academy Road had become my sanctuary, where I found quiet peace at night.

I had once assumed that my nightmares or, more precisely, my fears would dissolve with the passage of time. It seems I had assimilated all the depression, aggression, flight, withdrawal, suicidal thoughts, and many of the psychological disorders that the Home children had been treated for. My backyard had left quite an impression on me.

Yet none of these internal mental eruptions or my continual journey quest to sleep at night ever got in the way of my desire to uncover stories during my days. There was something about putting together the pieces of people's lives, their characters, and their development from childhood to their present that seemed my natural calling. I sensed that if I could put a life compactly together for other people and write about that, someday I might understand my own development. I became a journalist.

When I moved to Manhattan, my first job—after cheating on a typing test—was working as an assistant for *Esquire* magazine, where I dutifully fetched muffins, scones, and coffee for my bosses. A year later, I answered a job advertisement in *The New York Times* from a successful author seeking a research assistant to work on books and magazine pieces. I assisted best-selling author Gail (*Passages*) Sheehy as she deconstructed and analyzed the character of the presidential candidates for the 1988 election, which she wrote about for *Vanity Fair* magazine and later published in her book *Character.*

Less than two years later, I interviewed for a job at *People.* First paying my dues as a fact-checker, I then became a reporter, a writer-reporter, and eventually one of the two New York correspondents for the magazine. I interviewed countless celebrities, as well as normal people with strange jobs—including the

woman who owned and loved each creature on her leech breeding farm. One
bittersweet story, however, will forever remain my favorite.

I had pitched a story idea to one of my editors about an orphanage celebrating its first-ever reunion on the grounds of its former campus. Orphans,
mostly from the Depression era, were coming back to remember the grounds
they once walked when they were just little boys and girls some fifty years before.

It was the story of my old backyard. At last, I was allowed to talk to the
children who had once lived at the Albany Home for Children and ask them
questions about their experiences growing up there, even if they lived there
long before I was born.

Sitting on a Rainbow

Bob Wygant could honestly say, as he entered his retirement years, that his life had been full and complete. The day I met him at the Albany Home for Children's first reunion that September day in 1989, Bob was clearly a happy guy. Why else would he wear an ostentatious lavender suit to come back home?

And so it was Sally, not Dorothy, with whom Bob walked hand in hand throughout the reunion festivities. He was so pleased to introduce his new wife to his old friends, whom he had last seen so long ago, and to those who helped him plan the intricate details of the reunion, like his old friends from Lathrop Cottage including Edna and Caroline LeRoy, and a number of the Bettys.

As the reunion progresses, at four o'clock, everyone begins to gravitate toward the JCA gymnasium, site of the evening's program and the dinner dance. Before climbing the stairs into the gymnasium, the former children are invited to offer testimonials of their lives at the Home while being videotaped. When doing so, they laugh about an era that was long ago and far away from the contemporary world. Both the men and women get a bit choked up when they recall not having the love of a mother each day through their childhood.

As the camera rolls, Floyd P. Squires is all too eager to share his story about living at the home from 1912 to 1922. At eighty-two, he is the oldest returning orphan. This lively man with brush-cut hair and a dapper dark suit is hard of hearing yet still alert. His favorite memory is about how he and his fellow orphans survived the influenza epidemic of 1912.

Supported on one side by his son and on the other by his cane, Squires speaks into the cameraman's microphone: All 102 of us had it and we all went down to the Albany Hospital, but none of us died. People were dying all over the place. Jell-O and milk—that's all we ate for two whole weeks. Normally we would have oatmeal and cornmeal for breakfast in the winter and corn-flakes in the summer. I remember every Saturday the iceman would come around and put ice in the iceboxes in all the kitchens. Back then we wore one-piece union suits. When I graduated from Albany High, they gave you the diploma and sent you on your way, and said, Okay, now do the best you can!

After registering, the returning orphans find seats at the big round tables arranged around the floor. They are given handmade yearbooks containing Xeroxed copies of treasured childhood photographs. These were taken by boxy Kodak Brownie flash cameras as they were growing up and saved with loving care by their former houseparents and housemothers. Parsons Cottage girls pose playfully on their porch, three friends sit next to a jaunty snowman, volleyball games and gymnastics, dancing in the gym. Split-second moments from their childhood.

By five o'clock, everyone assembles in the gymnasium, continuing to catch up with one another and introducing their families to friends from their shared past as they make their way toward their tables. They scan the room for missing faces. It comes as no surprise that for every orphan who has returned for the celebration, there is another who's put the years spent at the Albany Home behind and shut the door.

Some who are absent have logistical reasons for not being there: They live too far away, or are too old now and unable to travel. Others are simply em-barrassed to let anyone know that they were placed at an orphanage. Some re-main so embittered that their parents abandoned them to grow up as orphans that they have vowed they will never set foot on the grounds again, even so many decades after leaving—even if it means never again seeing their childhood friends, who were so much like brothers and sisters.

My parents eventually end their afternoon stroll around the old Albany Home for Children. They feel it is best to leave the celebration to those who live on this side of the yard—so they say to me. Even though my mother is excited that I am reporting a story so close to our home, this story is too close to the situation of her own childhood. And just like when she played "Ave Maria" at Christmas to drown out the sorrow of her childhood, the reunion day pulls at her heart. My mother never would say, Let's leave, John. It's something he instinctively knows whenever she becomes too quiet. He is the tough side of her heart, the protective side. She is the soft and caring side. I don't think my mother could ever have survived this world without him. I see that in the way she looks at him so adoringly, and I see that same feeling of adoration returned by my father. It just hasn't come to me that my world would live or die without him. It most certainly would live or die without her. Although now twenty-eight, I know that whenever she dies, I will feel orphaned. Hers is the beating heart that matters to me. But on the day of the reunion, my mind switches from that fear that never goes away of losing her to trying deeply to concentrate on the story I am here to report for *People* magazine.

As I look around me, I see that like little kids, most of the alumni are too excited to eat the fruit cup medley and tossed garden greens, much less decide if they want the stuffed breast of chicken supreme or broiled haddock with lemon butter sauce.

One of the orphans who left the Home in the mid-1940s calls out, Hey, I remember that we always ate well, but nothing like this!

Laughter ripples across the room as the orphans call out their favorite—and least favorite—meals at the Home.

My God! Remember that lumpy oatmeal? one woman asks aloud.

Oh, yes, and we stuck it in our baggy green gym bloomers so our housemother would think we ate it. We had to clean our plates, someone else chimes in with a spirited laugh.

Before the music and dancing begin, Bob Wygant, the emcee for the reunion, stands before the assembled crowd to make a toast, saying to all present, It's okay to be a kid from the Home. Look at us now. We're all doing okay.

Then Bob introduces Coach Ronald J. Huddleston as the son of a gun who made us mow the big lawn. The crowd responds with a resounding standing ovation.

At seventy-seven, this gentle man stands proudly before the assembled crowd of men and women—the boys and girls he once led in calisthenics on the lawn. Though he can barely make it through his prepared speech as his eyes start to well with tears, he recalls the activities—the Girl and Boy Scouts, athletics—and accomplishments of his wards. He looks around the room and acknowledges how he remembers them: Betty Lappeus Johnson, best basketball player; Gail Lewis Elliott, best voice; Bob Wygant, best all-around athlete; Sue Dieckelmann, the first girl he gave away in marriage . . . He recalls all the great times he and Swannee had shared with them over the years. It has been two years since Swannnee has gone.

After Coach sits down, the lights are switched off and the room grows silent. Black-and-white images flicker across the screen, capturing a bygone era through eight-millimeter film taken in the 1940s by Charles Keck, who was the Home's handyman and the one who delivered groceries to the cottages where the orphans once lived. For this reunion, he has donned his fanciest suit and, though eighty-eight years old, has driven himself over for the festivities.

The orphans and their families are taken back as this living time capsule of their childhood years at the Albany Home plays out before them. There they are, shrieking with laughter as they run around the wading pool, grabbing their towels to run away, only to return moments later for another splash. Mr. Keck captured the boys and girls as they tended to their farm, weeding grass, saddling the Home's horse, Lady Marilyn, and feeding their chickens. They are even shown facing the doctor's big needle in the cold, sterile infirmary. As the film moves inside the cottages, children are memorialized as they sit at the table for dinner, where Keck has even filmed the little tin cups that they once drank from.

The orphans emeriti scream out in gleeful embarrassment as they see themselves as naked three-year-olds in the bathtub. They call out the names of their childhood pals and the adults they knew as houseparents.

In the course of the twenty-minute film, never once is an orphan seen crying. Not even when they are at Bill the barber's getting their hair shaved off for the summer, or at the dentist's to have a tooth filled.

The evening continues on, and the former brothers and sisters dance together to their favorite music from the Platters.

From the beginning to the end of the reunion, not one orphan appears devastated. It is as though by the end of the night, every face has been cast in a radiant smile. All that was bad was forgotten; only the good remains. The lessons they cared to learn have been instilled.

Close to midnight, as everyone prepares to leave, many eagerly exchange telephone numbers and addresses. They promise to have a reunion every year until they have all passed away. Everyone agrees the day was too short as they reluctantly head off to their cars with their families. They linger as if dawdling will stop time . . . so the reunion will never end.

Bob asks me about my day.

Did you get a story? he wonders, hoping I can make a story about a bunch of middle-aged and elderly people getting together again for a day to talk about childhood memories that didn't seem all that unusual to him.

It might be hard, Bob, I reply, smiling. It seems I tape-recorded one hundred stories. You know, I thought this would be a day full of agony for all of you. And I only found happy endings.

Not everyone felt the same way about this place, Bob said. Sometimes you have to search for happiness in sadness you may have faced as a kid. I think the people you met today found that.

I agree. It was a special day. And I believe what you say about finding happiness. After a pause I add, I wonder about the kids who grew up on my side of the fence and what might have happened to them. They obviously didn't live in our backyard for the same reasons.

No, he said. Not at all. But strip away whatever their problems were and are and you'll find a decent kid. A good kid. Now that you know about us, why don't you go find out about them? Maybe someday we'll have a reunion with everyone who lived here, whatever side of the fence we might have lived on.

In his final act as chairman of the first-ever reunion of the Albany Home for Children, Bob Wygant locks the gymnasium door and hands the key over to me so that I can return it to my father. I kiss Bob on the cheek and walk toward my home. I turn to see him embracing Sally and then, right there under the parking lot lights, he stops and kisses her before opening their car door.

I've got the world on a string,
Sitting on a rainbow . . .

Questions and Answers

When I came home from the reunion, I found my mother sitting outside on the patio in a low-seated beach chair, our black dachshund Mercedes with a brown-tipped nose curled up on her side. Marnie had hanged herself several years back after trying to jump out of a kennel's open top cage when our family went away to Cape Cod. The operators of the kennel had forgotten to take off Marnie's silver choke-chain collar. When she jumped because she wanted to come to the beach with us, too, no one at the kennel saw her try, so she dangled there until they discovered her dead body. When we came back from Cape Cod, we found a note on our door to call the kennel immediately. I suppose you always know what those things mean even if you haven't been through a death before, albeit a family pet. I hated that Marnie suffered slowly, the air chopped off at her neck. If she had to die, I wished it had been in my arms or my mother's because we were her favorites.

She had kept me company through my lonely childhood nights. Marnie was my instant alarm system. If I didn't catch someone breaking into our home, Marnie would have. And so many times, I kept Marnie awake through the night, tapping her little rump whenever she started to drift off to sleep because I needed her to be my *Adam-12* costar, and I would say to her, No sleeping, Marnie. One Adam-12. One Adam-12. We're on night patrol. Have a cup of joe, puppy, if you're feeling sleepy. We'll pull over at Denny's.

My mother loved our new dog Mercedes in the same way she did Marnie, maybe even more so, since my siblings and I were now all gone. Billy had married his college sweetheart, Ann Marie, Mandy lived in Baltimore, and Sarah had gone off to Amsterdam for a year after she graduated from college. Jimmy was living in Yonkers, training to be a parole officer.

Quietness surrounded my mother now, although she took such pleasure in seeing us come back home. There didn't seem to be a weekend when one of us wasn't here. Plus, she always had nearby her best friend, Aunt Mary, whom she'd visited several times a week ever since my uncle Ed had passed away a year before from lung cancer.

She left the sliding glass door partially open for me because I'm sure she could see that the lights had now been turned off at the JCA campus. It was a chilly night, and my mother wore a pink cashmere sweater draped over her nightgown. Her chair wasn't in its usual position, always looking toward the cottages to the right, making sure the children were sleeping soundly. Fire engines rarely came to the grounds anymore. A system had been installed where the fire stations could immediately determine if a child had triggered a false alarm. My mother's chair was turned at an angle facing a break in the trees to the left, which gave her a clear view into the darkness that shrouded the older campus of the former Albany Home for Children.

She had been waiting for me to come home. Dashing into the kitchen, I opened the refrigerator and grabbed two Molson Lights. I pulled up another beach chair beside her. Both of us stared at the old Home. I told her that our house was built on the place where the birch trees once grew, a little bit beyond the horseshoe playing field where the orphans used to play.

It was interesting learning about that side of our backyard and the history behind it, I told her. I never understood its true heritage.

Our backyard affected you, my mother offered in an honest manner I had never before heard. I think you were the only one of my children who was keenly aware that it wasn't just a playground with lots of open space, swings, and a pool.

You're right. But all these years after going away to college, I thought about our house as a home without a backyard. When I think of it now, our backyard was once a place that consumed my thoughts, but then as it expanded after I left initially for the University of Vermont, it slowly faded away into oblivion. I don't think I've told one person in my adult life that I grew up on the grounds of a children's home.

Are you embarrassed by it? she asked me with a degree of concern.

In high school, I was embarrassed to live here. But that was only true for a couple of years. It's hard to feel anything for a backyard that I didn't understand and that was kept at bay from me. There's no one for me to miss over there. It's different from all the stories I heard today. All those people I met had a reason to be wandering around their old property today. It was their home. Wandering around our property is different. I think of it now as more or less a child psychiatric hospital, and less of an orphanage.

Do you ever think about any of the kids you grew up with?

I was surprised by her question, and could have been sarcastic in my response—*grew up with?* I tried to be gentle with my mother, an effort I didn't always make with others. How could I answer this question with a degree of grace? I knew their faces without knowing their stories, I said. I wasn't supposed to know their stories.

No, you weren't to know their stories, because they weren't stories you could retell your friends. I know you heard parts of stories but I'm sure nothing added up to you.

You're right. And I suppose if I had heard the gory intricate details behind a placement, I could have used it like a game of telephone and told my friends.

It was hard for your father and me to keep things secret.

You did a good job, I said. It's strange how I turned out to be a reporter.

There's nothing about my backyard that I could even write about. I could only describe what it looks like now or what it looked like then. The stories of the children would just be blank pages. After today, I now have a book of material about the old backyard next door.

My mother's eyes teared up. I hated seeing her cry. I thought best to change the subject. As I started to ask her if she could make me blueberry pancakes for breakfast, she said something that stunned me.

It shouldn't be like that. Your father said everything was confidential. You shouldn't stop thinking about the faces you once knew. Those kids were special to me.

My mother now spoke passionately. Some of her sentences were told through her tears: But it was all so sad. It hasn't been easy to live here and know the children like I did, and see them go off into the world, often wondering if they would ever make it and be able to be accepted in the world because of their illnesses. I wanted that for all of them. But sometimes, it just didn't happen that way. I think troubled children become troubled adults.

She was right about that. But when she looked in my eyes, even if it was dark outside, she didn't see the connection.

Thinking about the stories I had learned through the course of my day, I thought I would ask her about one—just one child—from my backyard. It had been a long day but I thought about throwing the question out there. I figured she would say she couldn't talk about the children I once sort of knew. I was getting tired, and I knew my mother wouldn't be able to tell a story if it didn't have a happy ending. So if she really meant what she said about remembering my backyard, I thought I would put her to the test and ask her about a kid from the Home for my bedtime story.

Why did my old summer boyfriend Ryan live in the cottages? I asked. Except for his scars, he seemed normal.

My mother shook her head, looking up toward the darkening sky. Those letters he sent you . . . I hope you understand there was a reason your father couldn't let you read them in their entirety. They were too graphic. He was truly troubled.

Could it really be true that my mother was going to answer questions and unlock the secrets of my backyard? I pressed on.

...

The scars on Ryan's face were from the fire his mother set, right? But did that affect him here? Was he a good kid at all?

As I said to you, I would like to think they were, and are, all good kids. Your father used to say, Ryan was a bright and personable child. He had a lot of charm, but he could never get his mother's death out of his head. He reached out to her, in the fire that scarred him so. But only he was able to get out, so he probably felt guilty, let alone extremely lonely. The fire shadowed his life. Your father thought that his letters to you showed that he desperately wanted to be loved by someone. So he let him send them, but it was conflicting. He had to use a Magic Marker to blacken any sexual references. Ryan was trying to grow up quickly, and you were so young.

What did the Home do to make him better? I sipped my beer slowly, assuming her story would continue on, perhaps to its ending.

He wanted to fly, she said. On the swings or from the highest branch in a tree.

Where did he think he would go? I asked.

I don't know. He took life-threatening risks, which some interpreted as a desire to join his mother. He broke bones, but he always lived. Sometimes I would see him fly forward off the swing and he would flap his hands like he was Peter Pan. For a second in time, he could fly. But Ryan obviously didn't have wings, so he would eventually crash onto the grass near the swings or into the bushes and tall grass around the trees in the woods way out back. Then he would cry, not because he was hurt but because he was frustrated.

How do you fix a kid like that? I asked. Through drugs?

Ryan may have been on medications. But actually one of therapists back then decided to try an unorthodox experiment to treat Ryan's obsession with death.

What did they do?

As I turned to her, I could see my mother put her index finger on her lower lip and move it back and forth hesitating with her thoughts.

I can't tell you.

What? Why? You just started to.

It's just that I can't. Your father is right; every child has a right to privacy. Forget everything I just said to you. It's just that I want you to come to appreciate where you lived most of your childhood. I hope our backyard makes all of you sensitive to the needs of sick and troubled children. Good night, Sue. I'm just going to walk with Mercedes a little. Come on, 'Cedes. Come with Mommy.

There was no way I was going to let the story of the first boy who ever loved me, albeit a strange love, not have an ending. So I followed my mother, who was now nearing the small woods that separated our house from the cottages. If it was a happy ending, my mother would tell it to me with a full Disney-like treatment complete with white doves flying out of a wedding cake. Obviously it wasn't, so that's why she walked away.

As Mercedes elegantly squatted down for her before-bed pee, I stood beside my mother.

Mom? Ryan? Happy ending or not? I want the truth. You started a story. And every story has an ending, it doesn't close in the middle.

She continued her walk with Mercedes to the edge of our former bicycle-riding loop and didn't say a word.

Please tell me the truth. Mom, you're the one who taught us how to figure out jigsaw puzzles when Jimmy and I were just little kids. You told us that all puzzles come together. Tell me about Ryan's. Please.

My mother started to cry again. I knew my tone of voice was enough to confuse her into thinking she owed me the truth.

And so my mother completed a story without using the lilt that was always present in her voice whenever she called me during my college years or when she told stories during my childhood.

She got right to the point without dancing around like she was explaining *The Nutcracker.*

Ryan was administered last rites by a therapist that a psychiatrist brought in. But he wasn't dead, she said. It was the strangest ceremony I had ever been to, but it seemed to me that it made sense.

Last *rites,* I asked as we continued to walk around the loop. Yet he wasn't dead. Why?

Because he thought no one cared about him or loved him. What little boy doesn't want that? Anyway, they made Ryan lie on a table atop a white cloth like you would see at the altar of St. Teresa's. Then his friends and remaining relatives walked over to Ryan and pretended he was dead and told him how much they would miss him. Everyone in the room was told to say their good-byes and then leave.

I don't like funerals, my mother said, continuing her light crying. I've been going to them since I was three. But your father told me that Ryan liked me and that he liked you, too. But you would never be allowed to go to such a thing, so I believed I had to. I had to help this little boy. There wasn't one child over there that my heart didn't ache for. The ones who wanted to die broke my heart the most. So I went.

I don't recall my exact words but I do remember this. I did not pretend he was dead. I spoke to him knowing he was listening. And I said to him, I know how hard it is to lose your mother when you are just a little boy because I lost my mother when I was young, too. I told him that the hurt he felt for his mother would always be there but that I was happy now and like me, I told him, he would one day get married and have children to love him as much as he wanted to be loved. I asked him to hold on to his life, and to think about a future where he would one day rock a baby boy or girl in his arms to sleep. I told him that seeing your own child grow was life's Holy Grail, or maybe I told him it was life's Willy Wonka. I forget. Willy Wonka sounds more like me, I suppose. In the end, I promised Ryan that once a week, he and I would walk up to Stewart's alone and talk about how we both felt about losing our mothers if he promised me he would stop trying to take his life. If I could help anyone who experienced such sorrow, maybe it was up to me to open up to him.

Did you keep your word? I asked as we neared our patio, my father assuredly asleep inside.

Yes, but only a few times. The ceremony actually helped him, but I think talking about his mother depressed him, so I had to end our walks. Still, every week I gave your father money that I saved and told him to give it to Ryan so that he could take a friend of his choosing up to Stewart's, just the two of them. He was the only regular one. Sometimes when your father told me such disturbing stories of why children came into the Home, I felt so hopeless and the only thing I could think to do was let them choose their own ice cream cone at Stewart's. You might have seen eight children walking up the street to Stewart's if you were looking out the front windows or playing outside. Once in a while, they were the ones I had selected for Mrs. Carswell Treats. Knowing they were getting an ice cream made me forget maybe for a moment how horrible their stories actually were. It made me happy, even if it was just a cone that lasted five minutes. That made me feel like I could do something that would take them away from the pain of their childhood.

Do you know what happened to Ryan after he left?

No, I really don't. But please don't tell your father I told you Ryan's story. Promise me. Maybe one day, you and your father will be closer and he'll feel comfortable enough to open up more when he's around you. I've always wanted that. Your father helped you so much when you were a kid and you couldn't sleep—and look how successful you are today—but I knew I was always the one whom all of you had so much love for. You don't know him. Why would I ever marry a man if I didn't think he was my other half?

I didn't know what to say. My father was my father, but unlike her, he wasn't my friend. And she was enough of a friend, and overtly loving parent, that she made up for him, too. Maybe I only had it in me to love just one person, not two. And ever since I could remember, she was my greatest love.

If Ryan loved his mother as much as I loved mine, I don't blame him for trying to meet her again whenever he tried to jump toward the sky in the swings.

I would do the same.

Part Two

Up, Up, and Away

You forget, dear, it was only a dream. We grow far away from angels and fairies as we get old, I fear.
                —Mrs. Molesworth, *The Children of the Castle,* 1890*

---

* Mrs. Molesworth had seven children and was a children's author of note, writing more than one hundred books. She has been called "the Jane Austen of the nursery."

Places I Remember

My parents moved away from 60 Academy Road the summer of 1994. By this time, Jim and Bill were both married with families of their own, Mandy and Sarah were working in Boston, and I was still firmly entrenched in New York City.

Although we had always considered this redbrick house with its extended backyard our home, it had, in fact, always belonged to the institution. My parents now found themselves rattling around in too many rooms, too many memories, and a greatly diminished backyard due to the construction of so many new buildings as Parsons Child and Family Center continued to grow.

Besides, they had always wanted a house of their own, and they had saved the money to buy one. My father was also earning a great deal more money than his original starting salary of eight thousand dollars a year back in 1962.

The time was right for them to make the move to a spacious two-story condominium on a peaceful cul-de-sac across the Hudson River from Albany. My mother looked forward to her daily walks along the quiet streets of their new neighborhood in East Greenbush—not too far away from the home of Bob and Sally Wygant, with whom I exchanged Christmas cards. My father couldn't wait to get his hands on a brand-new garden.

After more than twenty-five years in the same house, my mother and father finally decided to throw a huge yard sale to dispense with the accumulation of clothing through the decades, skis, other sports gear, kitchen gadgets, and all the Tupperware that had accumulated in the basement since 1968, the summer we moved in. Since my mother never wanted to throw away anything that may still have some value—sentimental or otherwise—there were boxes and boxes of treasures, toys, books, just about everything.

Sarah, by this time in her midtwenties, drove over from Boston to act as cohost for the sale, hawking our junk with the same finesse she had used to sell Kool-Aid when we were kids. She even repeated her determined walk to the traffic light at the entrance to the Junior College of Albany, directing motorists to the detritus of our lives, now spread out upon the driveway and lawn.

Much like Carol Merrill stirred contestants into a frenzy over washing machines and La-Z-Boy lounge chairs on *Let's Make a Deal* in the 1960s and 1970s, my almost six-foot-tall blond sister didn't let a vehicle or pedestrian pass by until they paid her a dime for one of my mother's paperback romance novels or some other vestige from our past. Sarah was able to collect a quarter for my complete set of law school books and hustled fifty cents from our neighbors across the street for my foam-green Easy-Bake Oven, by then a vintage yet campy reminder of my childhood, when I baked my own cakes with the ulterior motive of enjoying an extra snack after school. The posters of Donny Osmond and David Cassidy that my mother once taped on my bedroom wall tipped the bank at a dollar.

By the end of the day, almost everything on the lawn had been sold or given away. By sundown, Sarah, now sweating profusely, was spent. Minutes earlier someone had asked to see the sofa bed, so she reluctantly obliged and opened it up on the front lawn to make the sale.

Then, lemonade in hand, she sat in the sole remaining folding chair, positioned squarely in the middle of the driveway to signify the sale was over. As she wiped her damp brow and neck with a cool towel, a potential customer asked if the chair she was sitting on was for sale. Sarah looked the woman directly in the face and curtly replied, No, even though a white tag placed clearly beneath the aluminum armrest had been slashed and was now boldly marked FREE. My sister was too weary to even stand up.

Collections from the Carswell home were eventually dispersed throughout the Albany area. What remained, carefully boxed and crated, were the valuable paintings collected by my parents, their accumulation of Oriental rugs and antique furniture, elegant china, silverware, Waterford crystal, and delicate vases they had brought back from Florence. Also making the move to the new house would be my mother's beloved hope chest and her new, locked jewelry box—which housed her collection of diamonds and rubies, along with her first pair of real pearls from Mikimoto—and, of course, the family photographs taken over the preceding decades.

One year later, on a warm evening in May 1995, my family gathered beneath a large white tent, set up in front of the old Parsons Cottage, to celebrate my father's retirement. After federal and state funding for social services had been cut and with what he perceived as a contentious board no longer supporting his vision for the future of the center, my father had abruptly resigned the previous fall.

I'll never forget my mother's phone call the morning he told her of his decision. She called me at work and said, Your father has decided to leave.

Leave what? I asked.

The Home.

I was shocked. I never thought I would see the day when my father would give up his efforts on behalf of troubled children. Besides, I had been home just the day before and he had given no sign of making such a momentous decision. My father had worked at the former Albany Home for Children, as we still called it, for thirty-three years, since I was just six months old.

The night of his retirement party, all my relatives, including my grandmother, and my parents' close circle of friends were there laughing away at the tables set for six or eight. Everyone seemed so happy for my father and mother. They knew my parents would bring their characteristic joie de vivre as they set off on this new adventure.

My mother and father were looking forward to traveling when the spirit moved them. My father could garden or golf as much as he wanted, and my mother could spend more time shopping with her sister, Mary, now legally blind. My parents would have all the time in the world to enjoy each other's company.

Many of the former staff members from the Albany Home, now retired, returned to pay tribute to my father in recognition of his service to the agency. I was glad to see Dr. Abbuhl, who had been the doctor on call to care for the children at the Home, and us as well. He was the one my mother had taken me to see when I was young and asked if I would ever be normal. We'll have to see, Elaine. We'll have to see. Dr. Abbuhl still had the same flattop haircut and colorful bow tie I remembered as a child. Now he was president of my father's lucrative Sunday-night investment club. Social workers who cared for children could indeed become wealthy, contrary to what my mother had said to me the second night we moved into the home, when she explained why we didn't have air-conditioning.

Before the dinner, I wandered around the grounds in front of Parsons Cottage and ran into many of my father's former colleagues.

Nadia Finkelstein stopped me as I was surreptitiously bringing another glass of Scotch to my grandmother. Mrs. Finkelstein was a young social worker fresh out of graduate school when she first came to the Home in the early 1950s. She told me how she remembered seeing the five Carswell kids at play in our backyard when we were little. She said, You were all awfully cute, and you looked so well cared for. As an administrator, I wanted all the little Home kids to look the way you Carswell children did.

Nadia went on to talk about how well dressed, well groomed, and obviously loved we had been. She explained that a child care worker who had to turn things over to another child care worker at the end of the shift could never provide the kind of attention and care that our parents had given us.

Mrs. Finkelstein credited my father's vision for the transformation of the Albany Home for Children to Parsons. As she said, He certainly recognized, with some of the rest of us, that having just a residential component of treatment wasn't enough. Keeping kids there for four or five years to get them cured wasn't working. You really needed a whole array of options.

She went on to explain how my father had implemented innovative foster care and adoption programs, as well as day treatment plans, well ahead of the rest of the nation.

When my father started at the Albany Home for Children in 1962, he was one of twenty-six employees. When he retired, almost four hundred employees, volunteers, adoptive and foster care parents were working either on the campus or throughout the community.

As I walked around the campus, I stopped to stare at the drips of paint on the nearly century-old bricks of Parsons Cottage. I remembered how one summer, when I was in college, my father offered me a job painting the cottage's porch. It didn't occur to him to ask if I knew how to paint anything other than watercolors. I didn't. My drizzles and drops of paint hit the brick instead of the white wooden porch and served as a constant reminder of the guilt I felt that I had permanently detracted from the beauty of the one remaining original cottage on the grounds now occupied by the center.

With her drink in my hand, I walked over to my grandmother, sitting in her wheelchair in the shade of an elm, not too far from the Van Alsytne Gym. After my grandfather died, she moved to be near us, or rather nearer to my father.

My grandmother still had a desperate need to share the latest gossip from her old town of Glens Falls or to talk in awe about Elizabeth Drew's weekly political essay from *The New Yorker*.

Her signature beehive hairdo was now as white as spun cotton, and it increasingly listed to the left. As I handed her a fresh, carefully measured shot, she growled up at me, Next time, tell 'em, Don't be so cheap with the Black Velvet. And remember, Sue, don't tell your father. He'll cut me off. She then pressed a ten-dollar bill into my palm, I suppose as a tip. It'll help pay your rent, she said with a wink.

Close to ninety, my grandmother was as irascible as ever, still a vocal supporter of the Democratic Party and quick to sling mud at anyone who disagreed with her politics. She had been perpetually radiant since 1992 when her party once again gained control of the White House.

Admittedly, my grandmother was in love that May as we milled around this garden party. Unfortunately, her new love lived in Washington, D.C., with his wife and daughter. This didn't stop my grandmother from dreaming. If only I was sixty years younger, she imagined. I'd be kissing Bill's luscious sweet lips. Then she shut her eyes and continued to fantasize about her desire beneath the elms.

Mind you, my grandmother was talking about President Clinton.

...

My father's retirement dinner was a bittersweet evening. Various city officials and my father's loyal associates congratulated him for turning an agency operating on a $150,000-a-year annual budget when he started into a highly respected residential institution for disturbed children with close to $20 million in federal and state funding at the time of his departure.

During my father's tenure, Parsons Child and Family Center had developed a national reputation as a progressive and innovative center for young people and their families. The number of troubled children continually increased, as did the number of dysfunctional and ill-prepared parents. Parsons now provided necessary support—through a wide range of educational, residential, and clinical networks—to almost two thousand children and five thousand family members across the state.

A large part of Parsons's growth was due to my father's extraordinary talents as a child care worker and administrator, and his unwavering vision that troubled children should always be cared for with respect and dignity.

Before the dinner began, Ray Schimmer, my father's successor, came over to the table where I sat with my brothers and sisters, shaking his head as he looked at us, and said, You all had a bird's-eye view of troubled children growing up. I sometimes wonder what it must have been like to live here as a family. Did it affect any of you?

He added, No one will ever again have that opportunity to see what you might have seen.

In the year since my parents had moved away, our house had been turned into the office for Parsons's residential programs. Mr. Schimmer and his wife and daughter lived far away from the campus, in an affluent Albany suburb. Like my sisters and me, his daughter also attended the Albany Academy for Girls.

As far as I could figure, all those children I had often watched in our backyard must have been in their midthirties by now, some nearing forty. I didn't know what happened to them, although I had learned from my father that most of those troubled kids now held low-paying jobs because they were years behind academically.

Some had become kitchen helpers; others cleaned houses or held seasonal jobs, such as selling frozen yogurt in a stand down by the state capitol during the summertime.

The successes, my father was quick to point out, included a woman who became a data entry operator, and a guy named George who was a reliable truck driver.

There were also the stories of those who became alcoholics and drug addicts. Some of their children now attended the Neil Hellman School at Parsons, or had been placed in foster families or group homes. These heirs continued their parents' legacy.

Others went off to jail for various reasons: John Willis Richards murdered a security guard—execution style, in 1989—not too far from the Home, down by the Port of Albany. Another boy moved downstate, and at seventeen he walked into the Yonkers Jewish Community Center where he started a pre-Christmas blaze that killed nine children and three adults. An investigator had stated the boy "had felt an urge" to cause excitement. He later got off because of his age. His mother died of cancer two months after he started the fire. The counselors who remembered working with him when he was at the Home recalled a boy who loved to make neat piles as he shoveled snow.

As my father said when he thanked everyone for coming to his retirement party, You wish you had a magic wand. You wish you had a secret to all of this and that you could write a script that has a happy ending.

My father was no Merlin. He was simply a guy with a heart who cared about overseeing kids and hoped they would find peace. He had loved his job.

By a strange twist of fate, I had run into Jodie, my favorite rowdy orphan from my backyard, when I was in my early thirties while vacationing with my parents in Aruba. We had been sitting and talking in the sand, our toes soaking in the warm water as it softly ebbed and flowed. Jodie and her adoptive mother, Nancy, were strolling along the beach when my father recognized them, jumped out of his chair, and called to them. Jodie had grown into an attractive, petite woman. Those big brown eyes that I remembered from my childhood seemed even bigger now.

My father looked at me and said, You remember Jodie, Sue, almost as if we had always been close friends. I nodded and said a simple, Hi. She did the same, with a shy smile. And then she turned her head away and sat down on the sand to talk to my mother.

I wanted to ask Jodie so many questions, but I didn't know where to begin.

When Jodie's mother died about two years later, my father received word that Jodie wanted to sell their condominium in Aruba. She had recently married and needed the money.

Two weeks out of the year, my parents now lived in Jodie's home.

As his retirement dinner neared its end, my father received a new set of golf clubs. Then I walked up to the podium and gave the keynote tribute, honoring him as a caring professional but, more so, as my dad.

My father once said he would have liked to have ten children. While he only had five, I don't think there was a child who passed through the doors at Parsons whom my father didn't care deeply for. He adopted hundreds and hundreds of these children in his heart and soul . . .

It was a hard speech for me to give, especially when I spoke about the possibilities of an endless horizon.

. . . Lately, I've been thinking about what the years ahead will be for my parents as they embrace my father's retirement. I've thought of all the oceans my parents have yet to cross on the cruises they take annually with their cherished group of friends . . .

My mother looked so striking that evening in a new red dress that complemented her hair, washed and styled earlier in the day by Louie, her long-time friend and hairdresser. As I spoke, she smiled at me, comforted, I suppose, by what she knew to be my fairy tale. In our own code, it was as if I was saying, *Don't worry. Everything will turn out fine. Promise.*

I was trying to give her a sign of hope. The day before, we had learned that my mother had breast cancer.

The next speech I gave before my family was less than two years later.

It was my mother's eulogy.

Mary Poppins's Umbrella

Three o'clock in the afternoon. The day before my father's retirement party. The telephone rang in the kitchen. This was the call we had been anxiously awaiting all day, desperate for news yet so afraid of what we might find out. My mother's soft cries confirmed her diagnosis as she spoke with her doctor: The cyst in her left breast was malignant, despite having a clean mammogram five months before.

I don't think I'll ever forget that moment—every detail of where everyone sat or stood, the terrified expressions on our faces as we waited with deep dread for my mother to get off the phone.

We had gathered at my parents' new home for the occasion of my father's retirement. Outside, my mother's beloved pale orange tiger lilies had just begun to bloom, and the nip of late spring was giving way to the warmth of summer, my mother's favorite season.

We were all there: my siblings—Jim, Bill, Mandy, and Sarah, my sisters-in-law Ann Marie and Kathie, as well as my future brother-in-law, Walter. When we heard my mother slam the telephone onto the table and scream out, crying, *Jesus, Mary, and Joseph!* we hurried downstairs with heavy hearts and hugged her, one by one. My father sat at the kitchen table. His strong hands now clutching his bowed head.

It was the first time I ever saw my father cry.

My family didn't know anything about breast cancer. We only knew people who knew people who had had it, and they all survived. My brother Bill, always practical and proactive, opened up the yellow pages in search of a special 1-800 hotline that could give us some answers to all the questions that we had about possible treatments. Stage-one breast cancer—from the sound of it—didn't seem like a death sentence. Still, we couldn't help thinking it might prove deadly. We instinctively knew that we had to act quickly before it spread. Bill discovered no listing under BREAST CANCER for us to call for help. And so my mild-mannered brother ended up crying in the ears of the operator out of desperation. Search again, he begged. Please.

The afternoon sun filtered gently through the sheer white curtains, which my mother had carefully chosen during her grand shopping spree to decorate the new family home. In its soft light, we sat around the kitchen table and clung to one another like children in a football huddle strategizing the next game plan. Even though we were together, we froze in fear at the thought that we might be losing the one who sparkled so brightly and held us together as a family.

We had no idea what would be in store for her, or for us. But first, we had to get through my father's retirement party.

In the fall of 1995, after my mother had successfully recovered from her lumpectomy and the subsequent radiation treatments, she and my father were on a plane the next day to Aruba, her favorite Caribbean island. My mother always looked forward to embracing the warmth of the sun-washed, tranquil cerulean sea. And she so anticipated the long walks with my father along the white sand, beneath the cascading glow of the moon and the boundless stars, always hand in hand, a gesture of love my siblings and I had always admired and thought would extend well into their nineties.

For a brief period, my family thought we were the lucky ones. We imagined we would be wearing pink ribbons in support of breast cancer research with a smile, as if to say, *There is hope; breast cancer is not always hopeless.* With my mother's cancer seemingly under control, our sleepless nights became easier.

For a time.

My mother's struggle grew more difficult when the summer breeze turned colder in 1996. As September leaves turned yellow and orange and began to fall, so did my mother. Even though it was diagnosed as stage one, her breast cancer quickly spread to her bones and her brain. After she began chemotherapy, strands of her red hair fell onto her silk pillowcase each night, until the day when her pillow was bare and all her hair had been washed down the drain. My mother then wore a light pink cotton cap every day, which she became attached to, even if it was just a cap. If it made her happy, it meant the world to us.

The ensuing complications of her cancer included shingles that caused her to scream in agony in a way we had never before heard as her children. When the shingles began, and if we were home, my siblings and I would scream along with her, one of us holding both of her hands, as the other set the three-minute egg timer, in the hope of drowning out her pain by the sound of our more powerful lungs.

As was her way, after the screaming was over, my mother would give us that reassuring smile that she would get over this hurdle, too.

My mother experienced every wretched side effect of cancer. Blood clots on one of her lungs and on her left leg caused her to be hospitalized for ten days in October at St. Peter's, the same hospital from which she had graduated nursing school. During her stay, my sisters and I came back to Albany, taking turns sleeping overnight in a small reclining chair next to her bed.

During the late night, she apologized to me when the lights came on in her room after she rang for the nurse. She would express such words of deep regret, thinking she had disturbed my sleep. What she didn't know was that since her diagnosis, I was being prescribed a potent level of Xanax in order to knock me out. She would apologize to the nurse for having to do such a simple thing as changing her disposable diaper.

My mother's struggle was valiant. In return, we could only shower her with our love, compassion, and commitment. The wrenching pain so visible in her eyes shattered pieces of our fearful hearts.

As fall turned into winter, we could do little for this gentle woman of quiet dignity.

We all felt robbed by my mother's impending death. My mother felt cheated as well. I knew how much she hated that notion of separation. She almost didn't marry my father because it had meant moving to Connecticut where he had then worked at an institution for delinquent boys. Marrying him, even if he was smart and handsome and she loved him, meant being far from her sister.

My parents met the summer of 1959. The child guidance clinic in Connecticut where my father was a counselor closed for a month every August, and unlike previous summers when he had taken a job as a waiter on Cape Cod during his time off, he decided to go home to Glens Falls. He spent most of his vacation swimming and waterskiing at Lake George.

One weekend, my mother was up from Albany visiting a friend from nursing school who had been at Glens Falls High School with my father. At the time, she was working in a doctor's office in downtown Albany, a position she had taken after caring for her grandmother for several months until her death around the time of, yet again, another holiday—Easter. After seven years, she had given up on marrying Rudy, a Filipino doctor. While he had asked her to marry him several times, he had never bothered to take the time to go out and buy her an engagement ring. As it turned out, he just liked coming over to watch her television set.

That Saturday afternoon, my father looked up from the book he was reading on the beach and saw his friend Barbara walking with a beautiful redhead. Barbara made the introductions, and John Carswell fell in love.

Within two months they were engaged, and within four they married. Even though Christmas had always been a season of loss for my mother, my father thought that perhaps by getting married at this time of year, she could grow to celebrate and enjoy the holiday. They married on the day after Christmas, 1959. My aunt Mary and my mother's childhood best friend Eleanor were her bridesmaids. My aunt wore a green taffeta gown, and Eleanor wore red.

Because it was Christmas, the banks of red and white poinsettias that graced the altar for Mass the day before were already in the church. They could take advantage of these flowers, cutting wedding costs considerably, and it would be a splendid affair.

My mother's father, sober—at least that day—came back into her life again, gave her away, and stood true to his word that he wouldn't touch a drink. Instead, he was the perfect host and father of the bride. One would have thought they had always been close. On and off the wagon throughout his life, he was one of the founders of Alcoholics Anonymous in Schenectady, New York.

Throughout all their years together, my father always thought of himself as my mother's Angel of Life. He was there to cheer her through painful holidays. He would comfort her as her children left to start their own lives. As for love, my father romanced her throughout her entire life. I can't imagine the shock and the pain he must have felt when she would plead with him during her most difficult times: John, please take me out into the fields and just shoot me.

Before her cancer took on monstrous proportions and left her in constant pain, my mother never failed to express her pure joy in spending time with her grandchildren. Even if she had to lie on the couch and just touch their heads, she saw her grandchildren as the repetitive image of my siblings and me when we were young. She now had five granddaughters—including a pair of identical twins, Maggie and Megan—with the same sun-bleached blond hair. Her then one grandson, John Carswell, had light brown hair just like Mandy's.

Her last Christmas, my mother rallied enough strength in her emaciated ninety-pound frame to dial the 1-800 number at the Disney Store. She placed an order for five Winnie-the-Pooh nightgowns and one set of Mickey Mouse pajamas. On Christmas Eve, right before my father read " 'Twas," Sarah and I helped my mother get up from the living room sofa, next to the Christmas tree. Then, supported by our strong arms, she walked over to the staircase where my nieces and nephew were sitting, one grandchild per step. They were all wearing her presents of whimsical sleeping attire, squealing in delight as they showed off for their grandmother, who just cupped her hands over her mouth in delight.

The cancer had spread to her eyes at this point, but she was able to squint and focus in on the sugarplum vision of these young children she so adored. This was a lovely fuzzy picture of the present, one that obviously brought up memories of the past, when her own five little ones awaited the reading of their favorite Christmas tale. Tears rolled down her cheeks.

There wasn't a day that passed since she had first learned of her cancer that she didn't say to my father, Oh John, you don't know how much I'll miss seeing my grandchildren grow up.

My mother faithfully crossed off every chemotherapy treatment on her calendar, making a bold *X* with her black Magic Marker as soon as she returned from the hospital. In February, however, her doctors stopped the treatments. They could do nothing more. As soon as he heard the news, my father left my mother in Aunt Mary's care and drove to St. Agnes Cemetery to buy two burial vaults inside a new mausoleum.

My family knew her death was near. Even so, we didn't think the day would come. Perhaps she had one week more, maybe two. Perhaps God would grant our wish for a miracle.

Then, each of us—her children, her husband, and her sister—had to let her know that we loved her so much that we could let her go and that she had our blessing to leave. That, in itself, is the hardest part of a child's relationship with her mother, a husband with his wife, and an older sister with her only, younger sister.

As for me, I had to break that pact that I had made when I was quite young to protect her always. I could not stand to see her suffer for another minute.

In preparation for the inevitable, my father called an emergency meeting of the whole family with the hospice workers the day before Easter. The night before, on Good Friday, my mother was very much present when she wished my sisters and me good night. The following morning, when we all woke up, after having slept on the floor in blankets we had placed next to her hospital bed, she said, Good morning, Sue, good morning, Mandy. And good morning, Sarah. She said it in that precise order. It was our birthright.

Precisely at 11 A.M., two lovely hospice volunteers gathered my extended family upstairs around my mother's bed and encouraged each one of us to speak directly to her, sharing our favorite memories. One by one, we approached her bed and held her graceful hands tightly in each of ours.

Jim and my sister-in-law, Kathie, along with my brother Bill and his wife, Ann Marie, thanked my mother for showing them how to be such loving and patient parents. They told her they would look to her as their guiding light and strive to be rewarded with the same love from their children, as my mother's six grandchildren, all under the age of five, grew up. They promised to always read their children stories at night and sing them the lullabies that my brothers still remembered from their childhood.

When it was Mandy's turn to speak, she said, This is going to be very hard for me, Mom, because I became the one most like you. I dress like you. I do arts and crafts like you. I became a first-grade teacher so that I could read to children and help them grow. All these things I learned from you. My sister then made a promise that when she married she would name her first daughter Elaine.

I think we were all a little nervous when Sarah took my mother's hand and confided a secret to her. Mommy, I've got something to confess, Sarah said. Do you remember those eyeglasses you bought me in sixth grade?

My mother nodded yes.

Well, I cheated on the eye exam because I wanted to look like Amy Carter.

And, as our mother had wished, Sarah promised to continue making plans for her wedding, three months away. She told my mother that when she had her own children, her grandchildren would come to know their kind, wonderful, and beautiful grandmother through the photographs of her and the remembrances that she clutched so dearly and close to her heart.

When I took my mother's hand, I spoke directly into her ear so that she could hear me clearly. I said, Mom, it seems we've only had you too short a time. I never thought the day would come without always having you here. I worried about this my entire life, and it doesn't make sense. Maybe this is about losing your mother when she was so young—and maybe she wants you with her now. Perhaps it's time for you to share special moments alone with her. You might have tried to hide it, but I always knew how much you missed your mother.

Shortly after the hospice workers left, I noticed how my mother started gurgling like a baby. Her only audible words were a quiet, yes, yes. Her head, still adorned with her favorite pink cap, was tilted even that much more toward the sky. It was as though she were listening to a symphony of harps playing far away. As the day mellowed into evening, the once distant choir appeared to grow louder, at least in her ears.

At seven o'clock, my mother's light breath became even softer. We gathered around her bed as the wind outside grew wilder. Downstairs the fireplace crackled, and since no one was tending it, the embers slowly died, and now just the sound of slight whistles came in through the chimney. As we each touched a part of my mother with our hands, we circled her bed. My hands were on the bottom of her left arm, just above her hand, holding on to her flannel nightshirt with its light blue daisy pattern. I had bought it for her just the day before at Lord & Taylor because it was manufactured by a company named Elaine and its logo was stitched onto the back, now pressing against my mother's neck.

Go, please go, we all said in a chorus to her, trying to help usher our mother, wife, and sister off to the band of angels we knew were waiting to escort her away from her pain.

It's okay for you to leave us. We'll look after one another just as you always looked over us.

At seven thirty-five—five minutes into *Jeopardy!*, her favorite game show, which played silently in the background on the TV—my mother let out her most powerful sigh that day. It was her last breath.

When we kissed her good-bye on her now still, soft pale cheek, it was my father who said, Good night, Sweet Princess. You will never be forgotten.

After I kissed my mother on her forehead, crying as I said good-bye for the last time, I immediately wanted something to hold to remind me of her. I walked over to the bookcase that was in front of her bed and took her copy of *Little Women*, which she had had since she was a little girl. I also took her talking Elmo doll, which I had given to her as a Christmas present. I had paid four hundred dollars for the little red puppet: Elmo was the most wanted toy of Christmas 1996. But when my mother had said she wanted one, I would have scoured the earth to find him. Instead, I took a taxi and found Elmo in Queens. When he was placed in my arms by the young couple who owned him but needed the money to buy Christmas toys for their own children, I embraced that toy in a fiercely possessive way, like I never had as a child.

My mother had lost her ability to smile around Thanksgiving, and although she couldn't laugh along with Elmo, I couldn't help but notice how she wouldn't stop pressing his belly to hear him giggle hysterically, especially when my nieces and nephew were present.

In the moments following my mother's death, I wasn't able to linger upstairs as the rest of my family did. I couldn't pretend it was simply okay to sit there and watch her, while waiting for the mortician to come and take her away in a black station wagon, zipped up in a heavy black plastic bag. When they finally arrived at our house, my father walked behind her body as it was taken down the stairs, past the kitchen table, and out of the house. He stood in the snow as the station wagon drove away. He could no longer be her Angel of Life, nor was he any longer his own mother's special angel, either. She had passed away in her sleep just three months before.

It seemed my grandmother's death, at the age of ninety-one, was inevitable. My mother's death seemed cruel and unfair.

Once I went downstairs, I never went back up. Instead, I made my way to the sliding glass back door and looked up into the cold, jeweled sky. I imagined my mother was now Mary Poppins, opening up her umbrella from the ground, pressing it upward as she held on to it tight, the wind blowing behind her as she headed to another place.

> It carried her lightly so that her toes just grazed along the garden path. Then it lifted her over the front gate and swept her upwards towards the branches of the cherry-trees in the Lane. . . . For she went sailing on and on, up into the cloudy, whistling air, till at last she was wafted away over the hill and the children could see nothing but the trees bending and moaning under the wild west wind.
> —P. L. Travers, *Mary Poppins*

There she went. I imagined my mother flying past the Amtrak station, just below the hill, crossing the Hudson River, and heading in a straight path toward 60 Academy Road. Once there, I'm sure she paused and wished all the children in the cottages down below good night before turning north toward Troy.

When she arrived at St. Agnes, I assumed she looked down on the gravestones of her mother, father, and grandparents. Perhaps, by now, she was then regaining her ability to smile. My mother always loved family reunions.

The next morning it was my aunt Mary's birthday, and Easter Sunday.

Looking over my family's history—especially my mother's side—it's clear that we are a family that has most notably seen its share of sadness on the day before or the day after a major holiday. This especially applies to the holidays most closely associated with family.

Already, I was wondering.

What happens when your biggest fear comes true?

Do you choose to live?

Ladybug

The day of my mother's funeral, our family rode in two polished black limousines. The streets of Albany were iced over from the unseasonably late falling snow. Like my mother when we headed to Mass on Christmas Day, no one spoke a word.

When we finally reached the church, the Carswell family, minus one, filed solemnly into the two front pews.

After the service was over, I held my father's hand tightly for the first time I could remember since the day he had walked me to my first day of school at the Girls Academy twenty-seven years earlier. Together we followed my mother's coffin from the church, the first two behind her casket. When we reached the door, he stopped to greet some of the 250 mourners, while I continued in the footsteps of the pallbearers. I had been a pallbearer months before at my grandmother's funeral, but I didn't want to be one now. I wanted to make sure my mother made it safely inside the long gleaming hearse.

When the funeral director had shut the back door securely, I stepped over and wiped the frost-covered window clean with my glove. Flattening my palm against the darkened glass, I quietly spoke to my mother. I wanted to keep her company until the hearse pulled away.

I watched as my mother left, until she was no longer in my sight.

The week after my mother's death, my father and I flew to Santa Fe, as I took a two-week bereavement leave from work. When we got there, I signed an employment contract to become an executive editor at a different publishing house. I wanted a change after working three years as a senior editor at a large publishing house that had lured me away from *People* magazine with double my salary after working there for six years. I didn't know where I was going with my career. Bigger titles just sounded better, so I jumped at new opportunities without thinking it would be nice to settle in somewhere. I wasn't a settled person, how could I ever be a settled employee? I just tried to act that way. When I was in Santa Fe, however, I decided that when I returned to Manhattan, I would give my editorial director my notice. I also needed to move on because I couldn't understand her not being understanding to me when I asked for more time off so that I could be around my mother as she lay dying. This woman had said to me, We all have deadlines to keep. And we all have our problems, Sue. I have to keep switching nannies.

Not too many people play golf in New Mexico that time of year, but we didn't mind the solitude as we whacked balls around the course, paying little attention to the location of the holes, let alone par. Instead, we knocked our white balls into the thick shrubbery that lined the course, or in the direction of the tumbleweeds that raced along the fairways brown with dried-out grass.

At lunchtime, my father openly wept when he tried to squeeze mustard on top of his hot dog. At night, he cried himself to sleep. I knew this because I was trying to sleep myself in a bed ten feet away. But once again I couldn't sleep, despite the high level of my sleep medications, antidepressants, and anxiety pills, which my psychiatrist had increasingly raised the dosage of as my mother became more ill.

My mother didn't travel directly to St. Agnes Cemetery when she left me standing alone in the snow outside the church. Nor was she buried near the plot of her parents and grandparents. Many years ago, the day after the reunion of the Albany Home for Children, I had told my mother the story of Irving Coffin, Bob Wygant's friend who died without a coffin and was buried on the adjoining side of the cemetery where my mother now lived. She interrupted me at one point, opening up in a way she had never before done. She said, My mother only had a marker until my grandparents died. That's when she finally got a headstone. When my father died after they found his body in a gutter, he was buried there along with all three of them. But his name was never etched into the dark brown headstone. Mary and I really should see to that. But then again, I don't think that would matter to him. It seems to me, he's exactly where he always wanted to be. He's finally sleeping with my mother. He's by her side. I think he's made peace with himself.

We sat in silence for several minutes. Then she spoke again. Her voice was firm. I'm sorry, Sue. Please keep going. But when I die, I want to be cremated. I don't want anyone thinking about my bones in the cold. I always want to be warm. Promise me you will remember that.

Precisely a month after her death, my family gathered at a new large indoor mausoleum at St. Agnes. My mother was reduced to ashes and sealed inside a jade-green marble urn with a narrow gold band. At its base were her initials, E.A.C.

After we said prayers, instead of looking down as most people do when coffins are lowered into the ground, we looked upward as a small crane operated by a uniformed cemetery worker lifted her small urn until it reached my parents' plot, E-19. My mother was then placed inside her crypt. I had bought the space above her two weeks before. When I die I will be buried in F-19. We will be eternal bingo balls together.

In the months after my mother was first diagnosed with breast cancer, I resorted to a variety of myths I had heard since childhood to make her well. I picked up pennies on the streets of Manhattan or left behind on taxi floors and clutched them tightly in the palm of my hand as I closed my eyes and prayed that this was the lucky penny that would make my one wish—that my mother would live—come true. I took care to stay away from cracks in the sidewalks, and if by chance a ladybug should land on me, I would blow it away with a strong gust of my breath and make a wish. I honestly believed that promises of childhood fables could prove true. You become that way when you're desperate.

For as long as I could remember, when my mother had so ingrained these impressions into my young mind, I deeply fell for the illusion of their promise.

But my world fell apart when her cancer returned. These beacons of hope, these powerful talismans, began to whisper away like a candle slowly losing the wick of its once bright flame.

Suddenly, the power of the penny, cracks in the sidewalk, and the ladybug became all that much more palpable in my mind, which was now clouded by misery and confusion. In a feverish pitch, if a penny was overlooked, or if I had forgotten about that damnation of cracks on sidewalks, or if a ladybug passed by unnoticed and I had lost the opportunity to make my wish, what would ensue would be the worst of days, creeping into sleepless nights and the haunting hollow sound of my cries in the darkness.

I left the fairy tales and nursery rhymes of my youth behind that Easter Eve of 1997. I tucked them away in a treasure chest no longer meant for me. I stopped paying attention to pennies and sidewalk cracks. Rather, I made it a point to spitefully slam my boot heel down onto crevices whenever I passed by. As for the ladybug, one landed on my hand and bit me in Santa Fe, and then boldly flew away. Perhaps it was disenchanted that I had ignored its purpose as the wish carrier.

As far as I was concerned, the one wish that I had prayed for since I was a little girl had not been served by these fairy tales. It seemed to me that their illusions were bereft of any real power and that they should be left for the young and innocent.

The June after my mother died, my sister Sarah married Walter Heffernan, a great guy who had just lost his father to cancer, and a sister a year before when she was only forty. Their wedding had been scheduled long before my mother's cancer had spread, and it had been her wish that nothing be changed.

My sister's wedding felt like a day that we had to get through, not a day that we were celebrating. Everyone tried hard for Sarah, but even she had to put on a face that belied a deep sadness. My mother's absence was everywhere. My parents had danced on the same floor at the Crooked Lake Hotel, nestled between Albany and the Berkshires, on their wedding day thirty-seven years before. The only other occasions we went to Crooked Lake as we were growing up was for celebrations, or on the way home from skiing at Jiminy Peak in nearby Hancock, Massachusetts.

During the ceremony, held outside by the lake, I avoided looking into the faces of my family and my mother's favorite friends lest I break into tears as Sarah and Walter exchanged their vows.

Toward the end of the service, as Sarah was lighting a candle in memory of our mother, a ladybug landed on the taper in her hand. As children, we often raced around the backyard, looking for ladybugs. We all had our own jars labeled with our names with holes punched in their lids to catch the ladybugs so we could bring them to her. We knew it would make her happy when she released them, smiling as she made her wishes.

I felt my chest relax as I released the tension in my jaw—the sole force that had held my sobs inside. Perhaps my mother was letting us know that she was there after all, in the form of a tiny red insect with a shiny round shell, her favorite magical creature.

I gave the toast at my sister and brother-in-law's wedding reception that night. I have become the one my family turns to whenever we want to talk about our memories and speak optimistically and yet perhaps full of nonsense about the future.

As the evening moved on, I looked out across the dance floor and got caught up in the sight of this new young love twirling before me. Throughout the evening, my father danced with my sisters, Aunt Mary, and me. Forever the dancer, he made sure that the widows in his circle of friends were not left sitting on the sidelines.

Not too many members of my family could make it through that one song, "Misty," when the band started playing. It had been my parents' wedding song.

On my own would I wander through this wonderland alone . . .

I looked around the room, alive with celebration, in search of my father and finally spotted him standing by himself off in the corner near the bar, tears once again welling up in his eyes. We had honestly believed my mother would have conquered her breast cancer in time for Sarah's wedding, that my parents would be the ones dancing to their song.

This remembrance of her tore us apart again, but she was always tearing us apart these days.

Keeping in mind that my mother would have wanted us all to be happy for Sarah on her wedding day, I went over to my father and asked him to dance.

I get misty just holding your hand

My father spent the rest of the evening dancing with, among other widows, Helen O'Hanlon, a longtime friend of my parents and his favorite dancing partner even when my mother was alive. Although my mother liked to dance, my father so enjoyed dancing that, had he not become a social worker, he might have preferred to work for Arthur Murray. On any occasion involving a band, my father was the first person to step out onto the floor. And in the middle of any party, my siblings and I always expected him to come running through the front door of our home, change his drenched shirt, and race back to the party. My mother could hardly match his dancing adrenaline. The only other person in their group who could keep up with my father was Mrs. O'Hanlon.

My mother and Gene O'Hanlon could often be found sipping cocktails while seated at a big round table and enjoying the company of their friends.

Helen also knew a great deal about what my father was experiencing, as she had lost her husband six years earlier to Lou Gehrig's disease. We had grown up alongside the five O'Hanlon children, who lived two blocks over, and my brother Jim had escorted her youngest daughter, Cindy, to his junior prom.

This had been a difficult night for all of us, but I was glad to see my father begin to relax and have some fun. He found it unbearable to live in the home he and my mother had moved into together. And he also missed his own mother. My father had become an insomniac, and his allergies had worsened—due to stress and his broken heart.

On weekends he played golf with his newest friend, Jeff Fairwell, the plot salesman at my mother's cemetery, when he wasn't driving back to Glens Falls to wrap himself in the company of his old high school friends.

A month later, my father called to tell me he had begun seeing Helen.

I wondered.

Had he forgotten my mother so soon?

How could he be thinking about a future when I wasn't even convinced I wanted one?

Where the Pink Dogwood Grows

I hardly ever went back to Albany. The streets, the stores, the little shop where she bought lottery tickets. Every place I went reminded me of my mother. As much as I enjoyed seeing my nieces and my nephew, it became increasingly emotionally debilitating for me to be there. I felt paralyzed. A black blanket enveloped my body.

On that first Christmas without my mother, I went back to 60 Academy Road, essentially to visit a tree.

My father dropped me off. He promised to pick me up an hour later. After he retired, and especially after my mother died, my father hardly ever went back to the grounds of the former Albany Home for Children.

I walked through the long entranceway, and then cut across the slope in our old backyard and made my way toward the bay window where I once lay on the sofa and watched the Christmas Walk of the Children. When I first peered inside, I noticed that the painting of an Amish family heading toward church in their horse-drawn wooden wagon, which once hung over our fireplace, had been replaced by a poster of a leopard. It was tacked onto the wall. Tacked. My mother would have been horrified.

After I turned away from the bay window, I saw that the trees in my backyard were now taller than the telephone lines. They completely blocked my view—except for one small dogwood sapling planted the previous summer.

The sidewalk where I had seen the Home kids make their annual Christmas Walk was gone, its place now occupied by the administration building joined by a walkway to Parsons Cottage. Still, I recalled how that sight once brought me such sadness every Christmas morning when I thought about how tough it must have been not to have a mother to share your excitement as you opened your gifts.

Now I knew just how it felt. Her death did not bring me closer to my father. I felt like an orphan myself.

I walked away from our old house in the direction of the little tree, plowing my way through the four-foot pile of untouched snow with my boots. As I trudged along, I looked to my right at the cottages and thought about all those sirens that had called my father from his bed and destroyed my sleep as well.

I saw no one outside. It was noon, yet it seemed as though everyone was still asleep. Most of the children living there now went home for Christmas, and those who stayed on campus were inside the cottages, not walking to the gymnasium to celebrate the day.

As I turned to the left, I could see that no one was home at the old cottages, either. The Junior College of Albany was on its winter break.

When I neared the new tree I imagined that its tiny branches, encased in ice so that they sparkled like dazzling crystal, could be swept away by a tempest wind. I desperately wanted to protect this dogwood so that its delicate blooms could open come spring. As I reached its side, I wrapped my arms completely around the little tree and hugged it, almost in the same way I had hugged Elmo the night my mother died. The tree and I shivered in the bitter cold. Then I knelt down and shoveled the snow with my mittens until I completely uncovered the black-and-gold plaque below in order to read it for the first time:

IN MEMORY OF ELAINE CARSWELL
WHO, IN THIS HOUSE, RAISED HER FAMILY,
WELCOMED HUNDREDS OF VISITORS AND STAFF,
AND EXEMPLIFIED THE MISSION AND VALUES
OF PARSONS CHILD AND FAMILY CENTER

Before I left this living testament to my mother's life, I snapped off a small twig from my mother's pink dogwood and I placed it in my back pocket.

A little more than a year after my mother's death, my father and Helen were married. Not long afterward, they moved into a large new home in Slingerlands, the Albany suburb I had once dreamed our family would move to together back when I was in high school.

The wedding was too soon for me.

When my aunt Mary received her invitation, she didn't bother to respond, vowing never to speak to my father again. My father had proposed to Helen on St. Patrick's Day, and they married on July 4. My aunt couldn't fathom how he could defame my mother's memory on her two favorite holidays—the only ones not associated with tragedies in our family.

Blind from macular degeneration, my aunt now spent her days with only her memories, sitting in her rocking chair on her enclosed porch, eyes shut, lost in thought about her sister and her husband. She remembered only the pictures of the past. She could not see the pictures of today, nor would she have ever wanted to see an image of my father kissing anyone but her sister.

As the wedding date neared, I told my boss at the second publishing house I worked at—where I specialized in nonfiction pop-culture books—that I needed to go away, as my father was getting married. Instead of attending the ceremony, however, I checked into the Topnotch Spa in Stowe. On his wedding day, I was getting a Swedish massage, a body wrap, and a salt scrub.

Many of my friends had told me repeatedly, in an effort to make me understand my father better, that widowers who had the happiest marriages always marry again, often within the year. But I was still mourning and grieving; nor did I care for celebrations. My mother haunted my medicated dreams.

There was one that always seemed to wake me up with a shock, every time its rotation came around.

There we are, my mother and me, sitting in the bleachers of my brothers' old high school way beyond the fields of the Home. We are watching them play football. My mother is cheering Jimmy and Billy on. I am eating popcorn. But then there is halftime and it is a wedding. My mother looks through her binoculars to get a closer view to see who is getting married. I already know the answer. I explain to my mother why my father is marrying again and her tears from those blue eyes just flow as she watches my father kiss his new bride and smile brilliantly. I turn to her and take her hand and tell her we should probably leave. I take her home to her new apartment in downtown Albany, where she lives alone and works someplace but won't tell me where. The next day I come by to visit her, and she's not there. After days and weeks of trying to find her, my mother finally makes her way walking down the street to her apartment building. She carries two bags of groceries. I ask her why she is never home, and she replies, I want to be by myself. Please stop following in my steps. When I'm ready, I'll come and see you.

But she never does.

Later that night, I reluctantly phoned my father and struggled with my words as I offered unenthused congratulations. I certainly hadn't prepared a wedding toast for this occasion. He asked where I was, and I replied Vermont. He laughed, seemingly embarrassed, and said, That's where Helen and I are heading for our honeymoon.

Luckily, we would be on opposite ends of the state.

Tell Me

That first year and a half without my mother, I felt like hibernating. I wished I could have been a bear, sleeping in a dark cave. I wished I could have been Rip van Winkle and woken up after decades had past. Perhaps by then my pain would have lessened.

The simplest task was a struggle. Even during the time of my breakdown in law school, I had never fallen so low with my emotions, nor had I ever felt this suicidal. It wasn't taking pills that worried me, or jumping out of windows; it was always about subways and whether I would jump into their path. When that idea was in my mind, I would flee the subway and catch a cab to get to work.

I was now seeing my psychiatrist several times a week, and she even checked up on me by phone throughout the day. I don't think my psychiatrist thought I would make it through my mother's death.

The week before my mother passed away, when I had been offered an executive editor position, perhaps I made the change too quickly. I wasn't myself. I couldn't think clearly, and my emotions were raw. After about a year and a half, I was summarily fired for failing to meet expectations. That's all that was said. My boxes and I were out the door, going back to my apartment where I lived alone, except for my dogs. I was horrible about relationships. No one mattered to me. My mother had been enough.

Between my mother's death, my father's remarriage, and losing my job, I didn't think I could sink much lower. I took my sleeping bag out of the closet and unrolled it next to the Baltimore card table my mother left me, then lay down on the red Oriental rug where Mandy had once cried on that day she was called offal. The rug now covered the floor in the foyer near the front door of my West Village apartment. This table had been my mother's first major purchase when she started her career as a nurse, bought with her inheritance from her great-aunt Amanda.

On this makeshift bed, I was only about twenty feet away from the sounds emanating from the elevator throughout the long night. Once again, I felt safe knowing somebody else was awake, even if they were unknown neighbors or guests in my building.

In the morning, I would discover that during the course of the night my two dachshunds, Edith and Maude, had jumped down from my bed and joined me on the floor. Like Marnie so long ago, they wiggled under my covers and nestled like badgers against my legs to keep me company. Even dogs can sense suffering.

I didn't need an alarm clock. Maude, the older dachshund by nine months, started licking my face at about seven o'clock. And that's how I began my workday—even if I was without work.

To busy myself and build a façade that I had a purpose, I walked out the door at 9 A.M. and headed uptown. I had decided to become a journalist again. Although I had no assignment from anyone, I decided that thinking back on my childhood and writing about my mother might somehow heal my emotional wounds, so that I could move on, too.

During the day, I shouldered my laptop and took the subway (on days that

weren't consumed by suicidal thoughts) up to 42nd Street and the main
branch of the New York Public Library on Fifth Avenue. Inside my new
office—the recently restored Rose Main Reading Room, a palatial hall with a
cloud-covered ceiling to rival Michelangelo's Sistine Chapel—I plugged in
my computer and set up my work space, midway down the back of one of the
long, polished mahogany tables, always parking myself on straight-backed
wooden chair Number 268. There, I typed in my rambling thoughts.

I imagined the regulars—for the most part, homeless people who chose to
spend their days indoors rather than on the streets—were my co-workers: the
woman who sported batteries entangled in her long, matted hair to fend off
beams from alien satellites; Ernie, who brought his luggage with him every
day and read the *New York Post* front to back, and back to front; and the
bearded man in the ratty tweed jacket who could have passed for a professor
were it not for the aluminum foil that stuck out from under his clothing.

I missed my mother more than words could express. When I imagined her
alive and so vivid, I often found myself putting my head down on the library
table. Within minutes, a security guard would come over, tap me on the shoulder, and say with authority, Ma'am, there is no sleeping allowed here.

I would look up, tears in my eyes, and ask, What about crying?

When the library bell sounded at 4:45 P.M., signaling the end of our so-
called workday, my co-workers and I headed out and down the massive marble stairs to go on our way to our next engagement.

At night, back in my apartment, I would sometimes telephone the people
who once lived or worked at the Albany Home. I wanted their help so that I
could better conceptualize and understand my backyard. I phoned Jodie, now
thirty-five and living in a trailer in Florida. She was divorced, after what had
been an abusive marriage.

After I introduced myself, Jodie responded, Well, this is a shock. We were
never allowed to speak to you *Carswell* kids. And your dad, well, he was supposed to be *God,* or else. But I didn't give a shit.

Jodie and I spent more than an hour talking on the phone about those
years so long ago when we once shared the same backyard. She told me how
she hated everybody and that she was hell on wheels. Jodie had lived in
twenty-one foster homes and three institutions before being sent to the
Home. She said that when she arrived there, she just wanted her freedom,
which finally explained to me her unending urge to flee.

She added, I used to love to swing at the Home. I would fly into the sky and pretend I was an eagle. That was really the only time I felt free. Whenever I tried to escape, I ended up tranquilized. The serum made me feel stupid and confused.

Then she asked, Did your mom ever tranquilize you as a kid?

No, I answered, Perhaps she should have.

When I asked Jodie if she ever received the Judy Blume books I had mailed to her, she responded almost in horror. I would never read Judy Blume or any of that shit. I like true crime stories—you know, stories like Ted Bundy and *Helter Skelter*. Right now I'm reading *Where the Bodies Are Buried*. Have you read it? It's a paperback about killer kids. Fascinating . . . Can't wait to finish it, because then I'm going to start another book about an eighteen-wheeler serial killer and severed relations—if you know what I mean.

I learned a lot about Jodie in the course of our conversation. She had been raped as a child by one of her relatives. Jodie met her biological mother for the second time since she was placed at the Home, in 1979, at her sister's wedding. Her mother had never once gone to visit her at the Home. When she first laid her eyes on the woman, Jodie immediately walked over and inquired, What did you ever do for me? Then Jodie balled up her fist and punched her mother in the face.

If she was tough as a child, she was even tougher now. She explained how she could blow up a car without leaving a trace, and that she could pick up her phone and have someone taken out just like that. But for all her bravado, when she spoke of her deceased adoptive mother, Nancy, Jodie grew quiet and, for the most part, cried. She missed the woman she considered her real mother.

My father had said of Jodie's new mom the day I met them both in Aruba, before my mother died, that she was one of the kindest women he had ever met.

Subsequently Jodie admitted, When I was adopted, I gave my mother one hard time. But she never lost her patience with me. When I learned she had cancer, I was scared she was going to leave me, so I walked out the door first. I joined the National Guard, but I couldn't stay away. I needed to be there for her as she had been there for me. She was the greatest mom. Your mom was awfully nice, too.

Whenever I tried to turn the conversation toward what she was doing now, Jodie always steered me back to her mother.

Although Nancy had now been dead for eight years, Jodie said that she had never been able to get over it, that she was still trying to pick herself up. As our conversation neared its end, Jodie told in lavish detail how she and her mother traveled to Camden Hills State Park in Maine every summer for two weeks' vacation. She added, When I die, I want to go back there. I want to be cremated and I want my ashes to be spread all around the park so I can feel free. I think my mom would like that.

She then asked me for a favor. Would you please tell your dad to remember that?

Like a game of telephone, I would track down numbers or an address of a former Home kid through talking to people who used to work at the Albany Home for Children. They were always happy to help one of John and Elaine's kids. Sometimes I would travel to spend weekends at their houses. I spent a long weekend with Mr. and Mrs. Cordes, who now lived in Maine: Cammy and Brad were married and had children of their own. It was hard looking at Mrs. Cordes because she looked like my mother's blond-haired twin. The two longtime friends had taken pride in emulating each other's clothing style. Once, I flew to Chicago to meet with my father's former boss through all my childhood, Mr. Millard, who was now retired and enjoying his condominium in Acapulco six months out of the year. I met with our former lifeguard of four years who then went on to work in the school. All of them and many more (whom I've left unlisted for reasons of privacy) gave me varying insights into their work at the Home and stories of the kids whom they cared for.

I finally learned more about Ryan from where my mother left off when she told me the story about how she bought him ice cream cones after attending his so-called memorial service. Ryan left the Albany Home for Children when he was fourteen. He was discharged to a group home and, like Bob Wygant, left to pursue his dreams when he was eighteen and had aged out of the system. But his ending wasn't like Bob's. In his twenties, Ryan gave up on at least my mother's hope of him starting his own family and decided to return to the arms of the one woman who loved him the most. Ryan finally figured out a way to fly to heaven in order to meet his mother, so that he wouldn't be an orphan ever again. He put a gun to his head, fired, and left his disturbing world behind.

And I learned that Eric, who was a test for how a Home kid might fare at the Boys Academy, had experienced a fate similar to Ryan's. After Eric left the

Home, he was arrested for a minor incident. He ended his misery with a noose he had made from the jail's stiff white sheets.

As for Sean, who couldn't seem to be cured of his proclivity for wearing dresses and playing with Barbie dolls, he was now working at an Albany mall in a women's clothing department. Like my mother's longtime hairdresser, he was gay and happy.

One day I spent the late afternoon with too-tall Tom, who had once frantically waved to his mother in a parking lot during the Christmas season when he was then living at the Home. Tom eventually left to go back to his real home, and he was so happy to be with his mother again. He could never forget how much he had missed her. As we sat outside on the deck of his pool in Albany, he told me how he had fallen off a chair when he was a young kid, and all of a sudden his thoughts were just slower. His parents didn't know what to do with him and they thought that living at the Home might cure him, and make his thoughts quicker again. Tom said that he felt he left the same way he came in, but he tried to hide his slowness from his parents by being diligent at what he did. He learned to concentrate on small things, even if they were complicated. When he had moved on to a new school, he was fascinated by the electronics of a television set and became a master at fixing them, so much so that all his teachers brought Tom their broken TV sets. And then Tom realized he loved the artistry behind making perfect cabinets, so he became a masterful cabinetmaker known for his perfection in detail and the special finish he used on them. As we drank a daiquiri by his pool, I realized he was the first Home kid I met whom I felt I could really talk to; who lived on my side of the fence. But even he admitted, he didn't know too many success stories. As he said, You just have to accept people for who they are—not send them away like a broken record to be fixed by others. As the evening moved on, his handsome blond-haired boyfriend came home, looked at me, and said to Tom, Does she know—to which he replied with a smile—No, you tell her, if you want.

Tom's boyfriend then said to me, I grew up at the Albany Home too.

And then we all just laughed.

When I thought about Jodie and Ryan, and Eric, and not someone who was able to adapt to society, like Tom, I finally concluded that contrary to my childhood presumption that they were just like my brothers and sisters and me—only without families—the children who grew up at the Albany Home had little in common with us. Our differences ran far deeper than how we were parented.

While I had my share of emotional problems, I had become a functioning and, although I was currently unemployed, college-educated, professional adult, unlike most of the contemporary children from the Home. Even when I was weighed down by emotional burdens, I had the resources and medications to move on.

Still, somehow I needed to find my way. I just wondered if I would be able to hang in and not give in as Ryan had. My salvation and my dignity came from my telling other people that I was writing a book about my mother. This made me feel less like a failure. On those rare trips to Albany in search of information about my past, I usually spent a couple of hours visiting my father and Helen, but I always stayed overnight with my aunt. I simply wasn't ready to stay in their home yet.

Helen had always been so nice to my siblings and me when we were kids. You never forget the nice ones. When I was growing up, I thought Mrs. O'Hanlon was a lot like my mother. She obviously loved her children dearly, and it was a love that was returned. It seemed easy for Helen and me to sit at the kitchen table and bring alive the memories of my mother. Whenever her name came up, however, my father nervously coughed and walked away.

For the most part, their new house was furnished in a strange fusion of half O'Hanlon, half Carswell memorabilia. No pictures of my mother were visible in the house—except for one family photo, taken in the early 1990s, that hung on the wall next to the guest room bathroom. Most photos from both families were packed away downstairs in the basement in storage. At their home, I didn't feel like I belonged.

Ever since our bereavement trip to Santa Fe, the only time my father and I ever spent time alone together was when he drove me to my aunt Mary's house. He always dropped me a block away since she didn't want to know that his car was parked outside. I now felt like I was from a broken family.

Every time I tried talking to my father directly about my mother, he refused to answer my questions and quickly changed the subject. The only comment he made was, I had to move on.

My father lost his mother when he was sixty-five. My siblings and I lost our mother when we were in our twenties and thirties. My father could not compare the weight on our scales of grief. He even admitted to me that he had that fault.

I was obviously closer to my mother than to my father. I suppose we all were. Sometimes I wondered if we weren't paying for that now.

When my siblings and I called home from college, or, later, when we lived in our own homes, my father rarely answered the phone, and when he did, each of us would say, Oh, hi, Dad, is Mom there? Calling home wasn't the same anymore because it wasn't really our home.

Still, through my difficult year after losing my job, my father was unwavering in his support as I tried to re-create the story of our backyard. He helped me find numerous children and former staff members who might talk to me about their experiences either living or working at the Albany Home.

My father was the one who spent weeks tracking down Jodie for me, calling a chain of former employees from the Home to get her telephone number. But whenever I asked him direct questions about my mother, who was so important to the story of my backyard and all those years they shared together, he would inevitably close down. Still, he did think about my questions, and I knew he did this because several days later, after returning to Manhattan, I would invariably receive a lengthy and elegant response from him about my mother by way of e-mail.

Apparently, this was the only way that he could deal with his grief.

My father and I had a long way to go.

But then one day he showed up unexpectedly, and I finally saw how much he missed her, too. That mattered.

Good Soles

Whenever I had come home from college or New York City and my weight had increased, my mother used to say, Sue. You've lost weight. Her words made me feel good, so I felt no need to go on a diet. At her death, I was a size fourteen. Two years after her death, I was a size sixteen, period. If clothes that size didn't fit me, then it was the clothes that were mislabeled. I didn't think of myself as out of shape because I had a gym club membership, even if I didn't go. I didn't have many mirrors in my apartment; nor did I have a scale. Only when I was almost strangled to death by a bacon string in law school did I fall to my mother's perfect size ten. She had loved it when I put on her slacks. John, look at Sue. She is so *thin*.

On a blustery cold Sunday morning nearly the second anniversary of my mother's death, I was eating a bagel and butter as I lazed about on my sofa staring at *The New York Times*. I was mesmerized at a full-page colored advertisement. It was an invitation to walk sixty miles, from Bear Mountain—near West Point—to Central Park at the end of August 1999 to raise money for breast cancer early detection, education, and awareness. By doing something "big, bold, and inspiring," the copy read, some forty thousand women a year wouldn't have to die from the disease that killed my mother. Other daughters wouldn't have to lose theirs.

Something about the photograph touched me. There was the all-too-familiar pink ribbon—breast cancer's signature reminder—as well as a shot of an empty, endless highway that appears to join the blue sky as it headed for the distant fleecy clouds. Another photo showed a sea of blue tents, side by side in a mobile city to house the two thousand or more participants over three days, and, finally, there was a picture of a pair of untied sneakers. This last image of the simple, well-worn shoes looked similar to the numerous pairs my mother had worn over her years.

The sneakers in the ad were meant to be filled, and I dialed the breast cancer organization's number, even if the notion of walking was the antithesis of me. Walking was my mother's sport.

When I was young, my mother would walk down the street to meet my sisters and me after school. She always stood there in the parking lot—arms outstretched just waiting to pull us into her heart. At night, she took long walks with my father, either on Academy Road or in the quiet streets where they lived before she died.

When we grew older and came home for a weekend stay, one request from my mother was certain: Please join me for a walk. She always spoke with excitement and hopefulness.

Mandy always said, Yes. Sarah usually replied, Mom, I'm going out. And I always shrugged and gave her a variation on the same line time and again. Walking is boring. Besides, there's a hill.

Several weeks after I registered for the walk, I received a breast cancer walk T-shirt—noting I was a participant—and an official walker's handbook. This included tips on aerobic conditioning and goal setting in order to get ready for the walk, which would involve traveling over a combination of public streets, highways, and hiking trails. I immediately put on the T-shirt and wore it to bed.

As for the manual, I peeked through it, saw drawings of proper stretching exercises, and read with dismay about how anyone caught consuming alcoholic beverages could be expelled from the walk. The tome also urged us to begin doing training walks, even if the sixty-mile walk was five months away. It suggested that we talk at regular intervals with our assigned personal walking coach, attend a shoe fitness clinic, go to a pitch-a-tent expo, and learn tips on fund-raising. Every walker needed to collect a minimum of eighteen hundred dollars in donations in order to participate. The handbook recommended that walkers consider throwing a party as a means of raising cash. I always enjoyed planning parties. I figured I could get in shape a month or so before the walk.

I can't begin to imagine what my friends thought when they received my invitation to a cocktail fund-raising party meant to pull at their hearts as well as their wallets.

Sue, walking sixty miles? Who's going to carry her?

The card—cast in a light pink and purple background—was a photo of Jimmy, then three, and me, then two, our blond heads shining under the Cape Cod sky as we clutched our mother's knees and pulled her forward to walk with us along the sand.

Inside it read:

Every twelve minutes a woman dies from breast cancer. On March 29, 1997, at 7:35 P.M., my mother, Elaine, was one of them. From August 27–29, I will walk 60 miles from Bear Mountain to Manhattan to help raise money for breast cancer education and early detection. I will be just one daughter in a group of 2,000 walking for three days, remembering my mom and hoping that my friends will never see their mothers, daughters, or friends die from this wretched disease. I need your help.

I eventually raised five thousand dollars for my walk. With my sister Sarah and my sisters-in-law, Ann Marie and Kathie, also participating in the event—Mandy wasn't able to raise the money needed—we as a family, in memory of my mother, raised more than twelve thousand dollars. I liked the thought that some of the money would support a mobile mammogram bus that made an annual pilgrimage to the Amish community.

. . .

With the party over, I began my training in earnest. Or at least I began to seriously think about it. The next few Sundays, I headed up to Central Park by taxi and walked the strenuous 6.1-mile loop around the beautiful park. Then I hailed a cab for the three-mile ride back home. Once, in mid-July, I added a 1.58-mile walk around the Central Park reservoir, bringing my distance level up to 7.68 miles for one day.

Countdown. The walk was approaching in late August. I decided it was time to rest my feet and shop for supplies—like nourishing candy bars, lip balm, suntanning lotion, stylish changes of clothing, and PJs for nighttime when we walked around tent city, all the accoutrements I needed—which brought my luggage close to a hundred pounds. There was a thirty-five-pound-maximum luggage allowance. My giant red duffel bag looked more like a traveling apartment. Thank God a platoon of Ryder trucks, driven by some of the volunteers and crew, would be transporting my luggage each day to that night's camping site.

The evening before we set off northward by bus, Sarah—who had taken a train in from Boston—and I made a toast to getting through the walk alive as we sipped red wine at Il Cantinori, my favorite restaurant in the city. Sarah described in detail how the French had conducted studies concluding red wine was good for your heart. So we drank another glass before dining on excellent *gnocchi di patate con pomodoro e basilica.* Carbs are very important before an endurance event.

As I drowned my Tuscan bread in olive oil, Sarah asked me, Are you physically prepared for this? I considered my sister's question and then ordered chocolate *tartufo.*

Later that night as I tried to sleep, I panicked about what lay ahead. Suddenly, I felt like my childhood goldfish, Orange, who only knew about life swimming around a little bowl with a plastic tree and colorful pebbles before I innocently set him free into a giant wave washing ashore the Atlantic Ocean.

But mentally, I was hell-bent on walking every single one of those miles in memory of my mom. I had given her my word, even if they were in my nightly talks with her from my bedroom window.

DAY ONE

En masse, 1,838 of us showed up for the breast cancer walk on August 27—the day after my birthday, my third without my mother. Sarah, my sisters-in-laws, and I all stretched our legs at 7:30 A.M. under low-lying fog and the prediction of torrential rains, in front of the Bear Mountain Inn before the opening festivities began. *Professional stretching,* I thought as I looked around copying everyone else's techniques, which included stretching hips, calves, groin muscles, thighs . . . thirteen more than the simple one I had mastered, the toe-stretch.

Before we stepped off, walkers from as far away as Los Angeles and Holland, and ages seventeen to seventy-six, all with their own reasons for being there, joined hands, bowed our heads, and were asked to think of those who couldn't be there with us that day. And then my sister, sisters-in-law, and I cried.

When the walk began, seven women representing the survivor's circle—those who had passed the seven-year mark after being diagnosed with breast cancer—walked by us, leaving a space between each of them, signifying those who hadn't lived through their own battle with the disease. I don't think the four of us could escape the thought that my mother wasn't a walker in this crowd. She would have been one of pinks, one of the 142 walkers who wore her favorite color on their T-shirts and baseball caps, noting they had survived.

As I began my sixty-mile walk to Manhattan, I looked to the sky and imagined her sitting in her favorite beach chair, side by side with so many like her who hadn't made it but rather, smiled, clapped, and cheered us on.

A mile later, I had shin splints.

As we walked along on the highway's shoulder, every car, van, or truck that passed us blew their horns in support of our chain of solidarity. With each honk, we waved back or clenched our fists—full of pride for what we were doing. It was the first time I thought I was doing something that might alter my life and inspire me to have a meaningful future even if it meant without my mother. By midmorning, I was beginning to see women pulling off the road, standing in front of their cars, and clapping. Some even stood on their hoods cheering us on when we approached the first mile-long hill of the day. Many yelled, Thank you. Others simply cried. Perhaps they had been through their own hell before. Every time I saw those women, some young, others in their early sixties, the age my mother died, my aching feet kept moving. I forgot my physical pain, the growing soreness around my knees, and the sun beating down on my skin.

By late afternoon, Kathie and I made our way into the woods. Cool breezes whispering through the trees offered some relief. I could no longer see Sarah ahead of us. Normally, I could spot my tall sister in a crowd, but she had appeared especially quiet during lunch. Sarah was my mother's baby girl and she rarely spoke of her after she died. Right after Sarah signed up for the three-day walk, her mother-in-law was diagnosed with breast cancer. Perhaps these things weighed on her mind as the small wind pushed her forth so she walked alone.

We reached the state park that housed our mobile city that first night, Kathie and I checking in at about 4 P.M. A motherly, friendly woman at the desk looked up at me and said, You look like you need a hug. She leaned across the desk and gave me one.

By midnight, I finally went to sleep inside my blue tent that Sarah had pitched for me before I arrived, lulled by a symphony of tired snores and the patter of light rain on the tent tops. Noises made me feel comfortable, and helped me sleep. And pushing my boundaries physically obviously helped, too.

I had never done anything like this before. Instead of taking a simple twenty-minute stroll with my mother when she was alive, today I had walked 19.5 miles because of her death.

I still had forty miles to go before making it to Central Park, where I knew my brothers, Mandy, my brother-in-law, and my friends would be waiting.

DAY TWO

By 7:30 A.M. on Saturday, August 28, we left the state park parking lot for what would be our longest day: 22.5 miles.

I cursed the fact that I had ignored the weekly postcards instructing us to bring two pairs of broken-in sneakers. I had brought one pair, and mud from the previous night's wet campground was seeping through my soles before I even left the site.

As I stared down at my now squeaking brown sneakers, the reality of the walk smacked me in the face. As we approached the hill that Kathie and I had sweated out yesterday but would coast down today, I saw a young woman, barely in her twenties. I had heard through a press representative I had befriended that she had had a double mastectomy. With her were her mother and her sister. Her mother was rewrapping the elastic bandage around her daughter's sprained foot. She was walking the three-day event on crutches. She was walking—although barely—because she still could.

Too young, my mother would have said.

I needed to walk alone with my thoughts for the greater part of this day.

There were two main rules that all walkers had to agree to in order to participate in the event. The first was to always say, Passing, when overtaking another walker. The second rule was to always be kind.

On the second day, hundreds upon hundreds of faster and more prepared walkers say Passing to me. They also ask me how I am doing. A young man says hello and reminds me to drink plenty of Gatorade. As he passes, I see a picture of his mother with her dates pinned onto the back of his T-shirt.

By late morning I trek through the beautiful streets of Nyack, New York, past the Runcible Spoon Bakery where the owners have draped their canopy with pink ribbons in honor of our walk. They stand outside their shop and hand each of us pink ribbon sugar cookies as we walk by.

During the early afternoon, my steps are even slower. I get scared when we walk on the side of a dangerous highway, cars speeding past one after another. Although Sarah and Kathie had waited for me at lunch, they had gone ahead because the temperature was now in the high nineties and they wanted to get to the second night's camp at a quicker pace in order to take a cool shower. I no longer saw anyone I knew.

Sometimes I staggered and I felt my heart beat faster. I was nervous. My thoughts raced. A rumor passed back through the throng that a walker had been hit by a car. This turned out to be false, but I still imagined it happening to me.

My stride became a shuffle by the time I headed in to pit stop number five at mile 16.2. I walked like my mother did in her final days of chemo, when it took her forever to creep down the short hallway to the bathroom. At this stop, I finally broke down. I headed directly for the medical tent, where I asked for an ice bag and took a seat in a folding chair. I leaned my head downward and cried. I can't do this anymore, I whispered out loud but to myself. I just can't.

A doctor came over and placed the ice bag on the back of my neck, and wiped aloe and sunblock on my blistering face. I felt sick to my stomach. My knees were spent and my toes now numb. He suggested I get in the sweep van for the walkers who couldn't make it in order to get quickly to the night's campsite. He said there was no shame in doing that.

I was confused. How could I break a promise that I had made to my friends who gave me their generous donations—but more important, how could I break a promise to my mother?

Suddenly, I turned my head and saw Sarah being drenched by a volunteer. She was laughing as he sponged her neck with cold water. My sister had appeared out of nowhere. For over an hour, she and Kathie had been waiting for me to make it to this point. They had described me as best they could to the other walkers who had passed me, many of whom replied, She's coming. She's on her way.

Sarah glanced toward the medical tent, walked over, and stood beside me. What's wrong? she asked.

There's nothing right, I replied. Admitting I had met my limit.

But perhaps something about my crying said something more to her. Look down the long road that we're on, she said. Look as far as you can see.

I squinted and looked down a long avenue in suburban New Jersey. I saw red lights and cars.

Do you see Mom?

What? I was losing it, but I wasn't that far gone.

Mommy, she repeated. She's all the way down the street, way past all those red lights. I'm walking toward my hero and it's what you have to do, too, Sue. That way you'll finish this walk.

That said, I asked the doctor if he would wrap my knees in an Ace bandage and medical tape. He tried as best he could to bandage the bleeding blisters covering my feet. I slowly put my sneakers on and left my chair.

In my jumbled mind, I remembered what the opening speaker had said to all of us the morning before about how walking three days straight would examine the way we dealt with adversity. In the moments you feel like quitting, you will be faced with a choice. Each of those moments represents an opportunity to define yourself.

All I had to do was recall my mother's hell and I kept walking. As we walked down the long avenue with the sun growing hotter, I turned to my sister and said, I finally see Mom.

At almost 7:30 P.M. that night, to the thunderous applause of more than a thousand walkers lined up to greet us late walkers, Kathie, Sarah, and I finally walked down the second night's victory path in triumph.

When the other walkers looked at me, some started to cry. I looked that battered and bruised. My face was so burned and tears poured down from my eyes in a way that I had never even cried at my mother's funeral. The white tape around my knees was now dragging down around my sneakers. I was being held up by my shoulders by Sarah and Kathie. My sister-in-law Ann Marie, who had come more prepared than anyone, completing it as one of the top thirty walkers the previous day, suddenly broke from the crowd with a look of horror in her eyes. Ann Marie took Kathie's spot in order to try to anchor me with her rested shoulder. Film crews and photographers suddenly noticed me, too. It seems we made a good picture, of one walker's saga to complete an agonizing day.

What's wrong with her? What's wrong with her? someone from the medical team screamed at Ann Marie.

She needs triage, she screamed back.

As I near the medical tent, nurses now taking me in, everything becomes a blur. The check-in nurse takes one look at me and orders another nurse, Get her to a cot, *stat*. Get a backup ambulance.

Seconds later, a doctor is checking my vital signs. A coordinator is furiously looking for my medical papers. Ann Marie keeps saying gently, You'll be all right. I hear the sounds of ambulances coming and going. The woman who was brought in ahead of me now lies unconscious on a cot across from me. All around lie exhausted walkers blanketed in sheets of thermal foil. People are vomiting. And when I move my head to look the other way, my thin cot collapses.

Miraculously, I tune out the seeming carnage around me. I calm myself down because I do not want to go off in ambulances anywhere. I am capable of getting through things. I desperately think of quieter times in my life. I think of swimming in my old pool.

The walker's manual clearly stated that we should eat before we were hungry, and drink water before we were thirsty, otherwise—bonking would occur: The glycogen stored in the muscles would be depleted, resulting in disorientation and a loss of body control.

On my second day, I had seriously bonked. But I pulled through. After my pulse settled down an hour and a half later, I took an invigorating shower. The next day we had thirteen miles to go before reaching the finishing line in Central Park. When I woke the next morning, Sarah had placed a pair of her newer sneakers in front of my tent. As I peeked out from under the flap of my tent, I saw Sarah disassembling hers. She looked my way and smiled, They'll get you there!

DAY THREE

My sister-in-law Ann Marie had checked in as Walker Number 31 on Day Two. I was closer to the end of our group: Walker Number 1,769. Ann Marie and her neighbor Margaret had trained earnestly for the three-day walk by walking ten to fifteen miles every morning the previous six months. Without fail, every morning they would wake up and walk through the dark streets of Albany at 4:30 A.M. Then Ann Marie returned home to wake my nieces and nephew and ready them for school. On weekends, she took several twenty-mile walks.

My brother Bill had made a playful bet with her. Considering all her training, he told Ann Marie that he wanted her and her friend to be in the first group of walkers to finish each day's leg. They had succeeded in doing that. But this wasn't a competition or a marathon, it was a breast cancer walk. And Ann Marie decided to slow her speed-walking down—way down—the previous evening when I hobbled in, looking so defeated yet willfully determined.

For the first two days, Ann Marie and Margaret had headed out almost an hour before Sarah, Kathie, and me. But as I began the thirteen-mile homestretch to Central Park, I saw Ann Marie and Margaret waiting for me. My sister-in-law then said, I'm going to show you how to do this right.

As we began the day's first climb, Ann Marie instructed me to take deep breaths and let them out slowly. She said to pump my arms and wiggle my fingers. As we walked, she showed me how to shift my weight, balancing it from one hip to another. With her coaching, I moved my arms and feet at a faster pace than ever before. I suddenly heard myself saying the one word I'd heard from almost everyone else the previous two days, Passing!

By the time I reached the George Washington Bridge and headed into Manhattan, I must have said it a hundred times. I had to smile. I finally got it right, this walking thing.

At about three o'clock, all the walkers, crew, and volunteers entered into

Central Park to the blare of "Chariots of Fire" and the roar of thousands of family members and friends on hand to applaud our efforts. We had walked sixty miles and we had raised more than three million dollars for breast cancer programs.

As we walked down the sloping grass hill into Central Park's East Meadow, I spied my entire extended family all the way down front. My nieces and my nephew all sat on top of adults' shoulders. I saw Jimmy and Billy. Mandy seemed especially taken by the sight of all of us, as I'm sure she missed not being a part of our journey. Suddenly, breaking through the crowd toward the makeshift fence separating walkers from the crowd, my father was shouting my name in order to get my attention. I headed in his direction. He had decided to come to cheer us upon our arrival, and he was there to remember my mother, as was Helen. My father wasn't the only one with tears in his eyes.

Hail the conquering hero, a friend wrote on a card attached to a lovely bouquet of pink roses delivered the day after my walk. But I was no hero. I was finally on my way to becoming more of a messenger of hope than I had ever been before in life. When they dried, I plucked the rose petals apart and placed them in a shoe box. On top of the petals, I put my sneakers, looped together with my plastic walker identification number, which had draped my neck throughout those three long days.

Then in late fall, I took a day off from my newest workplace—where I was employed as a contributing launch editor for *O*, Oprah Winfrey's magazine— and rode the train upstate to Albany once again, holding the brown box securely on my lap. My father met me at the depot, and we headed toward the cemetery.

Once more I was walking toward my mother, this time in the serene solitude of the mausoleum where her ashes lay safely. When I got beneath her crypt, I knelt down and placed the open box in front of her. On my sneakers, I had written in a black marker:

> *Mom, I walked sixty miles in memory of you. I would have walked thousands just to have you here again.*
>
> *—Love, Sue*

Then, holding my father's hand, we slowly walked away.

An Orphan and a Friend

Later that evening, after leaving my sneakers behind with my mother, I made arrangements to have dinner with Bob Wygant, a man whom I had grown very fond of after our first meeting almost eleven years before. It's nice to be around confident and optimistic people when you yourself do not feel a sense of complete balance in this world. Sometimes on an occasional trip to Albany, I would phone him and ask if he would join me for dinner. Bob's reassuring voice put me at ease. His gentle manner reminded me in some ways of my mother's. As we spoke, he always said, Can't wait to see you, Sue. It's always so nice to talk about the past.

I enjoyed learning more details of the children who had once lived in my backyard to the left of the fence. The backyard where I grew up brought up sad memories of a great family who no longer lived there on its grounds. Over the years, my family seemed to grow apart. Every summer we would get to-gether for a weekend in Cape Cod, where my father and Helen rented out six rooms for all of us in a motel. Our growing family spent three days talking about what we were doing now as my increasing number of nieces and nephews splashed in the ocean waves or dug castles in the sand around us. If anyone brought up a story that involved our mother, there was this startling si-lence between my siblings and me. We all just buried our feet into the sand and looked down. It seems we tacitly agreed to each remember her privately.

When Bob Wygant and I sat down together to reminisce, it was at Jack's Oyster House, not far from the capitol. When my mother and father had eaten here over the years to celebrate their anniversary, I remembered how my mother loved the shrimp scampi; my father, the prime rib; and they always got their picture taken with a Polaroid and put into a Jack's Oyster House paper frame. They continued this tradition until the last year, when my mother's ill-ness kept her from leaving the house. As Bob and I sat in my parents' favorite restaurant, I sometimes wondered if this had ever been my mother's seat when she came here, too.

As became our way, whenever I saw Bob, we hugged each other hello. Be-cause we talked in such detail about his childhood, he often left his wife, Sally, at home. Although we were meeting as friends, our conversations filled in the holes on his side of my backyard.

By the late 1990s, Bob had retired from his position as an educator and coach and was now an honorary board member of Parsons Child and Family Center—the old Albany Home for Children. A year didn't go by when Bob didn't attend the high school graduation ceremonies of the children, even if only a handful of kids were graduating and making their way beyond the des-tiny of Academy Road. At the ceremonies, you could spot Bob easily. He was the one standing, clapping and cheering them on like he was at an end-of-the-season football game.

Sitting across from me, Bob said, It's heartwarming to see any of these kids become successful. It's a different ball game for them, and I have to keep re-membering that. It may be hard for us to connect with these children, but as alumni we have to give it a try. That's why I go back to the grounds so often. I want to help those kids feel like they have a real shot at a future.

He smiled as he cut his steak with his still-steady strong hands, and added,

I'll tell you, if I win the lottery, I'll give it all back to the grounds where we both grew up.

As I looked at Bob, I sometimes just wondered if he and the other orphans might have been the lucky ones. Having never experienced the true love of a mother as I had, to have flourished in the beauty from her heart and the kindness of her soul, they would never feel the devastation I lived with every day, the sense of loss I felt magnified by the thirty-five years when I had my mother in my life.

I suppose every single person must develop the capacity to move on when dealt the unfairness of life's blows.

During our dinners, Bob expressed his disappointment that the annual reunion never really took off after the successful first one at the Junior College of Albany that fall of 1989. As the years passed, the numbers kept dwindling. Eventually, Bob and the other organizers took annual cruises together instead. But the cruises came and went as well. So instead of having their own reunion each year, the Alumni Committee of the old Albany Home for Children decided to join forces with Parsons Child and Family Center at their annual June Lawn Festival. They set up a booth stocked with memorabilia and now antique photographs and scrapbooks from their past to show attendees another era, another time when they lived there for reasons very different from why the children were there now. The orphan alumni were excited to talk to anyone who stopped by to ask them questions about growing up at the Albany Home for Children so long ago.

As the years moved on from that first reunion, Bob took steady notes on where people were living so that he could stay in touch with them through a newsletter. Lately, he had been getting a number of his newsletters returned in the mail, noting that many of the orphans emeriti of 1989 were now deceased. He admitted to me as we moved on to dessert and his favorite item on the menu, vanilla ice cream, Well, it looks like the orphans of another time are becoming extinct.

When I asked Bob how he was doing after losing his best friend just a couple of months before, tears welled up in his eyes. You know, Sue, I feel like I lost my dad.

Coach had passed away from a massive heart attack as he was putting gro-

ceries into his car. After many years of being on his own without Swannee, he
had only recently remarried before his sudden death in a hot parking lot in
Florida.

I saw Bob the following day at the Parsons Lawn Festival. The ground-
breaking ceremonies for a new gym and activities center were now taking place.
I walked away from the booth where some of the remaining alumni of the old
Albany Home for Children huddled over a previously unseen photo album de-
picting their days growing up there. An orphan who hadn't attended the first or
subsequent reunions had brought it to show. I made my way over to an area
right near our old swimming pool. Bob was almost ready to dig the ceremonial
first shovel of dirt. This new facility would be three times larger than the Van
Alstyne Gymnasium, where both Bob and I had played as children.

His shovel went down deep, and when he brought it back up, Bob Wygant
spread the dirt up into the sky until it fell onto the grass. I think Bob and I
both hoped the children of our Home's future would find at least some joy in
playing when they weren't drawing art to express their inner turmoil or going
through intensive therapy. At separate times years ago, Bob and I had both
loved running freely in our old backyard.

I walked around the area where they still had a hayride and where Mary
Fundis had held her nightly summer barbecues. Then I headed inside the cottages. I wanted to look into the eyes of the children who lived there through
adult eyes. The children were tugging at their counselors so that they could go
and have their faces painted. Looking into their brown, blue, black, or green
eyes, I saw children who looked pretty much like a child you might see anywhere. Nothing signaled that they were different. Over the years, the clothes
the children wore had gotten better, and they looked fresh and clean. I knew I
was seeing them on the day when their backyard was like a carnival, and
things were significantly different from their days before or their days after the
Lawn Festival, but all these kids were adorable. Nowadays, children at Parsons
lived on the grounds or in a cottage for only two or three years at the most. If
they did live there, the reasons for doing so must have been atrocious. Kids
with emotional problems were now mostly medicated at their own homes by
a mother or a father; they came here only during the day for special schooling
that concentrated on helping them deal with their attention and behavioral
problems.

Why the children lived here was none of my business. They had, as a journalist might write, off-the-record stories. To pry further would be breaking the confidence of an innocent child. I had finally learned that lesson. And so I walked away from the kids who live there now, to let them heal their wings until the day, I pray, they are healthy enough to fly again.

As Bob accompanied me to the entrance of Parsons, I saw another group of children eagerly trying to win the prizes at the watermelon-eating contest sitting on picnic tables not too far away from my old house. And as I walked on, I heard the aging Shriners play "What a Wonderful World."

I hear babies cry, I watch them grow
They'll learn much more than I'll never know . . .

As we neared Academy Road, walking over the old speed bumps, still humming the words to myself, Bob asked, You asked about Coach last night. But what about you, Sue? How are you doing without your mother?

I miss her like it was yesterday, I replied. I miss her every breathing moment of my day.

And how are things going with your dad?

Occasionally you just make up answers to be polite. My father and I sometimes had nice times together. He would be there for me at a moment's notice, but there were other times when I failed to understand why my mother loved him so. I believe he didn't even understand my decision to get psychiatric help and thought perhaps I wanted prescription drugs to make life easier without toughing it out.

What did he personally know about the need for counseling? I was the only one of his children who had ever reached out to ask for help.

So I answered Bob's question in a way that wouldn't open up any further discussion. Great, I said, we're going to a movie tomorrow. My father likes that. It kind of bugs me that he always takes my popcorn. I never understand why he can't get his own. He's always talking about calories and cholesterol.

And then I hugged Bob good-bye, always like it could be our last time together. His, or mine.

My Father's Story

About a year and a half later, after that last day in my backyard, I received an e-mail from my father inviting me to visit him and Helen for a long weekend. He asked if I'd like to go skiing up at Gore Mountain again and perhaps try Hawkeye, the black-diamond slope that gave me such tremors as a child. He also asked if he could provide more information or insight into my research on the Albany Home for Children. He concluded his e-mail by saying, If you want, you could even interview me. I've never told you my story.

I went to Albany. While nobody could fill my mother's place in my heart, through the years Helen had never once negated my mother's memory; nor did she attempt to replace her. Instead, if any of my siblings and I needed to talk, she was there. And she loved to feed us.

After the breast cancer walk, I had decided to actually use my gym club membership—instead of just paying the bill. I joined the diet plan my mother often encouraged my father to go on when we were young.

By my fortieth birthday, and after eight months of adhering to a strict regimen that found me at the gym doing kickboxing, sword fighting using a heavy wooden stick, Spinning, and body-conditioning classes some ten hours a week, and adhering to the Weight Watchers point system, I lost over sixty pounds. When I tired of the routine of my gym classes, I headed to Gleason's, a famous musty old boxing gym in Brooklyn located underneath the Brooklyn Bridge, where amid the smell of sweat and an overwhelming sense of power, a trainer would wrap my hands and size me up with boxing gloves, a plastic teeth protector, and a padded helmet. Inside the ring, after first learning how to jump rope for an hour straight, and shadowbox, I would go four rounds with guys who were hoping to compete in the Golden Gloves or other boxing competitions. I think that all the fury of my life came out when I used my right hook, because it often sent men much bigger than me flying back to the ropes. I earned the nickname Krusher. Reaching for my outer limits, I was exhilarated. When exercising on the ground became all too familiar, I took to the skies with a new love—skydiving—or to the ocean in Mexico to learn how to surf eight-foot-tall waves. A fearful girl for way too long, I became a confident and fearless woman who is prepared to take on the world, or any of the obstacles that get in my way. Oh, and there is another love I have when it comes to physical endurance. I once had a loop where I rode my bike in my old backyard. Today I have a bike that I often ride around the perimeters of the city that I so love. Manhattan, as it turns out, is also a loop full of children riding alongside me on my quest, or off to the side playing basketball, or even splashing in a pool. One size smaller than my mother, I am now in the best shape of my life.

I took a day off from my hectic job as a story producer for ABC News's *Good Morning America*. It seems my professional career, along with my mental state, is a work in progress. I was always a news junkie, ever since those days my father and I watched the local and national news together. To be right on top of the news, and watching it break, made the world feel less intimidating to me. My mind was more tranquil when chaos surrounded me. And so on that day we skied Gore Mountain, my father—now seventy—and I made our way toward Hawkeye, the wind pounding the top of the Adirondacks with such fierceness that it pushed us toward the trail whether we wanted to go there or not. At the top, I thought back to those weekends when Jimmy and I shimmied down the steep slope on our rear ends, clinging to a tree on one side until we shimmied down to the next tree. But now Hawkeye looked like the bunny hills I so relished as a kid.

After the first New Year's Eve without my mother, later that January, my brothers, my father, and I had skied in Zermatt, Switzerland, with the spectacular view of the mythic blue, snow-draped Matterhorn always at our side. Maybe I had not exactly loved skiing as a child, but because my father started teaching us so young, he prepared us for the most challenging mountains in the world. My father, and my brothers, and I have now skied not only the Swiss Alps, but the French, Italian, and Austrian Alps as well. There is no place in the world I'd rather be when I travel, and there is no other sport that generates the excitement I feel when I race down these awe-inspiring hills. The beauty, whiteness, and serenity of the Alps take my breath away every time I see the chain of mountaintops. Sometimes I think how lovely it would be to retire there.

For some thirty-six years, ever since I was four, my father always led us down the mountain. But on the day we ski Hawkeye, he seemed bothered by the way his skis were moving, and annoyed that his boots were too tight. I waited for him at the bottom. As my father aged, he no longer charged down as the hero of the mountains that he had once seemed to us. It felt lonely at the bottom of Hawkeye, waiting for him. Perhaps I shouldn't have skied so far ahead. The rest of that day I slowed down my skiing, and headed down the mountain following in my father's path. Later, when he asked if we could leave early, something we had never dared ask when we were young—always staying at a mountain until the lifts closed—I replied, Yes, of course. I want you to be rested for our interview tomorrow.

Saturday morning, I awoke at nine o'clock, still jangled from my hectic week, and shuffled sleepily into the kitchen. Sipping his second cup of coffee, his doughnut long finished, my father was already waiting to begin the interview. He had placed my tape recorder on the table right in front of him and taken the cellophane wrapping off all the cassettes I might need.

Even before I got settled at the table, my father began talking about his early childhood. Growing up in Glens Falls, he said he was such an active child that his parents put him in a halter similar to those used to constrain a dog and, with a long rope, tied him to a tree near the sandbox in their backyard. As he grew, his mother threatened to send him to the Albany Home for Children whenever he misbehaved, which was often.

The thought of being sent to an orphanage frightened him so much that when his father was being considered for a job transfer and there was a possibility that his family would move to Albany, he didn't want to go. He feared that if they lived nearer to the orphanage, his mother might actually carry out her threat.

Sitting down in the seat across from him, I asked, Really?

I knew what that place was and it scared me, he replied.

He talked about his lifetime love of reading. Considering I had no idea of where our conversation would lead, I didn't ask any questions. It seemed to me he just had a story he wanted to tell.

As a teenager he was particularly attracted to books that had to do with the social condition of the country and the history of the union movement. He was on the organizing committee that brought Eleanor Roosevelt to speak at the University of Vermont. He found her fascinating. He was also particularly impressed with John Dos Passos, and the class wars between those who had everything and those who had nothing. My father had always been interested in human behavior, in the same way I was interested in uncovering stories.

His father, much older than his mother, was a conservative Republican, born in the late 1800s, and his mother a liberal Democrat. Even as a child, he remembered being impressed by the Democrats, who took care of the underdog. As he said, he was swayed by the victims, never the aggressors. He gravitated toward his mother, who seemed more like-minded, and he had difficulty dealing with his father's views, most particularly his prejudices.

His parents were always at each other's throats. His mother was an instigator who relished the thought of making her husband jealous. Even as a boy he knew that when he married, he hoped to find a soft-spoken and kind wife.

His mother was so attractive that he was frequently embarrassed by her flaunting her sexuality. Every time they went to church together, she insisted on sitting in the front pew because she wanted to be *seen*. She liked the idea of walking down the aisle and having all the men in the church staring at her sexy legs.

During summer break from college after his sophomore year, my father was working as a mason's helper. One afternoon, he was on the roof of a building right across the street from where his mother worked. One of the other guys he was with screamed out, Oh, my God! Look at that *thing* coming down the street! I've never seen such big tits!

When he peered over the wall, my father was mortified. The woman his coworker was ogling was his mother.

After his first year at college, his mother insisted he change fraternities because he was partying too much and he was in danger of flunking out of school. While at the University of Vermont, he had no idea what he was going to do when he graduated.

Because one of his roommates was going to veterinary school, he thought he might do the same. Since he wasn't the best student at the UVM, when he applied to the veterinary school at Cornell, he received a letter stating that his application for admission would be reconsidered only after he first worked on a farm for six to ten months. So my father went to work at a dairy farm outside Hudson Falls, New York. He got up every day at 4 A.M. and stopped working at 9 P.M. While the experience gave him an appreciation for farm life, my father decided that having the letters *DVM* after his name was not for him.

And so, after only a month on the farm, he thought he would be an insurance salesman. But after working in that field for a few months, he then decided, Why not try law?

Then my father thought he would be a zoologist and teach. So off he went to the University of Rhode Island, stayed for about three months, and dropped out.

As he said to me, I guess I knew what you were going through when you dropped out of law school.

After running through various career choices, my father decided he might be wise to see a career counselor. He wanted to take aptitude tests in order to figure out the job he was best suited for. A couple of days after taking the test, the results came back and the counselor called him in. He said, John, it looks to me like you should be a farmer.

My father replied, No thanks. He asked if there was anything else the test identified that might give him some direction.

The counselor replied, Yes, you have some positive marks beside the category of social work.

To that, my father inquired, What's that?

After learning more about this burgeoning field of study, my father enrolled in the graduate school at Boston College. He also worked with programs that dealt with single mothers and their children.

He couldn't stand the notion of a family being separated or not being able to care for their offspring, so with many of his cases, he would write up authorizations for a variety of goods—like a bassinet for a new baby, or a new stove—to help them get by. His supervisor was semi-blind and couldn't read the paperwork my father put before him, so he always signed off on the purchase orders without question. He assumed my father was an honest man. To the single women and their children, he was a savior.

After receiving his master's in social work, my father's first professional job was working at the Child Guidance Center in Waterbury, Connecticut, a place that closed for the month of August. The first summer, he waited tables at Cape Cod for the month. The second summer during his August break, he fell in love with my mother at Lake George.

I interrupted my father. You know, Dad, I sometimes wondered how you were able to get inside the mind of a child who was troubled. You spent your entire career working with disturbed children, yet I've often wondered—do you really know what emotional suffering is? And what do you really know about depression if you've never experienced it yourself?

My father reached his arms up into the air and locked his fingers on top of his head. After a long pause, he asked, Haven't I ever told you that there was a period in my life when I was very anxious?

No, I replied, shocked that he would even say those words.

It was before I got married, and I had all these anxiety attacks and I got jittery whenever someone screamed at me. I would just freeze with anxiety, so I went into therapy.

My face paled. *You* went into *therapy?* I was stunned.

Everyone I worked with in the clinic was in therapy. I realized that if I wanted to be a good therapist, I had to be in therapy myself. Plus, I needed it.

I saw a psychoanalyst, sometimes four or five times a week. I found it helpful. I worked out a lot of the problems I had with my parents. I used to bitch about them all the time, and I think I got a better perspective of who they were. I eventually left therapy after I met your mother.

Did you ever tell Mom? I asked.

No, he replied, and took a long time before he said the one thing about him I needed to know to conclude my book and my personal story.

I never told anyone I had fears, my father said. I just had them. But now I'm telling you.

My father and I had made a connection. It has given me more insight into my emotional heritage. It remains to be seen if we will ever become close in that way that I was with my mother. I don't think we will. Once was enough.

I had always believed that I inherited my anxieties from my mother. My life was filled with fears, born in the backyards of my childhood. Our first—until I was three—was a backyard with a slaughterhouse to the left and a cemetery to the right where I once feared Casper the ghost was not so friendly. In my second backyard, and only one hundred feet away from our house, trains blared their horns through our windows at all hours. That was also the backyard where, when I was five years old, Jimmy told me I could no longer be his best friend because he wanted to hang out with the other boys. It was a crushing blow to me because even as an adult, I can remember being three and four and so adoring of my older brother. When we moved to my third backyard, the summer I would turn seven, I especially feared the night—tempered by the charged emotions roiling in the cottages behind our house on Academy Road. When I learned that my predisposition came from both of my parents, it became even clearer that I was the one of all of their five children who had taken their combined fears and anxieties as a direct hit.

For so many years, I had thought that my strong, decisive father had looked down on me for reaching out for help; that he considered the medications I took were just a phase. After a lifetime of feeling disconnected from him, I have now learned that, just like me, he had reached out for help when he needed it, too. That made me feel better. And the reality is I *am* better.

It once seemed unfathomable to me that my parents, but more so my father, could not have noticed how much a child of their own could have benefited by some of the treatment offered to the children who lived at the Home. The signs were there. I can still remember the day when I was seven and I lay on the living room rug with a knife in my hand, threatening to cut my wrists because I felt so out of place.

Surely the breakdown that prompted my leaving law school, only to return to Albany and stare blankly out the window, should have indicated a deeply troubled emotional state.

Sometimes I think perhaps my father, the professional who dealt with troubled children every day, took a dangerous chance by not seeking treatment for me as a child. However, I am sure that both my parents felt that, since I was their blood, I would make it. The truth is that, against insurmountable odds, my mother had survived her childhood of losses and my father had been able to work out his internal conflicts. Certainly, they must have thought that I would eventually pull through just like they did.

Recently, my second longtime psychiatrist, Dr. Ann Campbell, of almost ten years, decided to leave the profession. Seemingly out of the blue—at least to me—Ann wanted to do something more creative with her life as she neared sixty. She was excited to study languages and learn the art of calligraphy. When I first heard the news two months before she closed her office and moved to Copenhagen, I felt my psychiatrist was leaving my emotional state abandoned, and it felt like a great loss. Ann was the one who had seen me through my mother's death. In the past couple of years, she had become my safety blanket. Still, while she prescribed my medications, it came to be I really only saw her two or three times a year to talk about things that were bothering me. After almost twenty years of therapy, sometimes I feel like everything has been said. And so I finally wished her well on her new adventure in life.

Through the help of my two longtime psychiatrists, whom I saw most of my adult life, I learned how to get through my life troubles. I am no longer paralyzed by the thought of my mother's death like I was throughout my childhood. I no longer believe I can't move on without my mother. It's so contrary to write this, but my biggest fear of her dying, and then her death, one day led me on a path to my first feelings of internal peace. She's always there, of course. Photos of her are everywhere in my apartment. The dark red rocking chair where she once sat by the fireplace full of enthusiasm as we opened our Christmas gifts, and where she listened as I told her I was going to die of breast cancer and that I was growing hair under my arms and becoming a Jimmy, now rests in my living room diagonally across from my sofa. I can always look there and remember her alive, my beautiful mother.

Right before my psychiatrist went away, I asked her, because I never really knew, what exactly I suffered from and how she would explain it in a medical way. She wrote me the following in a letter, and then attached a two-page list of all the medications that I have been on combining my first psychiatrist's list with hers.

Dx: lifelong history of anxiety, with occasional panic attacks, and insomnia—waxing and waning of symptoms led to adjustments in dosages and sometimes medications; episodes of depression/dysthmia and violent suicidal ideation with an occasional manic or mixed flavor at other times suggest the possibility of bipolar spectrum disorder, but brief trial of Lamictal inconclusive and such episodes are now rare; ability to withstand life crises and maintain high level of function has only increased over the years.

Flickering Images

I turn off the flickering screen of my computer that has made it possible for me to retrieve the Technicolor childhood memories—the good and the bad—that came with the story of my backyard. Sometimes the images of my mother are so real that I have the urge to reach out and touch her familiar face once more.

But they are just memories, fading pictures from my former backyard.

As I get up from the chair by my desk, I remember her as I do on all special occasions—Christmas, her birthday, St. Patrick's Day, and especially this day, March 29, the date of her death.

I put on my increasingly tailored-down dark blue Armani suit, and an elegant pair of high-heeled black Clergerie boots. Then I spritz on my mother's favorite perfume, Eau de Calandre, kept on the nightstand beside my bed. I open up my mother's old jewelry box. Three things are inside: her mother's engagement ring, so small it fits only my pinkie; her strand of Mikimoto pearls; and a copy of the prayer to St. Jude she clipped and pinned to her nightgown when she was very ill.

I don't usually wear pearls, but I wear them as I make my way—walking thirty-nine blocks—today to St. Patrick's Cathedral in her memory.

Inside this great church, I quietly make my way down the long center aisle. Sitting, I listen to words from a priest, which I have never really understood. When the Mass ends, I walk to the first statue of a saint to the right of the entranceway. There I stop and tuck a crisp one-dollar bill through the slot of the bronze collection box—just as my mother taught me when I was so young at the same cathedral. I light a votive candle and then say a prayer as I kneel before the first of many giant marble saints that loom around the vast sanctuary. I do the same before every saint around the perimeter of the church, asking each of them to watch over my mother.

When we were still young, my parents bought an eight-millimeter movie camera and projector to show us the home movies they took of the faraway places they visited when they went off on their own vacation every year, just like honeymooners. I suppose that's when my brothers and sisters and I became aware of the greater world beyond Academy Road.

Even if we never left our living room, when my father flipped the switch to start the projector, we traveled the world with them. We saw Barbados, where my mother learned to play steel drums with the dark men of the island. And we saw the redwood forest with its trees so big they made the elms along Academy Road look like twigs.

In all the images, in each frame, whether it was in Ireland, where a flock of sheep surrounded their rented car on a winding country road, or Rome, splashing inside the Trevi Fountain, or London, in front of Buckingham Palace, what I distinctly remember most is our mother waving to us, her children at home.

My father, holding the camera in one hand, would direct my mother to walk in the direction of whatever landmark, vista, or monument they were visiting, turn and smile at the camera, and then wave to us. Since he was also the sole cameraman, he was in none of the pictures. Sometimes we would see my mother retrace her steps and then wave again—because she hadn't done it *exactly* right.

Whether it took one or five takes, she kept on smiling. It was just such joy to be there, even if it had taken great strength for her to leave us.

As I think back on those home movies, one place in particular I will never forget. Her wave was of such intensity that I knew even then that it must have meant the world for her to be there, more than any other place that she had ever visited before. In the early 1970s my mother stood outside Notre Dame Cathedral, right there amid the pigeons. Churches were always special to my mother, but it was obvious that Notre Dame held even more meaning to her than St. Patrick's.

I imagined my father caught her jubilant spirit in only one take. As she waved to us, my mother turned around, away from the camera's lens, and pointed directly to the sky above the cathedral's imposing spire. It was almost as if she was trying to say, *Look at this. This is the church that is closest to heaven!*

I have found that by retracing my mother's steps, visiting the places that she traveled, I feel connected to her again.

And so I went to Paris for the first time last Thanksgiving. Once I reached Notre Dame, I stood on the same spot where I remember watching her point to the cathedral and heaven some thirty years before. I pulled a plastic bag, containing red leaves that I had taken from my mother's dogwood tree on my last visit to Albany, out of my back pocket. Then, as dusk settled about the regal Gothic cathedral, I twirled around and tossed her leaves into the sky. As the leaves were caught up in the autumn breeze, I spread my mother's memory around in front of this magnificent church that had held such special meaning for her. To me, these leaves are living pieces of my mother, and I was bringing her back to this majestic place.

I place dollars in the collection boxes at St. Patrick's Cathedral on the special days of the year meant for her, as that was how my mother remembered her own mother. I also honor her in my own way, by spreading her leaves, keeping her memory alive every place I go.

My mother is the sum of my spectacular joys, and most treasured memories.

All that is me goes back to my yard. Yet all that I miss is my mother.

Acknowledgments

Seven years ago, on the back pages of whichever book I happened to be reading at the time, I started jotting down thoughts of my mother. The first word I wrote was her name, Elaine. From those back-page scribbles in *The Color of Water, The Professor and the Mad Man,* and *The God of Small Things,* I began a comprehensive examination of my childhood, as well as the greater story of my former backyard. Writing this book has been a seven-year journey from grief—from how utterly dejected I was after my mother's death—to redemption. I have come full circle, finding a place in my heart where my mother's kindness and optimism have now become a part of me.

I am profoundly grateful to my family and friends, who have stayed so steadfastly loyal—not only in the period following my mother's illness and death, but throughout my entire life, which has had dramatic ups and downs.

Three people in particular were extraordinarily helpful in allowing me to interview them, imparting wisdom and insight into a time period unfamiliar to me. I am thankful to the poignant recollections of my charismatic friend Bob Wygant; to my wonderful aunt and confidante, Mary Schuh; and special thanks and much love to my father, John W. Carswell, a tireless crusader for children even today, and the master and commander of my former backyard. Without these three gifted storytellers, and the tireless attention of Claudia Cross, my agent and longtime friend, this journey from idea to finished book would have been more of a lonely struggle.

I would like to thank my supremely good-natured brothers and sisters for enduring this foray into the way I observed our backyard—to Jim, Bill, Amanda, and Sarah, and to their spouses (respectively) Kathie Carswell, Ann Marie Carswell, Philip Smith, and Walter Heffernan. And to my lovely stepmother, Helen O'Hanlon Carswell: the right one—the second time. And I also send fond gratitude to my *older sister,* cousin Laurel Colasurdo, and my *niece,* Chelsea.

My close circle of friends are all so very kind by nature that they remind me in different ways of my mother. I admire all their patience and steadfast loyalty. In alphabetical order (to be fair, in the way my mother would have been), a thousand thanks to Susan Bornstein, Victoria Gotti, Lisa Halliday (my first friend that I entrusted to read my manuscript and champion it onward), Tina Johnson, Elizabeth MacDonald, Joanne Merrigan, Walter Owen, Susan Reed, Elisabeth Rohm, Nancy Seifried-Miller-Shaw, and Sara Switzer. And to the gentleman who each year serenades my birthday song, Darryl Brantley.

Special appreciation to my bicentennial friends, Theodore and Stratton Bouloukos. And to my faithful financial adviser (even without those finances), Richard Blonstein of Broad Wealth Management, Inc.

To journalists and idols about whom I've written stories in past years, and who then demonstrated many kindnesses, assisting me in getting job interviews, offering references, and just being there; namely, Katie Couric, Cynthia McFadden, and the legendary Liz Smith.

Many thanks to my good friend Sallie Batson, who assisted in the research of my book's early stages, and who has remained the very devoted friend of my beloved Edith and Maude on all the streets they've walked, as they now enter their golden years with enthusiastic and worn-in paws. And to Bob Scarry, who sets out on a new journey with them each day through rain, snow, sleet, and the hot sun. Thank you both for showing such love and protection to my pups.

To my parents' good friends from the old Albany Home—Ralph and Marlene Cordes, as well as Bradley Cordes, for inviting me to their home in Maine. And to my father's debonair boss, the late Edwin Millard, with whom I spent time in Chicago. I am so grateful that all of them were able to bring my backyard vibrantly alive again with their own memories, as did Nadia Finkelstein, an expert on the separation of children from families.

From the Albany Home for Children (Parsons Child and Family Center) past and present: I am indebted to Orissa Healy, who founded the original orphanage as The Society for the Relief of Orphan and Destitute Children in 1829. She heard the "Macedonian cry" to help impoverished children, many of whom were then living in garbage cans outside of Albany's fine restaurants, and being turned away from the Almshouse where their mothers sought refuge. Thank you, Ray Schimmer, a truly decent man who forges ahead where my father left off; my gratitude to the now deceased Dr. Lenore Sportsman, a psychiatrist who made the leap from child to family center therapy; Dr. Wander Braga, a pioneering child psychiatrist; Bonnie Morrison O'Shea, my favorite lifeguard; and to Jim Hudson and Tom Walsh whom I fondly recall from their early days at the Home as dedicated child care workers. I would also like to share my gratitude to Lynn Pauquette for loaning me almost two centuries of photos so that I might imagine my former backyard and its original namesake from its beginnings, and I am appreciative to the invaluable look into the world of foster care as told to me through the eyes of Elaine Person, who now sits on the board of directors at Parsons. Much appreciation to my father and Ray Schimmer's executive assistant, Elizabeth A. Waite.

Also from the days of the Albany Home for Children, I would like to thank Mary Fundis and *cousin* Marge McGraw for feeding us special treats during the many years my siblings and I lived on the grounds; and to the late Dr. James Bell, who never missed a birthday, Christmas, or graduation and brought generous, thoughtful gifts.

To David Curley, I gratefully thank you for sharing your papers and tapes with me. Your research was invaluable. And to the late John Maguire, who left behind a wonderful historical paper titled, "The Hapless Children," about the origins of a Home that this year celebrates its 175th anniversary.

To orphans gone by, whom I originally met in 1989 for my *People* magazine article and then who continued to let me interview them about their side of the fence over the years: Mr. Wygant—again and again (and my special liaison, Bob's wife, Sally Wygant), Edna LeRoy Hornachek, Caroline LeRoy Commisso, Betty Lappeus Johnson, Dorothy Bunshock Crowley, the late Betty Elder Bruni, the late Betty Sherwood Turner, and finally, Mary Martits Jr., who also lived with her family on the grounds of the old Albany Home for Children under very different circumstances. Thank you all for inviting me into your world or your homes and opening up your hearts about a lonely time in your young lives. And a very special thank-you to the insights of John Garzia.

I am beholden to the detailed research that Virgina B. Bowers, Albany's city historian, generously provided me.

I am appreciative of the motivation provided by my fitness sensei, Ilaria Montagani and her Powerstrike classes—without her, there would be much more of me. And to Weight Watchers founder Jean Nidetch, who in the early 1960s began inviting friends into her Queens home once a week to discuss how best to lose weight. I swear allegiance to both of your programs.

And to the two women who literally saved my life, the now retired Dr. Mariannne Horney Eckardt and Dr. M. Ann Campbell: a most sincere thank-you for all the hours I sat across from you in the chair and poured out my heart. I appreciate the patience, wisdom, and guidance you both so generously offered over the course of almost half my life.

A kind thank-you to Lydia Wills, who, with remarkable grace, insisted I start off on a course to write a book about my backyard. I would like to thank the late great and far too young Sarah Pettit for teaching me how to write and trust my voice.

In my professional life, I am deeply grateful to the countless friends I have made and treasured over the years, ever since those early days working at *People* magazine. A special thanks goes out to my assigning editor there, Dick Lemon, who let me write a story about a bunch of orphans having a reunion; to the friends I made at Pocket Books; *O, The Oprah Magazine*; *Good Morning America*; and my newest friends at *Vanity Fair*, especially the brilliant and larger-than-life Graydon Carter, the very kind John Banta, and the lovely, awe-inspiring and mannered Punch Hutton. Thank you to my dear friend, the irreplaceable Beth Kseniak, whose loyalty is unparalleled. She recommended me for the *Vanity Fair* job, which has taken my career back in the right direction, even if it is where I once started so many years ago.

I am grateful for places where a writer is allowed to go and tap out their thoughts, namely the Rose Main Reading Room at the New York Public Library on 42nd Street and 5th Avenue. To The Writers Room and Doma Cafe on Perry Street with a special thanks to its proprietors Evie and Michael Polesny; and to Il Cantinori on East 10th Street, where I sometimes worked on the varying drafts of my manuscript through several courses of dinner, sitting at a table alit with bountiful candles to illuminate the pages of my book. To Frank Minieri and your kind coworkers, *grazie tanto* for all of your gracious, welcoming attention, and for your friendship and continued interest in my book. And Frank, during those days when I didn't have a dime, I can never thank you enough for always saying, Don't forget, Sue, staff dining hours are at 5 P.M.

To my four editors along the way. Thanks especially to my acquiring editor, Joanne Wyckoff, who saw something in a rather long-winded 150-page proposal. I am indebted to Dan Smetanka, who inspired me to be more impressionistic with my writing; and to the delightful Allison Dickens, who valiantly took up the cause of my book and shepherded it through a lengthy process. I owe much to the guidance of lovely, gentle Dana Edwin Isaacson, who took my manuscript, ripped it apart, and then put it and me back on a new track.

To the Ballantine team—led by my partner-in-crime from my Pocket Books days, senior v.p. and editor in chief, Nancy Miller—for their enthusiasm and support; publicity and public relations savants Carole Schneider and Thomas Perry; Kim Hovey, marketing director; Lisa Feuer, the production director who approved my pretty-much-begging request for rough-cut pages; detail-savvy Laura Jorstad, copyeditor; Crystal Velasquez and Alexandra Krijgsman, managing editorial; Erin Bekowies, production manager; Libby McGuire, associate publisher; sales director Anthony Ziccardi; Ingrid Powell, editorial assistant; designer Dana Leigh Blanchette; art director Gene Mydlowski and his jacket design team, including Krista Vossen.

Finally, I would like to thank Gina Centrello, my publisher, literary maestro, and friend—who signed off on my book contract back in 1999, and then wisely insisted that I take the necessary time to bring my faded pictures alive more vividly.

To all of you, as Mademoiselle Tribot Laspiere once taught me at the Albany Academy for Girls, "Merci beaucoup." (And yes, that is a quote mark.)

About the Author

SUE CARSWELL is a reporter/researcher at *Vanity Fair*. She has worked as a senior story editor for ABC News' *Good Morning America*, a contributing editor for the launch of *O: The Oprah Magazine*, an executive editor in book publishing, and a correspondent for *People*, where the story of the orphans from her backyard was originally published in December 1989. A graduate of the University of Vermont, Carswell lives in Manhattan's West Village with her dachshunds, Edith and Maude. This is her first book.

About the Type

This book was set in Caslon, a typeface first designed in 1722 by William Caslon. Its widespread use by most English printers in the early eighteenth century soon supplanted the Dutch typefaces that had formerly prevailed. The roman is considered a "workhorse" typeface due to its pleasant, open appearance, while the italic is exceedingly decorative.